HISTORY OF WORLD CIVILISATION

N. JAYAPALAN

ATLANTIC
PUBLISHERS & DISTRIBUTORS (P) LTD

ATLANTIC
PUBLISHERS & DISTRIBUTORS (P) LTD
7/22, Ansari Road, Darya Ganj, New Delhi
Tel.: +91-11-4077 5252, 2327 3880
E-mail: orders@atlanticbooks.com
Web: www.atlanticbooks.com

Reprint 2018, 2021, 2023, 2024, 2026

Published by Atlantic Publishers & Distributors (P) Ltd.

Printed & bound in India by Atlantic Print Services

Preface

It gives me great pleasure to place this book 'History of World Civilisation' in the hands of the readers. The book is quite comprehensive and covers all aspects. The book covers the entire syllabus prescribed by several Universities.

I have narrated all the events Chronologically from the beginning to the end. I have also made a serious and sincere attempt to present the matter in a simple and lucid manner.

There is a plethora of books on the 'History of World Civilisation' in the market. Indeed, most of them are bulky. I have written this book in a sizable volume *i.e.* neither too small nor too big.

My experience of teaching the subject at the college level for several years has prompted me to write this books for the students of Indian Universities mainly to fulfil their requirements. In addition to this, it has been designed to meet the requirements of the examinees of Civil Services Examination in History. I hope that the present book will prove to be most useful to the students.

I am thankful to the M/s Atlantic Publishers and Distributors, New Delhi for readily agreeing to publish this book and bringing it out expeditiously and efficiently.

Suggestions, if any, for the improvement of the book in the subsequent editions will be highly appreciated.

N. JAYAPALAN

Contents

	Preface	*iii*

ANCIENT PERIOD

1.	Origin and Growth of Civilisations	1
2.	Paleolithic Age	5
3.	Neolithic Age	9
4.	Egyptian Civilisation	13
5.	Mesopotamian Civilisations	20
	(i) Sumeria	20
	(ii) Babylonia	23
	(iii) Assyria	27
	(iv) Chaldea	31
6.	Ancient Persian Civilisation	34
7.	Hebrew Civilisation	39
8.	(i) Hittite Civilisation	43
	(ii) Phrygians	46
	(iii) Lydia	49
	(iv) Phoenicia	52
9.	Greek Civilisation	55
10.	Roman Civilisation	67
11.	Asian Civilisations	75
	(i) Aryan Civilisation	75
	(a) Early Vedic Civilisation	75
	(b) Later Vedic Civilisation	79
	(ii) Buddhism	84
	(iii) Jainism	88

12. East Asian Civilisations 92
(i) Chinese Civilisation 92
(ii) Japanese Civilisation 98
13. Civilisations in America 103
(i) Maya 103
(ii) Aztec 105
(iii) Incas 108

MEDIEVAL PERIOD

14. Legacies of Christian Religion 113
15. Byzantine Civilisation 117
16. Rise of Islam 121
17. (a) Feudalism 128
(b) Manorialism 133
18. Holy Roman Empire 136
19. Contribution of Papacy to World Civilisation 144
20. The Services of Monastic Orders 151
21. The Crusades 158
22. Rise of National States 166

MODERN PERIOD

23. Renaissance, Reformation and the Counter Reformation Movement 170
24. Geographical Discoveries 183
25. Age of Enlightenment—Enlightened Despotism 187
(i) The Age of Louis XIV 187
(ii) Frederick The Great 191
(iii) Peter The Great 196
(iv) Catherine The Great 201
(v) Joseph II 206
(vi) Tudors In England 209
26. Era of Revolutions 211
(i) Causes of Revolutions in Europe 211
(ii) Glorious Revolution of 1688 212

(iii) American War of Independence 215

(iv) French Revolution 223

(v) Industrial Revolution 239

(vi) The Agrarian Revolution 241

(vii) Russian Revolution 243

27. Romanticism in Art and Literature 252

28. Rise of Nationalism 255

(i) Europe 255

(ii) Africa 259

(iii) Asia 262

(iv) Indian Nationalism 264

29. World Peace Movement 267

(i) The League of Nations 267

(ii) The United Nations Organisation 268

30. Contemporary Civilisation and its Features 272

Index 277

ANCIENT PERIOD

1

Origin and Growth of Civilisations

Historians of the ancient period simply recorded the accomplishments of their kings and ignored those of the rank and file. But soon it came to be realised that the culture of the people was more important. It is so because the kings pass away while the culture and civilisation of the people stay. Culture must be distinguished from civilisation to have better understanding of those two terms.

A group of people living under a political organisation with a certain moral code, a religion and some economic way of life is said to have developed a civilisation of their own. New inventions would radically change their way of life. Freedom from want would encourage them to launch cultural pursuits in art and architecture, literature and philosophy. Civilisation of the people could be seen through the modern factories, educational institutions and so on. Hence, civilisation is the external environment in which man finds himself.

But culture of the people is the inward condition of their mind. It is represented through art, architecture, literature, religion and philosophy. That is why Mathew Arnold considers culture as "the study of perfection and of harmonious perfection". That perfection lies in man's attempts to be something rather than possessing something. So culture is a study of what man is and civilisation is a study of what man has.

Besides, a same object may have both cultural and civilisational features. For instance, Sucheendram temple represents a feat of civilisation in so far as it is a place of worship and an object of culture on the point of its beauty.

(i) Culture is an expression of our nature and spiritual cravings whereas civilisation is the reflection of physical needs.

(ii) Culture cannot be measured with standard measurement whereas civilisation can be measured in terms of their power to satisfy human wants.

(iii) Culture is subject either to progression or regression. But civilisation advances steadily unless hampered by disasters.

(iv) Culture is transmitted selectively whereas civilisation is transmitted from one generation to another. The culture can be compared to the steering wheel of the society while civilisation is compared to the driving force of it.

Growth of Civilisation

Man is constantly trying to find out the origin of this universe. The traditional view was that it was a product of civilisation. Copernicus, Galileo and Charles Darwin were branded as heretics because they challenged the traditional view which were shielded with alleged divine sanctity. The recent geological discoveries suggest the evolution of this universe.

There are two outstanding scientific theories which explain the origin of the universe. They are the Nebular Theory and P.lanetesimal Hypothesis.

According to the Nebular theory of Laplace, there was a huge revolving gaseous mass. It gradually cooled and contracted. Each ring became a planet and the lesser rings, became satellites. This theory is highly untenable.

The Planetesimal Hypothesis suggested by Professors Chamberlain and Moultan of the University of Chicago in 1900, seems to be a more plausible explanation of the origin of the universe. According to this hypothesis, our sun was approached by another star. It pulled into space a great quantity of matter through gravitation — the particular of the matter were united to become planets. Our Earth is such a one. Vapour that surrounded the Planets condensed and fell as rain. The water made possible the development of plant and animal life on the earth.

Sir Charles Lyell, in his principles of Geology (1833) established scientifically for the first time the fact that the earth's surface is the result of evolutionary natural causes. He divided the history of the earth into the following geological periods: Primordial, Archezoic, Protezoic, Paleozoic, Mesozoic and Cenozoic.

In the Primordial Age, the flaming earth cooled down forming stratified rocks. The steam condensed into heavy rain which formed rivers and seas. There was no sign of life.

The Archezoic is the first well-defined geological age. There were volcanic eruptions which had buried the forests deep in the earth to form the later coal mines. Yet no direct evidence to show that life existed in this period is available.

The Protezoic period also lasted for hundreds of millions of years like that of Archezoic Age. Numerous mountains were formed in this period. Evidence of life could be seen through fossils available in places like Grand Canyon.

In the Paleozoic age, Fossils increased in number and variety. Australia and India had obtained their present form. It was rather an age of fishes. Primitive seed plants and farms are found in the great coal beds.

Animal life was abundant in the Mesozoic age. The first birds, flying reptile, flowering plants and various other types of vegetation also existed in abundance.

In the last age namely Cenozoic age, Mammals reached the apex of their variety *i.e.*, Man. The early human was ugly and unattractive with his body covered with shaggy hair. In this period the Great Fourth Ice Age came. Man was forced to seek shelter and to make clothing for protection from the cold. Many tropical plants and animals perished in Europe and northern North America and new plants and animals that could withstand the cold appeared.

The earth's surface is under going constant changes. For example, the Mississippi river adds a mile to its delta each 16 years; the Yorkshire coast in England is being eaten away at the rate of 7 feet each year, and Niagara Falls recedes, on the average of 3.7 feet a year. Deserts have extended and Earthquakes have resulted in the formation of new islands.

Origin of Life: The explanation of the origin of life is one of the most complicated and disputed problems in the study of the history of man. The primitive stories of creation attempt to prove the superiority of man over the other animals and to establish immortality. Many of the early accounts of the creation try to prove that man was made of clay through the handiwork of a God.

Such stories are absurd. Hence, the scientists had tried to unravel the secrets of life. There are two scientific hypotheses. One is the vitalistic theory of Lord Kelvin which explains that the life came to the earth from some other planets. Another is the mechanistic theory to which most scientists subscribe. They explain the origin of life through evolution. Charles Darwin (1809-1882) advocated the theory of "natural selection", of fitness to environment : the camel for the desert, the fish for the sea and birds for the air. He put forth his theory that all organic life is developed from one celled bodies to man, the most complex, and that man descended from lower primates. His two books "The Descent of Man", and "The Origin of Species" became most popular in this field. In the evolutionary process, man got the power of articulate speech that gives him the decided advantage that has enabled him to develop in culture. He has the ability not only to create, but also to preserve and transmit culture, which the lower forms of animal life have not developed. Men have taken intensive efforts to develop their culture and civilisation in the past and thus attained the present stage of civilisation.

2

Paleolithic Age

No documentary or other historical evidence is available with regard to the life of the earliest man and his culture. Hence we are forced to depend solely upon the material remains of the primitive tribes to make a study about the prehistoric culture of human beings. This can be broadly divided into the Paleolithic or Old Stone Age and the Neolithic or the New Stone Age.

Paleolithic Age: The word 'paleolithic' finds its origin from the Greek words 'Palaios' and 'Lithos'. The former means 'old' where as the later means 'Stone'. Thus, it means old stone age. In the evolution of man kind, Paleolithic age played a very great role and can be characterised as a land mark.

Paleolithic Period: The exact span of this period is a matter of controversy. Any how it is believed that this was the largest period in the human history of mankind. Some scholars are of the opinion that this period covered about 90% of the total span of time. Prof. J.E. Swain fixes this period by saying that it began roughly 300,000 years ago and ended about 15,000 years ago.

Despite the long span of time for the paleolithic period Man did not make much progress and it was at a dead slow pace. The causes for such a slow rate of progress could be attributed to the following factors:

(1) Four glacial ages intervened between the old and new stone age. Every glacial age had wiped out whatever progress was made by the primitive man.

(2) Man had to live at the mercy of powerful animals. He had no security of life. He was completely preoccupied with the prime duty of protecting his life rather than making any attempt towards his progress.

(3) The rapid changes on the surface of the earth caused insurmountable hurdle towards the path of progress of primitive man.

Physical Growth of Man

The Neolithic period reflects the gradual evolution of man. Before attaining the present shape he had undergone various stages which could be inferred from the archaeological excavations made at different places of the world.

1. The South African Ape Man: They are said to have existed over a million years ago. They are considered to be Austropithecus man. Since they were unaware of the use of tools, some historians do not consider them as men of this paleolithic age.

2. Java Ape Man: The Java Ape Man lived 500,000 years ago. He was halfway between that of a Chimpanzee and that of a man. The head was set far forward on the neck. The thighbone of this ape man was well adapted to standing erect. He had a height of five feet six inches. The remains of this type of man were found in Java in 1894.

3. Peking Man: The Chinese Paleontologists had found out the remains of the oldest known specimen of a type similar to man, in 1929. Evidences indicate that he must have lived more than 500,000 years ago. It appears that he could some what stand upright. Traces, of fire and stones used as tools are found in the same stratum of excavation. They are the first known human artifacts in history.

4. Heidelberg Man: The remains of this type of man were found in Germany. They are considered to have lived 300,000 years ago. They possessed teeth that were strikingly human. But their chins were poorly developed and it is ambiguous whether they had the power of articulate speech.

5. Piltdown Man: The skull bone of this type of man was found in Sussex, England in 1911. His brain capacity was much bigger than the Java man, but much less than that of the modern man. He had an unusually powerful lower jaw and possessed a very thick skull bone like that of the Ape's. Some crude stone implements were also found in the same stratum which indicate that the Piltdown man had made considerable progress.

6. The Neanderthal Man: Material evidences about the Neanderthal Man are amply available. He belongs to period of 100,000 years ago. It is believed that he was the real ancestor of man of today. He had a large brain and still looked like an ape. He had a long sloping forehead, heavy jaws and teeth, slightly developed chin and protruding jaws. He lived in caves, used fire, killed animals for food and clothing. He made crude stone axes.

7. The Cro-Magnan Man: The remains of this type of man were found in France. Since he resembled the modern man, he too was included in the group of Homo-Sapiens. He lived about 35,000 years ago. Caves were his dwelling places. He was a great hunter. He was about 180 cm high, of good complexion, broad faced and had long legs. He used bones as needles and also known the use of needles for sewing the skin of animals which he used as his clothes. He had artistic talents. Pictures with columns still distinct can be found on the walls of caves that he occupied. Body ornaments made of teeth of wild animals and shells were extensively used. It appears that the fat of animals was used for light in the lamps.

Paleolithic Culture

The Paleolithic man was a nomad and a hunter. He lived in caves, made stone tools, designed clothing from skins of animals. His chief tool was the 'first hatchet'. Later in the Paleolithic age, bone and home tools came to be used. It is interesting to note that most of these tools were found along the river banks.

During the later part of this age, man learnt the art of making a fire either by rubbing together pieces of wood or by striking a flint producing sparks. The fire revolutionised his mode of living. He could cook his meat and preserve it longer. He could have used it to keep off the wild animals in the night and thus made his life comfortable.

The use of bones as needles and skin of animals as a cloth was also a significant features of this age. He became conscious about the need and necessity of putting on something on their body. They now did not like to remain nude and naked.

Later on, Paleolithic man began to hunt bigger animals like the wooly mammoth hippopotamus, European bison and the steppe horses so common in central Asia. It is inferred that man must have lived in organised communities and must have co-operated in hunting big animals.

The men of this period developed art through cave paintings and sculptures. Forms of animals were painted on the walls of caves or engraved on tools and weapons. Later came paintings of human beings. Men were usually painted in the nude form while female forms were covered with shirts made of skins of animals. It shows that man had reached a creative state on his road to civilisation.

Another step of improvement in the life of the Paleolithic man was the basis he laid for the need and necessity of a language for the posterity. Of course, the very idea of a language and its development had its beginnings in this period. Despite the vocabulary was very limited, it formed the root for the growth of a language.

With all the above features of the Paleolithic man, one can perceive that he had developed a social order, a law, justice and religion. He produced art, told stories and played his games. Of course, the progress was very slow. Yet definite advancement was made in this age. His invention of fire, stone tools, use of bones, paintings etc. are some such useful important efforts that really contributed in the advancement of mankind during subsequent periods.

3

Neolithic Age

Origin of New Stone Age: Neolithic Age is another important land mark in the history of the world civilisation. The word 'neolithic' derives its origin from the Greek work 'neos' meaning 'New' and 'lithos' denoting 'Stone'. In this age, the weapons and equipments were well finished and polished, a definite improvement over those Paleolithic age which were rough and crude.

Period of New Stone Age: The New Stone Age began about 15,000 B.C. and ended with the commencement of the Metal Age. But this transition from Neolithic age to Metal Age took place at varying times in varying Places. For instance, Copper was used in Egypt about 4000 B.C. but it was not available in Scandinavia and in Britain it appeared only after 2000 B.C.

Centres of New Stone Age: Of Course, New Stone Age culture appears to have been widely dispersed, but its earliest evidences were seen in North Eastern and South Western Africa. It developed all over the world slowly and gradually but the centres of its development were the Nile Valley, Tigris and Euphrates rivers in Mesopotamia, Indus river, Hwang Ho river, Crete islands, Andes Mountains and Yucatan Peninsula regions.

Salient Features of the Neolithic Age: The Neolithic man profited from the experience of the earlier culture. He polished stone implements with sand and made beautiful knives. The invention of the bow and arrow made hunting easier. The axe became heavier and was fitted with a wooden handle. Instead of depending completely on the skins of animals for clothing, the Neolithic man used flax and wool from which threads were spun for weaving them into cloth. He built houses from hewn logs. Villages were constructed in lakes on long wooden platforms, supported by thousands of piles, to afford protection from enemies and wild animals.

Agriculture: His most important achievement was agriculture. Until then, animal flesh, wild fruits and wild vegetables formed his staple food. But now he made wooden ploughs and hoes. He started cultivating wheat, barley, millet, fruit and flax. In the neolithic period, Man began to settle down permanently. This kind of transformation from the life of a nomad to that of a farmer is one of the most striking features in the whole history of man. When life became settled, society became orderly and this became the starting point of human civilisation and culture. In this period women did most of the farming works while men did the fighting and continued to hunt.

Rearing and Domestication of Animals: The Neolithic man began to rear and domesticate certain animals for his assistance. The domestication began with the dog as one of the first, followed by the cow, the sheep, and the ass. Pig, camel and fowls were the other animals. He also began to keep herds and for feeding them, took to nomadic life. The dog helped him in hunting and also for protecting their cattle.

Development of Arts and Crafts: Art of pottery and earthen wares were developed quickly. Beautiful colours were applied on the potteries which assumed graceful form. Textile weaving and basketing were the new crafts of this age. Vegetable fibres were used for the purpose of weaving. They made rope nets for fishing purposes. The most important invention of this period was wheel. The cart with the wheels became his chief means of transport. This invention accelerated the pace of progress and communication between different groups became quick and feasible.

Society: As there was plenty of food, the population increased. The head of the family now enjoyed great respect. People had an elaborate political organisation. The tribe was divided into a number of clans, which in turn were divided into a number of maternal families. The tribe was ruled by a chieftain and the various chieftains represented their respective tribes in a league, which became the governing body of the confederated organisation. The principle of division of labour among the people also emerged in this period. There were farmers, miners and traders and others. But the mining and trading works were in rudimentary conditions.

Communal Life: When people had settled life, the community life also began among them. They built houses from hewn logs. Villages were constructed in lakes on long wooden platforms, supported by thousands of piles. Such constructions provided them protection from enemies and wild animals. They made boats by burning the inner parts of the long logs.

Such boats were used for going from one place to the other in the rivers. Gradually, group and family life began to emerge. They lived in organised societies governed perhaps by a council of elders. Their activities and relationships were governed by customs which was law for them.

Religious Beliefs: The New Stone Age man had belief in the supernatural powers. They developed a sort of crude magic. They worshipped Mother Earth and Sun. The excavation of a temple for sun proves this fact. Human sacrifices were offered to propitiate the Gods. They worshipped ancestral spirits and some ceremonies were performed at the time of death. There are signs of elaborate burial ceremonies, which is an indication of belief in future life. They erected stone monuments consisting of either single pillars called Menhirs or groups of pillars called Dolmens. Dolmens consisted of three or four stones supporting another. Some of them were surely tombs, while others might have been places of worship or memorials of great events. Religion became part and parcel of their life. Every action was begun with religious ceremonies. Slowly, Gods took the place of these spirits. Polytheism, thus became a common feature among them.

Language Developments: The primitive men might have imitated natural sounds to express their thoughts. Sometimes they must have gesticulated with appropriate cries. It marked their early speech. Modern languages arose out of these rudiments. The picture working like the Egyptian hieroglyphics mark the beginning of writing. It took many centuries before writing became an art. The invention of writing was the most important event in the history of mankind. It helped the growth of government. Laws of a country could be put into working. The officials could make periodical reports to the rulers and also receive orders from them. The technique of writing had exerted a remarkable effect on business life.

Advancements Made By Neolithic Man: Neolithic man used beautiful and sharp equipments. He was also aware of the use of metallic equipments. He started living a settled life and hence there was no necessity for him to be roaming like the nomads. He made agriculture as the main occupation in which ploughing was one of the processes. He developed a flair for art. He applied colours in the potteries. Colours were used for making flowers and animal faces. He started weaving cloth and was using clothes. His invention of wheel was the most remarkable one which had revolutionised the communication system. Since they had a settled life, they were able to develop a social system and a cultured life. They had orgainsed family life by obeying to the commands of the head of family. Organising themselves in to tribal clans was also started. Besides, obeying to the tribal chiefs had paved the way for the monarchical type of political set up in the future.

Conclusion: Thus, the Neolithic men had made definite advancements in their way of life and thereby registered gradual improvements in their civilisation. Because of several far reaching improvements made in this period, it was charterised as Neolithic Revolution by certain scholars.

4

Egyptian Civilisation

Egyptian Civilisation was one of the ancient and most advanced civilisations of the world. It was called as the "Land of the Pharaohs", "Land of Pyramids". It was also called as the "Gift of Nile" because Egypt owes everything to the river Nile without which it would have remained as an extension of the Sahara Desert. Hence, it was called by the name the "Daughter of the Nile". Because of various congenial natural conditions the Nile Valley had been made as the "cradle of civilisation". The various monuments that are available in Egypt bring to lime light about this marvellous civilisation.

People: Nothing is known about the origin of the Egyptians. Some scholars are of the view that they were crossbreed of Nubian, Ethiopian and Lybian elements. Others say that they were a Semitic people or Armenoid immigrants. Perhaps people from western Asia might have migrated into the country between 4000-3000 B.C. and their inter marriage with the original inhabitants would have resulted in the Egyptian people.

Sources: There are umpteen sources to make a study about the splendid features of this ancient civilisation. They are Pyramids, Sphinx, Obelisk, Temples, Tombs, Mummies, Inscriptions, Paintings and written works of Greek historians. Each monument speaks volumes about this wonderful civilisation.

Kingdom of Egypt: There were three kingdoms during the period of the ancient civilisation. They were known as: (a) Old Kingdom; (b) Middle Kingdom and (c) The New Kingdom.

Old Kingdom: During the period of Old Kingdom, Egypt was divided (i) Upper Egypt and (ii) Lower Egypt. These two vied with each other in order to achieve supremacy over the other. Menes, a most powerful pharaoh combined these two Egypts in 3000 B.C. and established his capital at Memphis. Menes and his successors ruled over this kingdom with absolute power and control and the people looked upon them as partly divine. They loved art and sculpture. Earliest pyramids were built by the rulers of this dynasty. The people were much influenced by the religious ideals. Their art and architecture came to be expressed only through their beautiful and massive Temples and Pyramids.

Middle Kingdom: During the Medieval Kingdom, authority of the Pharaohs had declined and the power and prestige of the feudal lords ascended. This happened especially after the death of Pepi II the pharaoh in 2644 B.C. But after a lapse of four hundred years, authority of the Pharaohs was restored by another valiant ruler namely Amenemhet I. He made Thebes his capital. His son Sonusret I, established a strong administration and built a great canal connecting Nile with the Red sea. After Amenemhet III, the country was plunged into another period of chaos and confusion owing to the invasion of Hyksos from Asia.

New Kingdom: Thutmosis I over ran the Hyksos and founded the New Kingdom. He was a great conqueror. He built a powerful fleet and invaded the near East and the adjacent island of Cyprus. His daughter Hatshepsut then ascended on the throne. She was the first great woman ruler in historic times. She was more interested in having great temples built and in developing commerce than in fighting wars. On her inscription, she was called "Son of the Sun" and "Lord of the Lands". She maintained internal peace and saved the country from foreign aggression. She was succeeded by Thutmosis III sometimes called "The Napolean of Egypt". He was said to have ruled for a long time from 1479-1447 B.C. His reign was filled with glorious exploits, accounts of which are preserved on the walls of great temple at Karnak. In 525 B.C. the Persians conquered Egypt and thereafter Egypt ceased to exist as a powerful kingdom.

Political Conditions

The Pharaoh: The King Pharaoh was considered as the representative of God on earth. He was absolute in authority. He was leader of the nation both in peace as well as in war. He was an autocrat and all national resources were at his disposal. He used to maintain powerful army. He was the final court of justice. He was advised by a Council or Saru of the oldest of the courtiers. His claim of divine descent and "Alliance with the Gods" were the secrets of his prestige.

Government: The scribes formed the bureaucracy and the provincial nobles were in charge of local administration. They took the census, examined the tax returns. Some of them estimated the agricultural yield by measuring the rise of the river with the help of Nilometres. Civil and criminal law was highly developed. There was a gradation of courts from those of the "nanes" to the Supreme Courts at Memphis. The cases were argued in the courts through writing. Torture was sometimes used as "midwife to truth". Beating with a rod, was a common punishment. The worst punishment was by embalming with natron. Vizier was the head of the administration. He was the Prime Minister, head of the treasury and chief justice. He was the court of the last resort, but only next to the Pharaoh himself. He was not to make distinction between the rich and the poor.

Economic Life

Agriculture: Agriculture was the main occupation of the people. Herodotus gives us a vivid picture about the plight of the farmers in Egypt. Every inch of land belonged to the Pharaoh and the farmers cultivated it as his tenants. Major portion of the land was possessed by the nobles. The tenant farmers paid 10-20 per cent of their crop by way of state revenue.

The farmers though poor, led a contented life. Besides his usual revenue from the lands, the farmer was subject to forced labour as he was required to dredge the canals, build roads, till royal lands, carry the stones for building monuments, palaces, temples and pyramids. Meat, fish, wheat and vegetables formed his chief diet.

Industry: Besides agriculture, people were engaged in industries also. The construction of Pyramids and palaces necessitated a large group of trained technicians. Granite quarrying, Brick making, Masonry, Metallurgy, Wood craft were important occupations. Mining of Copper and Gold also became other professions. Ship building became an important trade, as well as pottery making and cloth weaving. Their cloth looked like genuine silk. Beautifully glazed and painted clay jars, furniture, vessels of gold and silver found in the tombs manifest the superior level of technique attained by the Egyptian craftsman and their aesthetic appreciation of beauty.

In the field of trade and commerce, Egyptians were quite well advanced. Their ships went to Asian countries. A canal was constructed across the isthmus of Suez. Trade Provided the most important source of royal revenue next to Agriculture. The workers included free labourers and slaves. The son used to take up his father's profession.

There was a regular postal system. A high way passed through Gaza and linked Egypt with the Euphrates. Coinage developed slowly. Taxes were collected and salaries were disbursed in kind. Royal Treasuries were merely royal granaries where goods of all kinds were stored up.

Moral Principles

(1) It became customary for Pharaohs to marry their own sisters and daughters in order to maintain racial purity.

(2) Every Pharaoh had a select harem.

(3) Divorce was practised.

(4) Adultery was punished with immediate dismissal.

(5) Egyptian woman was endowed with full liberty.

(6) Woman was the mistress of the house and all estates descended through her.

(7) Dancing girls were welcome in the families to entertain guests.

(8) Religious prostitution was practised.

Manners

(1) Egyptians loved humour and played many public and private games like dice. They enjoyed wrestling, boxing and bull fights. The paintings portray the people as vigorous with a muscular body, broad shoulders, narrow waists, full lipped and with black curly hair. The women bobbed their hair and men shaved their lips and beards — Both men and women wore wigs.

(2) The women painted their lips and eye-brows, and coloured their nails and perfumed their bodies. Their burial remains show toilet sets, mirrors, razors, hair curlers, hair pins and other beauty aids.

Clothing was simple in the beginning but became elaborate with increase of wealth. The farmers and servants contented themselves with a loin cloth. They wore plenty of jewellery.

Education: Education was the key to open the world of professions. Priests offered instructions in schools attached to temples. From Temple Schools, students went to the government schools where they received instructions in administration. They made paper from the papyrus plants. This was a permanent contribution of the Egyptians to this modern world. They painted pictures with a reed pen. Egyptians borrowed their pictography from Asia. From this picture writing or Hieroglyphics, the Egyptians developed the 24 alphabets. This alphabet then spread to Greece and Rome.

Literature: Most of the Egyptian literature was written in praise of Gods and Goddesses. The earliest text was "Pyramid Texts" engraved on the walls of Pyramids. The early libraries contain papyri scrolls packed in dry jars. "The Book of the Dead" and "Coffin Text" are two important literary works of this period. Other important literary pieces were, "The Story of Shipwrecked Sailor" and the "Tale of Anupu and Bitu". They also wrote love and short stories and stories about ghosts during the Middle Kingdom. History was an old form of writing in Egypt. Official historians accompanied the pharaohs in their campaigns.

Science and Medicine

(1) Throth was the God of knowledge in Egypt. Immensely in the construction of the Pyramids, they developed a system of survey which became the basis of modern geometry.

(2) They had a curious numerical notation system. They represented fractions, but their numberator was always one. Thus, ¾ was represented as ½ + ¼. Their multiplication and division tables were as old as the pyramids. They produced a decimal system.

(3) They developed astrology, but scientific astronomy was neglected except for star tables. Yet they observed the planets and distinguished them from stars.

(4) They worked out a systematic method of recording time on the basis of the Solar year. Their year had 365 days with 12 months of 30 days each and five feast days at the end of the year.

(5) They excelled in medicine. Embalming gave them experience in the study of anatomy. A papyrus dating back to 1600 B.C. refects to 48 diseases and their treatment. They prepared a large number of drugs. Baldness was treated by rubbing scalp with the animal fat. They tried to promote health through public sanitation.

ARTS

Architecture: They had marvellous achievements in the field of art in which they excelled every country except Greece. Simplicity and massiveness were the chief artistic qualities of the pyramids. As pure monumental structures, pyramids have not been surpassed. The pyramid of Gizeh built by King Khufu and Pyramids built by many other Pharaohs still astonish the modern architects. Egyptians were the first to use square block masonry and the Pyramids design in architecture. The beautiful columns of the temples of Karnak and Luxor are still praised by our people. It is said that it took 2000 years to complete the temple of Karnak. The Hall of column is 180 ft. long and 138 ft. wide. On the walls of the column of the Great Hall are recorded the important events of Egyptian Kings.

Sculpture: Sculpture occupies the second place in Arts. They used wood and stone for sculptures. Realism and permanence were given priority in it. The sculptures are rigid in postures. Some of the master pieces that grace this period include the fine granite bust of the queen, the statue of Thutmosis III, the lion sphinx of Amenhotep III, Ikhnaton in lime stone and granite, statue of Ramasser II. Lion Sphinx of Amenhotep III which has been cut from a solid rock, is a beautiful example of Egyptian culture.

Bas-reliefs abound in Egypt: Painting became a handmaid to architecture, sculpture and bas-relief. In the Middle Kingdom distemper painting becomes prominent. During the period of Empire, painting became prolific. The paintings are true to life and their colour and movement make it a pleasing art to the eye. Music did not become a fine art. But still the rich refreshed themselves with melodies played on lutes, harps, flutes and lyres.

Religion: Egyptians were religious minded people. Religion guided every aspect of life of the Egyptians and determined his attitudes. Their belief in an after life and the care that they gave their dead are responsible for the preservation of a considerable part of the knowledge that is available about the ancient Egyptians. They preserved the bodies of the dead with such success that, after thousands of years, some of the Pharaohs have been identified from their mummies. They worshipped a large number of gods and goddesses. Each God had its own temple. Usually a God had a human body with an animal head. Amenhotep IV made a bold attempt by locking out the temples of many Gods and ordering the people to worship only one Sun God 'Ra'. But he was overthrown by the resented priests.

The priests enjoyed a place of honour and respect. The Pharaoh stood at the head of the organisation for the control and administration of religion. He himself was a God, son of Amon-Ra, who ruled by divine birth, as well as by divine right. As chief priest, he presided over religious ceremonies and festivals of the Gods.

Sun God was quite commonly worshipped. Their other important deities were Osirius, Isis, Horus and Troth. Sun God 'Ra' was considered as great creator and destroyer. God of Nile was Osiris and it was also highly respected. God 'Set' was known as the God of destruction.

Decline and Fall: Egyptian civilisation began to decline after passing on to successive civilisations a priceless heritage. The reasons for the decline were as follows :

(1) The reign of Ramasses II was the last flicker in imperial rule before Egypt sank into dust. His reign was full of wars. He had

several hundreds of wives and left behind a progeny of 100 sons and 50 daughters. His progeny was so numerous that for the next 400 years Egypt was ruled by one or the other member of his family.

(2) Exploitation of the lower classes and religious intolerance had a retarding influence.

(3) The priesthood sapped the people of their material wealth and discouraged independent thinking. Bulk of the revenue enriched the coffers of the temples. While the royal treasury was depleted, the temple treasuries became replete with revenue.

(4) Egypt was confronted with formidable rivals more efficient in the art of war. Assyrians, Persians, Macedonians and Romans subjected Egypt in the order mentioned.

(5) Assyria, Babylonia, Persia, Greece and nations on the northern coast of the Mediterranean wrested trade from Egyptians. Thus, Egypt lost its trade, its gold, its power and finally its pride too.

(6) In 48 B.C. Julius Caesar captured Egypt's new capital Alexandria and gave Cleopatra a son and heir to the throne. Egypt could never be independent any more. In 30 B.C. Rome made it its province and Egypt, the land of the Pharaohs sank into oblivion.

5

Mesopotamian Civilisations

(I) SUMERIA

Geography: Mesopotamia is a land of ancient civilisations situated in the river valley of Tigris — Euphrates in the modern Iraq of South Western Asia. This fertile land looked like a crescent and hence it was known as "The Garden of Eden". Professor Breasted named it as "Fertile Crescent". Due to its fertility, nomadic peoples poured into this region from the various surrounding deserts. The most important group of people that inhabited the eastern part of the Fertile Crescent possessed a Semitic culture. It is believed that Mesopotamian civilisation developed in about 3000 B.C. Mesopotamian civilisation actually consists of three civilisations namely the Sumerian civilisation, the Babylonian civilisation and the Assyrian civilisation.

Rise of Sumeria: From all the accounts it appears that the Sumers were the settlers of the lowest parts of valley of Tigris and Euphrates. The Summers should have gradually settled over in this region only after 4000 B.C. Excavations about this civilisation were made by Paul Emele Botta and Sir Leonard Woolley. The latter based his whole study on the clay tablets of the period.

Sumerian tradition tells the story of a long period of prosperity and a well developed, orderly society. There are records of floods that destroyed the cities and accounts of the rebuilding of these cities. Greatest among them were Ur, Lagash, Uruk and Nippur. The Sumerians drained the marshlands and developed a powerful political system that lasted almost 1500 years.

Political Conditions: City state of Sumeria was ruled by a King who was called as Patesti in the Sumerian language. He acted as "the tenant farmer" of the God. His 'lease' was renewed each year, during a great festival held in honour of the God.

also developed. Most of their tools were made of flint. But copper, iron and tin tools were also known. Weaving and Pottery were also carried on. There were government overseers to supervise the weaving.

Sumerians had good trade relations with India and Egypt. This is evident form the available seals. Barter was the chief medium of exchange. But there was a recognised system of credit Social Life : Society was divided between the rich aristocrats and the poor people. The rich lived in palaces with all luxuries where as the poor lived in houses made of adobe. The middle class included small businessmen, scholars, physicians and priests. There was proper drainage and sewage system.

Marriages were regulated by laws. The wife had an exclusive right to the dowry given to her. She enjoyed equal rights on her children and property. But man remained the Lord of the house for all practical purpose. Women were also attached to every temple either as menials or as the concubine to the priests. The women were expected to give many children to her husband and the state. Sterile women were divorced. But the woman of the upper classes enjoyed freedom.

Law: Sumerians had respect and regard for the laws of the land. They had a well developed code of law which touched all aspects of their life. It was not based on brutality but on reasonability. Ur. Engur and Dungi earned the credit for giving code of laws to the people, which subsequently became source of inspiration to Hammurabi. The code of laws protected the poor from exploitation. The priests also performed the duty of the judges.

To conclude, we can very well perceive that the Sumerians had a well developed civilisation. Their love and taste for the fine arts is reflected by copper statue of bull excavated at Tellel-ubiael and that of silver cow head excavated from the grave of Queen Shabad. The invention of bronze and wheeled war chariots are a proof of the advancement the Sumerians had made in civilisation.

(II) BABYLONIA

Rise of Babylonian Civilisation: The Sumerian city states were invaded and conquered by the nomadic Semitic people from Akkad in 2900 B.C. About 2300 B.C. their authority too decayed and the Sumerians got an opportunity to become independent again. After about 100 years, however, another Semitic people, the Amorites from Syria again invaded the Sumers and under their able ruler Hammurabi, they again conquerred both the Sumers and Akkadians. They made Babylon as their capital and the civilisation which they gave the world is known as Babylonian civilisation.

Hammurabi (2123-2081 B.C.) was the greatest of the Kings of Babylon. He attained fame more as a ruler and organiser than as a warrior. He governed with an iron hand. He derived his authority from The Divine Origin. There are two chief sources of information for the study of Hammurabi's rule. They are a collection of 55 of his letters, and a monument bearing the code of laws.

The Code of Hammurabi: The code of laws is the most famous of all the remains of Hammurabi's rule. It is carved in stone shaft in which Hammurabi is depicted as receiving the laws from the Sun-God. He tried to make his subjects believe that the laws were divine. It is clear that Hammurabi did not originate all the laws for many of them appear in old Sumerian records. He simply codified and put them into force. This code, the oldest known in a complete form, is modern in several respects. Through this code an attempt has been made to reduce the influence of theocracy on the pattern of justice. Hence, Judges were appointed to try cases by the State in order to establish that it was the responsibility of the State to give justice.

Hammurabi's Code contain 285 laws and it covered all the classes of the Society including the highest and the lowest.

The whole code of conduct aimed at deterring the people from committing crimes. Accordingly punishments awarded were harsh. The Code was arranged under laws dealing with (a) Personal property; (b) Real Estate; (c) Trade and Business; (d) Injuries and (e) Labour. As regards criminal law, it was provided that the system of 'eye for eye' should be followed. The people who were well placed and prosperous were given harsher and severe punishments as compared with the low placed people. It was made clear to all that no body could take laws into his own hands. For the first time the slaves were given a legal right to amass wealth and buy their own property.

The laws were enforced and the punishments were executed under the supervision of the state. If a house collapsed and killed the son of a house holder, the builder must suffer the loss of his own son. Death penalties were common. Conviction for adultery meant death for both parties concerned. Harboring a run away slave resulted in capital punishment.

Women were conferred equality in owning the property, right of divorce and right to bring law suits. They could engage in business and become professional scribes. Justice to the widow and the orphan was assured.

The law also regulated prices of necessaries and the wages in all professions. Under the law of inheritance the sons became equal heirs. There were no lawyers in Babylon except priests who could become notaries. The accuser had to bear the consequences, if he failed to prove the guilt. The early judges were priests and the secular courts also had begun to appear. But the King remained the final court of appeal.

Babylonians After Hammurabi: After Hammurabi's death, Babylonia was conquerred by the Kassites about 1700 B.C. The Kassites destroyed much of the Babylonian civilisation. Anarchy and chaos prevailed every where. But Kassites were driven out by Nabopolassar. A brief but brilliant revival of Babylonian civilisation was brought about by his able son Nebuchadnezzar II (604-562 B.C.) He was the greatest warrior, Statesman, and builder of all the rulers after Hammurabi. Babylon regained her lost glory and splendour under him. He made it very beautiful, prosperous and magnificent. It was during his reign, that beautiful tower of Babel was constructed with 288 ft. wide base. He also constructed a beautiful palace with Hanging Gardens in the vicinity of this great tower. The Greeks had included this Garden among the seven wonders of the world. He constructed this for the pleasure of his wife, a native of mountainous country.

Social and Economic Conditions: Inequality among the social groups and special privileges to the select were recognised. There were three social groups. The wealthy could exact retaliation in kind for personal injuries; and paid heavier fees and fines. The second group had to accept payment of injuries and the third group the slaves were treated as personal property. Workers of various kinds were guaranteed of their rights. The craftsmen were to maintain the quality of their work by their skill.

Agriculture was the chief basis of economic life. Most of the land was filled by tenants or slaves. Nebuchadnezzar was said to have constructed a lake 140 miles in circumference. Wheat, barley, date and fruits were produced. The Grape and the olive were cultivated and later introduced into Greece and Rome. Trade was brought under governmental supervision. Business contracts are mentioned in the code. Deeds of settlement, leases and land deeds, promissory notes, interest rate, were all standardised and defined. People carried trade with the Indus and Nile Valley people.

Art and Architecture: Art was not that much developed as that of the Egyptians. Architecture has completely disappeared. Only literature furnish information about the temples. The tower temples known as Ziggurats were built in stages, like small artificial mountains. One such pyramidal structure was 650 feet high and built in seven stages. On the top of the tower were a shrine and rooms for the home of the God. The brick walls were covered with rich woven carpets, coloured tiles and mosaics, giving the structure beautiful appearance. Absence of columns are noteworthy.

Babylonian scriptures were inferior in quality and quantity to those of the Egyptians. Men and animals were carved in mixed profile. The development of seals, which they borrowed from Sumerian was their greatest artistic achievement. Every man in Babylonia from the commoner to the King had his own personal seal. The seals furnish an interesting source of information.

Literature and Learning: Learning was respected much by the Babylonians. Men were trained in temple schools for clerical work. Other types of cultural pursuits were also encouraged. They followed Sumerian cuneiform writing with slight improvements but it never reached the alphabet stage. The priests supervised and passed upon the written clay tablets before they were preserved in the temples. Mathematics, algebra and geometry were first developed by them. The Babylonians had opened schools where the students were taught arithmetic, business techniques and religion. They had also made considerable progress in astronomy, medicine and movements of the Sun, Moon and other Planets.

The great 'Epic of Gilgamesh' contains several different Babylonian myths. The whole epic, by comparison stands in literature as one of the magnificent portrayals of the struggles of mankind in war, in love, and in death. Some of the descriptions in the epic remind one of Milton's "Paradise Lost".

They had invented Sun dial and time was measured by water clock. In Mathematics, different signs had been invented which were used for commercial purposes. Mathematicians worked out tables for multiplication and division and for the halves, quarters, thirds, squares, and cubes of the most important numbers.

In addition to epics, there was a large amount of writing called "temple literature". Psalms, hymns, and prayers Epigrams replete with wisdom and Philosophy were common; "Avoid vulgarity and hatred", "Do not hasten to speak in public".

Religion: Babylonians were religious minded people. Marduk, god of Babylon was generally recognised as supreme. Ishtar was the goddess of fertility of masterhood and of creative principle everywhere. She had control over reproduction among plants, beasts, and human beings, commanded almost universal attention. Tammuz was her husband god of Vegetation, who died each year and went to the lower region. Ishtar always went in search of him and, while they were gone, vegetation died, but when they returned it revived. This explained seasonal changes.

Babylonians did not believe in personal immortality. Like the Sumerians they could never trust their gods beyond the grave. So they prayed to them for earthly pleasures and a long life on earth. The art of divination, the ability to foretell the future was granted to chosen individuals by the gods. A diviner used sheep's liver, the stars, an the planets, to foretell the future. Fear held the people in subjection, and the element of love, as a dominant factor in worship was lacking. Babylonians were relatively uninterested in after life, which they considered dismal at best. They concentrated on improving man's existence on earth.

Each temple had a priest. They got heavy amounts in offerings. They rolled in wealth and were the most influential money lenders. Being rich, they exerted considerable influence over the government. Sometimes they were even more powerful than the king.

Estimate: The importance of Babylonian civilisation is just beginning to be fully appreciated. Archaeological excavations of Germans have highlighted this culture. It is realised that most of the succeeding civilisations in South Western Asia and even Greece owe much to this civilisation. Babylonians studied the past unhampered by the idea of future life. They preserved many legends which present an interesting background for the Hebrew Bible. Science made a real beginning under their critical and analytical observations. They developed units for the measurement of length, cubic capacity, time and weight. In literature they developed the epic, psalms, fables and proverbs. The foundation of mathematics, astronomy, archaeology, history, medicine, grammar, lexicography and philosophy were established. Their intellectual contributions guided many a scholar in centuries that followed..

(III) ASSYRIA

Geography of Assyria: Assyria, the hilly country to the north-east was different from the plain of the two rivers. It had a good climate and did not need the careful irrigation of the Mesopotamian plains and it had a regular rainfall and was well watered by Tigris and its tributaries.

Early History: Assyria was occupied by a Semitic people in about 3000 B.C. Constant danger of invasion of the neighbouring warlike tribes made Assyria, a military state. Gradually it conquered the cities of Elam, Sumeria, Akkad and Babylonia and established its hegemony over Egypt and Phoenicia. The origin of this civilisation was Sumerian, developed by Babylonia and was borrowed by Assyria.

Assyria grew out of four cities Ashur, Arbela, Kalakh and Nineveh. The ancestry of the city unearthed near Nineveh goes back to 3700 B.C. The early kings of Assyria came from that city state. Ashur became the patron diety of the state. Sargen II (722-705 B.C.) and his son Sennacherib (705-681 B.C.) conquered the whole of the Fertile Crescent and extended the Assyrian domain from the Taurus to the borderlands of Egypt. Ashurbanipal was the greatest Assyrian ruler. He came to power in 669 B.C. During his long reign Assyria achieved its unprecedented glory and prosperity. He claimed that he was a great peace giver. He was also a great builder and Patronised arts and letters. About 22,000 clay tablets excavated throw much light on the rule of Ashurbanipal. After his death Chaldeans and Medes reduced Nineveh to nothingness.

Political Administration: The government was very highly centralised. The king was really a general, directing the affairs of the state, both civil and military, personally appointed governors and messengers kept him in close touch with all the important centres of his empire. Bigger cities enjoyed a degree of autonomy and the conquered people were left with their own religion, law and rulers. The Signs of revolt were always present and hence Assyria had to remain always armed. Military organisation was one of the chief contributions of the Assyrians. Their soldiers were among the first to be equipped with iron weapons, battering rams, and war chariots. The army was divided into corps of infantry, charioteers and engineers. The army was the state; everything centered in it.

The church was another prop on which the state depended Rulers lavished their wealth and even gave a part of war spoils and slaves, to the peoples. All laws were the commands of Ashur and all taxes were collected in his name. Religion of Assyria was borrowed from Babylonia and Sumeria and was adapted to the military needs of Assyria.

This adaptation was seen worth regard to law. The punishments had a tinge of martial ruthlessness. They varied from forced labour, 20 to 100 lashes to sliting of the nose and ears, castration, pulling out the tongue, impaling and beheading. In general, Assyrian law was less secular and more primitive than the Babylonian code of Hammurabi which apparently preceded in time.

Imperial governors were placed in charge of local administration. They collected the taxes, supplied the forced labour for public works, raised armies and led them in person in royal campaigns. That form of provincial administration was adopted by the Persians, who bequeathed to Rome.

Violence was one of the causes of the decline of the kingdom. There were frequent revolts in the provinces. Wars of succession often resulted in the assassination of the ruler.

Economic Conditions: The economic life of the Assyrians was practically the same as that of Babylonians. The rich Assyrians were rich landed aristocracy supervising their estates. Same system of irrigation and same types of weights and measures were used. Assyrians mined metals or imported it from foreign countries. By 700 B.C. brass was replaced by iron as the basic metal in industry and armament. They cast the metals, dyed their textiles and carried on glass industry. Sennacharib constructed an aqueduct which carried water to a distance of 30 miles.

Social Life: Society was divided into five classes. They were (a) the patricians; (b) craftsman organised into guilds; (c) the unskilled but free workman; (d) farmers and (e) slaves. The slaves had their ears pierced and heads shaven to distinguish them from the rest of the society. Like all military states, Assyria encouraged a large population. Abortion was a crime and woman who aborted was impaled on the state. Prostitution was a recognised institution and was regulated by law. The cuckolded husband could murder the paramour of his wife. The women however, were allowed to go about unveiled.

Religion: Religion did not exert any refining influence upon the brutality of the Assyrians. Infact it considered the needs of the state. Ashur, was a solar deity who was supposed to take delight in sacrifices of prisoners. It trained the people to be patriotic and at the sometime docile. Human sacrifice and magic were considered to be the way for securing divine favours. They believed in a world of demons and were armed with incantations and talismans to ward off their evil influences.

Science: The Assyrians borrowed medicine and astronomy from Babylonians. The stars were studied for the purpose of divination. They added some practical knowledge to chemistry in making glass and in the preparation of ores. They contributed for the growth of botany through their lists of plants. Large number of words like hanger, gypsum, camel, plinth, naptha, sesame have become part of the English language through the Greek.

Literature: The claim of greatness of Assyria depended on her libraries containing clay tablets. Ashurbanipal's library at Nineveh had 30,000 tablets. Mostly they were official records, astrological augural observations, prayers exorcisms, and geneologies of kings. Only a few were the literature of the country. Assyria did a great service in preserving the literary records of Babylonian. But for this service, much of Babylonian achievements would have been a closed book for the modern people.

Art and Architecture: Of course the Assyrians borrowed art from Babylonia but they excelled the Babylonians in bas relief items. Arterial prosperity of the country encouraged the artists to produce Jewels of all kinds, cast metals with dexterity, made beautiful furniture studded with gold, silver bronze and precious stones. They were not good at pottery. However, Assyria excelled intempera painting in bright colours over a thin glaze.

Bas — relief became an efficient art during the key days of Sargon II, Sennacherib, and Ashurbanipal's Animals were portrayed more successfully than men. Human figure are stiff and coarse, with large heads, long whiskers and invisible necks. Horses and lions seem to have been favorite subjects. The horses of Sargon II on the reliefs of Khorasabad, the wounded lioness from Sennacherib's palace, the dying lion from Ashurbanipal's and the resting lioness are still recognised as master pieces in bas-relief.

But in sculpture they remained mediocre. However, the sculptures of Assyrians were more realistic and life like than that of the Babylonians. The carved animals are full of power and majesty. This is evident in the case of winged bulls at Khorasabad. Another distinguishing master piece is the statue of Ashurbanipal II, now lying in the British museum.

In architecture, they cared more for the size than the beauty. The mighty rulers of Assyria were also great builders. Tiglath Pileaser I rebuilt the temple of Ashur. Sargan II constructed his palace at Dur-Sharrukui. Its gateway was flanked with winged bulls. He built a Ziggurat of seven storeys, topped with silver and gold. Ashurbanipal II constructed a beautiful palace at Kalakh and ornamented it with bas-reliefs praising piety and war. Sennacherib raised his "incomparable" a royal mansion at Nineveh.

Decline of Assyria: The magnificent and grand civilisation of Assyria vanished immediately after the demise of Ashurbanipal the great. The main factor for the decline of Assyria was its exclusive reliance on foreign wars and conquest, for its financial needs. So, they were not able to bear with any decisive defeat. Another factor was the neglect of agriculture due to their military preoccupations. All alien people in the country created hostility to the nation. The far flung frontiers were exposed to barbarian attacks which exhausted its resources in an endless defence of the country.

Ashurbanipal died in 626 B.C. After a lapse of fourteen years, a Babylonian army under Nebopolassar captured Nineveh and razed it to the ground. Assyria was erased from history. Near East remembered Assyria as merciless unifier of weaker states. The Hebrews remembered Nineveh as city full of lies and robbery. In fact, when the power of Assyria was broken there was a general sigh of relief.

(IV) CHALDEA

One of the magnificent and most remarkable civilisations that emerged on the eastern region of the Fertile Crescent was Chaldean civilisation. Perhaps it was the last in the series. The martially splendid civilisation of Assyria was revaged by Babylonian ruler Nabopolassar with the aid of Medes and Seythians. Nineveh was razed to the ground. Babylon was restored once again. Chaldeans were the last Semitic people who established their paramountcy in Mesopotamia. Under their aegis, Babylon once again ruled the Tigris — Euphrates valley with great pomp and pride.

Geography of Chaldea: Chaldea was located in the Southern Iraq of the modern day. The southern part of the ancient Babylonia was formed as Chaldea. Bible calls Chaldea only by the name of Babylon. Strictly the name Chaldea should be applied to the land bordering the head of Persian gulf between the Arabian desert and the delta of the Euphrates. This part of the region was called as Kaldu by Assyrians, as Kasdu by Babylonians and as Kasdin by Hebrews.

Emergence of Chaldea: No reliable and authenticated source are available to know about the origin of Chaldea. But it is known that a certain semi nomadic race of Arabia had settled in this region and captured the coty 'Ur' and the adjoining areas.

Early History: Only scany historical sources are available to draw a outline of the early history of Chaldea. Not even archaeological evidences are available to augment the data collected already about them. But the majority of the materials are derived from the life sketches of the contemporary rulers of other countries.

Early references about the Chaldeans are found in the life history of Ashumasirpal II (884-859 B.C.) Yet this region was referred as "Sea

Lands" in the references earlier than that of Ashum, asirpal II. Assyrians had categorically segregated the Chaldeans from their north Babylonian neighbours, Aramaic people and Arabians. By 850 B.C. Shalmanesar III, the ruler of Assyria plundered Chaldea and conquered the regions up to the Persian gulf which he called by the name of "Sea of Kaldu" or "Bitter sea". But his victories were only short lived. His successor Shamshi Adad V had to intervene into the internal affairs of Chaldea and thereby had to renew his authority over them. At that time, the Chaldeans were extending their support to the rebellious leader Mardukbalatsu — Iqhi of Babylon. But the later ruler Adadnirari III (810 B.C.) claimed that Chaldeans were one of his feudatories. Chaldeans were not under the suzerainty of Assyrians for a long period. Because the ruler Tiglath Pileser of Assyria (745-727 B.C.), who went on a military expedition had to face the revolts of the Sheiks of Chaldea.

Achievements of Chaldean Kings: While Sargan II (722-705 B.C.) ascended on the throne, the ruler of Bit-Yakin region of Chaldea was Marduk Ilabina II. He attacked Babylon and captured it at that time. It is this king who so referred as Merodach — baldan in the Bible. He retained Babylon under his control for a period of ten years (721-710 B.C) despite the stout opposition from the Assyrians. He also tried to instigate the western kings. This information also is referred in the Isaiah's account of the Bible. Moreover, he sent has embassy to Hesekiah king of Juda in order to derive his support for his conspiracy. But after a brief span of a single year of rule over Babylonia in 703-702 B.C. Merodach baladan had to run away from the country. Hence, his native land of Bit — Yakin was brought under the rule of person nominated by the Assyrians.

Conquests of Chaldeans: After the decline of Assyrians the governor of Chaldea Nabopolassar tried to establish his sovereignty in the northern region. By 626 B.C. with the approval of the people, Nabopolassar assumed the religions of the government of Babylon. Thereby he commenced the rule of Chaldeans in Babylon. This Chaldean dynasty ruled up to 539 B.C. when the Persians invaded into this region. The successors of Nabopolassar were Nabu — Kurriusur (605-562 B.C.) and Nabonidus (556-539 B.C.). They ruled the country with fame and name. Since the Chaldeans had acquired such a high esteem among the people of Mesopotamian region, they were regarded on a par with Babylonians. Both of them were considered to have belonged to the same race. During the regime of Nebuchadnezzar II (597-586 B.C.), he subjugated the kingdom of Juda and captured its capital city Jerusalem.

Estimate of Chaldeans: The fame of the Chaldeans could be derived from the scholars of the later periods also. For instance, Herodotus, Diodorus, and Strabo of Greece, had referred about these Chaldeans in their works. In the Book of Daniel and in the list of Priests and Persons educated in the classical Babylonian literature are also they found a place. The achievements of Chaldeans were referred in Astronomical and Astrological traditions. Ancient accounts of scholars had also provided the information about the Chaldeans and their expertise in magical incantations.

Scholars were of the view that the language of the Chaldeans were nothing but Arabic language. This was the estimate upto this twentieth century. But the truth is that it is only a regional language of Babylon.

6

Ancient Persian Civilisation

Introduction: By 1000 B.C. a group of people from the northern steppes, east and north east of the Caspian Sea, settled on the borderland of the eastern part of the Fertile Crescent. They are Indo-Europeans. Among them Medes and Persians were the two most powerful tribes who entered into the South Western Asia. The Persians lived for centuries in the high lands over-Europeans. Among them Medes and Persians were the two most powerful tribes who entered into the South Western Asia. The Persians lived for centuries in the high lands over-looking-the Tigris-Euphrates valley.

Persian State: By 549 B.C. Cyrus a ruler of Anshan of Persians seized the throne of the Medes and established the Persian Empire including Asia Minor and the entire Mesopotamia valley. Soon he conquered Afghanistan and Punjab too. But in 528 B.C. he was killed in a war against the Mesegatae tribes. Except for his military victories little is known of Cyrus who earned the title "The Great". He respected and preserved many of the ideas of the conquered states.

He was succeeded by his semi-mad son Cambyses. He had a very brief period of rule between 528-521 B.C. But his successor Darius I (521-485 B.C.) revived the Persian power with greater grandeur. Darius, was a great military genius and a great religious and political organiser. He managed to reunite the old empire of Cyrus and extended his realm into India and Africa, and across the Bospharus to Thrace. His first reverse came at Marathon where his army was routed by the heroic Athenians under their King Miltiades. But his son Xerxes (485-465 B.C.) continued the struggle but reverses came one after another from the rising power of the Greek city state. Alexander the Great put an end to the glory of the Persian state in 331 B.C.

Provincial System of Darius: He was the greatest of the Persian organisers. He set an example of one-man government. He made himself king of Egypt and Babylonia and divided the rest of his territory into 20 provinces. Each province was called a Satrapy ruled by a governor called a Satrap. The Satraps were responsible to the king and also directed the civil and military administration of his Satrapy.

In order to keep the Satraps under control, Darius sent a general independent of the Satrap to command the provincial army. Further, a secretary was also stationed in the capital of Satraps to observe and report about the actions of the officials to the king. In addition to that a Special Agent travelled throughout the empire in order to keep the emperor informed. He was known as "The king's Eyes and Ears". Military Roads and canals were constructed for the movement of troops to suppress any rebellion.

The will of the king was the law of the land. The laws were supposed to be inspired by Ahura Mazda and hence were considered to be divine. In the beginning the priests were the judges and later on there emerged a class of lawyers who expanded the law to the litigants. Speedy Justice was assured by fixing a time limit for deciding cases. Cambyses assured the honesty of the Judges by flaying alive dishonest members. Flogging was the punishment for minor crimes. But serious crimes were punished according to the gravity of the crime. Death penalty became barbarous and it formed a heritage of Perisa to prosperity.

Zoroastrianism, their religion formed the basis of their administration. It taught them that the rulers were responsible to God. It also ordered them that they should govern wisely, justly and piously. The citizens too started the same spirit and considered it their duty to help the king in administration.

Social Life: Persians were the most handsome people of the near Eastern regions. They were vigorous and hardy people with well developed features. Both sexes were fond of cosmetics and fragrance. Though the Persians spoke many languages, the court language was something like that of Sanskrit. They borrowed the cuneiform writing of the Babylonians. But they reduced its 300 characters with 36 signs from which the modern alphabet was developed. Since they considered writing as a feminine work they did not produce literary master pieces.

Economic Life: Persians were engaged mostly in agricultural works. Their main crops were wheat and barley. Meat and wine were their favourite food items. It was said that Cyrus distributed wine to his army before war. The council commenced their discussions after tasting wine. Haoma Juice formed an important item of sacrifice to the Gods.

Handicrafts were encouraged by the states. Transport system was well developed in Persia. Metal roads were laid in order to connect all the farfetched areas with the capital city. One such road connected Sardis with Susa which had a distance 1500 miles. Distance was measured in the unit of parasangs and at every four parasangs there was a serais. It served as a post house and rest house for travellers. A relay of horses was kept ready to carry the orders of the government to the officials. The roads served as highway of trade and a media for the propagation of ideas, customs and superstitions of man kind.

Persians hated the trade since they considered market as a place of breeding ground for lies. Herodotus wrote that the Persian fathers taught their sons three things to ride, to use a bow and to tell truth. "Better death than to he guilty of a falsehood" was a common proverb among the Persians.

Art: Persians did not excel in art and architecture for their religion exerted inhibitive influence on it. Hence, they adapted the art of the people they conquered for their own monuments and decorations.

Yet remains of the palaces of Cyrus and Darius at Pasargadae and Persepolis give us some idea of Persian architecture. The main buildings were erected on a hill. At the top stood colossal winged bulls. The winged bull was used as a decoration for the capitals of columns. The tomb of Cyrus is comparatively well preserved at Pasargadae. It was built in Pyramid shape with six terraces, at the top of which is a gabled house.

The tomb of Darius at Rustam was carved out of a single mountain rock with its gate looking like a palace facade. On the top is carved the image of Darius praying to Ahura Mazda and dais borne by the prisoners of war. His palace at Persepolis had disappeared. But the flight of steps that reach the palace is so spacious that ten horsemen could easily ride abreast simultaneously.

People lived in beautiful villas surrounded by luxuriant gardens. Tables studed with gold and silver, couches, floor carpets for various colours adorned their houses. People generally had a great passion for poetry and romantic writing.

Religion: The most interesting legacy of the Persians was their religion. Originally they followed animistic cult but later Zorastrianism as became their accepted religion. The Persian tradition say that the founder of Zorastrianism, namely Zoraster was born of a heavenly inspired priest and a pious lady. Further, Ahura Mazda the true and all powerful God was said to have appeared to him while he was a young man and gave him the Avesta and bade him to preach it. As such, Zoraster, started preaching Avesta, the Bible of the Persians. But he was ridiculed and finally persecuted. Darius found in the religion an instrument to strengthen his authority and so he made Zorastrianism as the state religion.

Avesta was a digest of the precepts and prayers of Zoraster. They were complied by his disciples. They indicate the influence of Rig Veda and the elements of Babylonia and Iran. The world is considered to be a state of struggle, running for 12,000 years between the great god, Ahura Mazda and the devil Ahriman.

His allegorical conception of God and devil clearly point out the basic principles that man's soul is the battle ground between good and evil. Zoraster exhorted the people to fight and destroy the evil with the blessings of Ahura Mazda. This concept was centred round the golden rule. "That nature alone is good which shall not do unto another whatever is not good unto its own self". Avesta laid down three important duties of man. (a) make an enemy friend; (b) make the wicked righteous and (c) make the ignorant learned.

Piety was the way to achieve it. Honour and honesty were only next in merit. Piety being the first virtue, it became the duty of every one to worship Ahura Mazda with prayers and sacrifices. Temples and Idols had no place in this religion. Fires were lit on hill tops or in palaces or in the heart of cities.

Zoraster vividly narrated about the perpetual joys of paradise and the eternal sufferings of hell. The end of the world would be marked by the arrival of three prophets who would preach the faith again. The last judgement would follow. Ahura Mazda would come in all glory and majesty and ruin the power of Ahriman. All good souls would he united with their old bodies and would live a new life free from all cares and worries.

Zorastrianism served as a high standard of conduct for Persians for centuries. It had its impact upon other religions. Jews borrowed their ideas of hell and satan from the Persians and passed it on to Christianity and Mithraism. Even Islam was influenced by it. But later on in the hands of the priests, this religion suffered a lot. Soon, the superstition appeared and other gods like Mithra were included in their Pantheon. Hence, gradually this religion faded away.

Estimate:

(1) The Persians improved on the Assyrian system of political administration and made possible a period of peace and prosperity that lasted nearly 200 years.

(2) Their religion the most original of their accomplishments marked an important step in the attempt to satisfy the spiritual desires of man.

(3) One outstanding achievement of the Persians was that they succeeded in bringing the various civilisation centers under one rule.

(4) This work of unification began under the Persians, was carried forward with considerable success by Alexander the Great.

7

Hebrew Civilisation

The Hebrews established their kingdom in Palastine of the South Western Asia. The fertile and prosperous northern part of Palestine was called as Israel. But the southern part Judah was a land of barren rocks and suffered from the lack of rainfall. Naturally, the Israelites enjoyed affluence where as the Judeans experienced abject poverty.

The Hebrews incorporated many of the ideas of the people who lived in Palestine before their arrival. As such they initiated the houses of canaanites and followed their woolen dresses also. They learnt the art of warfare from the Philistines and improved their language with the influence of the Aramaeans.

The Hebrew State: Since the Hebrews migrated and settled in Palestine from the desert in a very long period of centuries there could arise no central authority to unite all of them. Besides, the pugnacious Philistines who lived in the south west corner of Palestine also prevented the possible unity among them. Saul was the first king who united the Hebrews. But the Philistines conquered them soon. David defeated the Philistines and reunited the Hebrews and other scattered tribes. His son Solomon had a period of plenty and prosperity and became the most renowned ruler of Hebrews. Later in 930 B.C. the kingdom was divided between northern and southern sections. Hence, the central government became weak. It was administered on the lines of an ecclesiastical organisation. Hebrews believed that it was God who ruled them all. A king was considered to be a necessary evil in order to maintain order, protect freedom of speech and develop trade.

Defeats and Downfall: Since the Hebrews were divided as Israelites and Judeans, they could not withstand the attacks of Assyrians. In 722 B.C. Israel was conquered and people were taken as captives. The Judeans thought that they were safe under the protection of their god. But soon in 586 B.C. the Chaldean king Nebuchadnezzar, attacked and destroyed Jerusalam. Some of the Judeans were taken as slaves and others took shelter in Egypt. They were guided by the Prophet Jeremiah while they were in Egypt. He was promising them on greater glory in the future. When the Persians defeated the Chaldeans in 559 B.C. the Hebrews returned to their native land. They developed a religion on the basis of their rich experience they had during their wanderings. Christianity emerged on the foundations of this religion.

Art of the Hebrews: Music formed a integral part of the religious ceremonies of Hebrews. Horp was an important instrument which accompanied the vocal songs. Though references are made about the orchestra, and choir, in connection with the religious service in their temples, nothing is so far deciphered. Excepting the "Songs of Soloman" in the old Testament of the Bible, no other Love Songs and dances are traced out.

The Hebrews' contribution to architecture, painting and sculpture is negligible. They had a high sense of imagination but they had not developed beautiful monuments. Their temple too had only simple structures without decorations. The basic reason for this was their religious instructions. Their prophets asked them to demolish all their images in 622 B.C. Besides, they were asked not to portray either earthly or divine figures in the artistic forms.

Literature of the Hebrews: Most part of the literature of the Hebrews is concerned with their religion and religious documents. They have both spiritual value and literary value. One among them, namely the "Old Testament" is the most beautiful piece of literature. It can be compared to the works of Herodotus and Gibbon in their historical value and to the works of Shakespeare and Gibbon in their poetic excellence. According to traditions, "the Book of Exodus" is an autobiography Moses.

Talmud: This is a collection of Laws of the Hebrew religion and the commentaries on them. It consists of the wisdom of the greatest thinkers of Hebrews. It is considered to be a library itself because it is a wisdom and mysticism of a period of 800 years. It is something like a New Testament to the Christians.

New Testament: Though New Testament was written at a later date, it is really a legacy of the Hebrews. It portrays the life and teachings of Jesus Christ through the gospels and Epistles of the Apostles. Paul is the major contributor in this book. His Apocalypse is a mystical work in which there is a promise of the Holy city, to succeed this sinful world. New Testament is a great work of imaginative and philosophical interpretation of life.

Contribution of Hebrews to Culture: Their contribution to culture is very meagre. Much of their literature is baseless. They used borrowed alphabet. They neglected all kinds of sciences. Their whole life was centered on God. They had developed metaphysics to a greater level and this can be considered as their significant contribution.

Religion of the Hebrews: The seeds of their religion were sown while they were living a nomadic life in the deserts. It attained its consummation with their ideals and their activities. Hebrews accepted many of the gods of Canaanites, Aramaics and Babylonian nature gods. Tammyz, the god of vegetation was the most important pastoral God. Later on the Israelites became more materialistic where as the Judeans kept up the spirit of their old traditions and built up a wonderful and philosophical and ethical religion on these foundations. Their cultural contact with the advanced people helped them in the development of an advanced religious philosophy.

Jehovah: Jehovah was the God of Hebrews and he was evolved from many sources. He was considered to be a god of war who would guard his people from their enemies. Prophets like Moses, David and Hezekiah worshipped Jehovah as a god of war. Jehovah was given the human form. The chief manifestation of the divine will was seen in the experience of the social process. Hebrews were given a history with a religious meaning. They considered that whatever happened to them, had significance in terms of Jehovah's purposes. It was Moses who gave the Hebrews their loving, all powerful and ever just god. He introduced the principle of one god. Moses took his people Hebrews to the Mount Sinai where God had made a covenant with the people and also gave 10 commandments. God promised them that they would be protected as long as they observed those commandments. Before Isaiah, Jehovah was considered to be a god as one among many lesser gods but Moses and Soloman considered him as "Great among all other gods".

Services of the Prophets: The Prophets of the Hebrews had rendered the work of formulation and codification of their faith. They placed Judaism upon a sound ethical basis making it a religion of morality. A prophet was one from whose mind the will of god can be deduced. Amos (760 B.C.) was the early prophet who considered that man's unique position was to he able to know and serve god. He believed that god had no material form but one could see, hear and feel him in spirit. He declared that oppression and social injustice was the sins of the nations. He was much worried over the oppressed people. He predicted the fall of Israel because of materialism and it came true.

Isaiah (724-680 B.C.) continued the work of Amos. He founded a prophetic principle which formed the foundations of Christianity. He guided the Hebrews at the time when the Assyrians invaded them under Sennacharib. He gave to his depressed people the Mesianic hope that a Redeemer would end their political divisions and end their misery and also introduce an era of brotherhood and peace.

Prophet Jeremiah (625-586 B.C.) established a monotheism and of Judaism. To him, god was super naturally great, omnipotent and holy. Ezekiel (6th century B.C.) another prophet advocated a rule of right conduct for every individual. He repudiated the idea of collective responsibility. Every one is responsible to his own misdeeds.

Thus, the prophets reformed Judaism and developed Jehovah from a Jealous god into an omnipotent God of love. They associated Jehovah's law with a Just Society. Under a Just God, social injustice would not exist. But through the mistakes of man miseries could be brought. Gradually, the concept of 'One God' was developed into an ethical monotheism.

Hebrew Religion After the Prophet: Hebrews accepted the idea of Jehova's being a universal god and they also clung the belief that they were the chosen people of god. They considered that by disseminating the knowledge of their god to the world they could convert the whole world into a paradise ruled by "The Prince of Peace" their own Messiah. It inspired them to the path of progress. But soon the priests occupied the place of prophets. They lost much of the spirit of the teachings of the prophets and became corrupt and worldly. Any how the idea of the coming of a Messiah was cherished by them.

Estimate: The most important legacy of Hebrews was their religion and religious literatures. Old Testament stands as the most precious legacy of western civilisation. Their monotheism, a god who ruled through love, and the high moral code of the people served as example for future ages. They believed that god had endowed every man with a knowledge to distinguish between right and wrong. An element of individualism could also be seen among the Hebrew conviction which became the germ of individual liberty.

8(i)

Hittite Civilisation

Hittites were a race of people who lived around 2000 B.C. in central Eastern regions. Hattushash was their capital city. It was situated in the central Anatolia near by Bogazkoy, a village in Turkey. They were akin to that of Indo — European language speaking people. These Hittites might have migrated in the western Anatolia regions from the Balkan areas sometime in 2500 B.C. Even though there is a controversy over the migration of these people, it is said that the Assyrian traders saw a race of people speaking Indo — European language when they had been to central Anatolia before 1900 B.C. That race of people were considered to be Hittites.

Old Kingdom: By 1650 B.C. a certain king called Hattusilis was said to have attacked the Hittites, captured their capital city Hatushash and established his sovereignty. A period of 150 years that followed is referred as a period of old kingdom.

Hitties wanted to monopolies the trade routes. Because, the raw materials for metals and minerals and the trade routes determined the development of a nation's economy. Their trade with Assyrians on the eastern direction was stopped since the trade route through Anti Taurus mountains was blocked. Hence, the Hittites had to recourse to another route that led to Northern Syria. They had to have contacts with other countries in this new route. Hathursilis tried to capture the Northern extreme commercial route from Aleppo but failed in it miserably. But his son and successor Mursilis I, conquered Aleppo and went on an expedition to capture Babylonia in 1595 B.C. But his expedition attempt ended in fiasco. Hence, he returned to his country without accomplishing his plans. People murdered him out of frustration. A period of anarchy ensued.

Middle Kingdom: Telepinus had tried to restore the failed pride of the Kingdom and tried to strengthen it. But during this period, (1500-1450 B.C.) a race of people called Hurrians had established a kingdom at Mitanni and captured northern Syria from the Hittites. Simultaneously, Egypt also had developed an interest over the eastern coastal regions of Mediterranean Sea.

New Kingdom: By 1450 B.C. Tudhaliyas I established a new dynasty and helped the Hittites to reach the apex of their greatness. He recovered the Northern Syria and conquered the eastern Isuwa. Suddenly, there was a slight deterioration in their power and authority. However, by 1380 B.C. Suppiluliumas had managed to recover Isuwa. He also conquered Mitanni. More or less the entire Egypt was brought under the suzerainty of the Hittites during the time of Suppiluliumas.

The credit of having conquered Western Anatolia goes only to Mursilis II. The period of his reign may be fixed in between 1345 to 1310 B.C. He established an efficient administration, based on sound principles and strict legal system. He also took care to implement all such legal codes in the day to day life of the people. He was highly cautious of the conspiracies hatched out by the Egyptians in the North Syrian border in order to launch an invasion into the borders of Hittites. Hence, he enforced rigorous regulations in the home land.

Ultimately, Hittites had to encounter the Egyptians at Kadesh on the banks of Orantes river. Hittites were led by their King Muwatallis. Egyptians were routed in the battle. Eventhough the Egyptians withdrew form the war, Assyrians now began to intervene in the Euphrates affairs and tried to establish their authority.

Hittites were affected much when their trade routes on the North Western area were closed. But, their power was completely destroyed when their trade routes on the south western regions were blocked. Thus, Hittites were eclipsed by cutting all their commercial contacts through which they were flourishing.

Kingship: Frontier areas were under the control of those who were related to the King. Landlords were regulated by the feudal laws. Local authorities, feudatories and provincial governors were bound by the contracts made with the king. The chief of the people was considered to be their king. Gradually, his power increased and ultimately he became a despot. It was believed that the king attained divinity after his death. Queen assumed the powers of the king when the latter expired.

Art and Architecture: The archaeological excavations made in the Hittites region had brought to limelight the colossal fort walls constructed for the protection. The fort walls and the temple were all made of mammorth designs. Such gigantic constructions could also be seen at places like Mersin, Alaca Huyuk and Yazilikaya. The sculptures in these places indicate their rudimentary levels but their attraction lies simply on their ragged and coarse nature. The statue found in the interior rooms at Yazilikaya exhibit their inner feelings.

Such a condition of rudimentary nature could also be witnessed in the seals of the kings, figurines and pots. Most of the pots unearthed were not ornamented. But they were polished with colours. Large jugs with mouth for outlet and vessels made in the figure of animals especially oxen were very beautiful.

Religion of Hittites: Their religious faith was more less based upon the Anatolian people's religion. They worshipped the female deities of the Anatolians. One among them was Arinna. Her consort Was Hurrian, the God of Storm. People worshipped Hurrian also. Besides these Gods, they had a pantheon of Gods. During their final days, many great Gods were called by the name of Hurrians. The main item of worship was begging the Gods for favours and the enjoyment of such benefits derived from them. They had developed a kind of sorcery by which they were able to predict great disasters and devastations.

Literature of the Hittites: There are mythologies and legends along with the above religious rituals. Epics of Human, Canaanites and Babylonians are read with intense interest just for the sake of their literary flair. Among the literature of the Hittites, the annals and chronicles of Kings of the Hittites were known for their literary style. They are much useful for studying the history of the Hittites, surveying the cause and effect of studies, and to learn things in the present from the past experiences.

8(ii)

Phrygians

Phrygia was a country in the Asia Minor and it was a plateau region situated on the west of Halys. The name Phrygia is generally used to refer to a race of people rather than that of piece of land. The land here is cut by several valleys. The western part of Phrygia was very fertile. Gold was available in plenty as it is narrated in the mythological story of Midas.

Political History: It is said that an ordinary labourer namely Gordius had founded this kingdom by 800 B.C. The names Gordius and Midas, the daughter of Gordius are frequently found in the Genealogical tables of Phrygians. But these statements cannot be tenable. In fact, there might have been a Phrygian civilisation previously. It might have spread over Lydia, Cappadocia, Lyconia and Phrygia and it might have evolved beautiful art and architecture. They also might have laid a great net work of road transport system. These roads were utilised by Persians later on. Their contacts with Greek city states in Asia Minor started in the 9th century B.C. They contacted with Greeks of Europe through their settlement in Sinope. But after a lapse of 100 years, the Phrygian Kingdom was destroyed by the invasion of Cimmerians in 680-670 B.C. The Phrygians were enslaved by Cimmerians in 620 B.C. then by Lydians, Persians, Macedonians and Pengamus successively. Ultimately, in 90 B.C. they were brought under the control of Romans. They were popular slaves under the Greeks even by 5th century. B.C.

Economic Conditions: Only very little sources are available which throw light upon their social and economic conditions. As per the oriental traditions, the priests who were endowed with autonomous powers were also owning the majority of the lands. It is so because temples were endowed with large tracts of lands. Society was based upon the feudal system. Though the word Phrygia literally means "free" they were sent to Greece only as slaves. The aristocratic Phrygians who were intelligent and highly cultured were said to have lived in places like Gordium and

Midas. They knew the art of reading and writing. Further, they were talented to have a flourishing trade and handicrafts.

The main occupation of the people was sheep rearing. Through this they manufactured woolen items which were purchased in large quantities in trade centres like Miletus, Pergamum and trade centres of Greece. Phrygian woolen costumes were world famous. It is generally believed that these Phyrygians were the first who started the embroidery works. Their excellence in embroidery works could be seen in the dresses of Urpalla,·the King of Tyana. The Statues of the Kings are seen in places like Ivriz and Bulgar Madan.

The forest near by the town Midas provided all the timber necessary for the Phrygians. Since they were exercising authority and power over the natives of their land, they had to necessarily learn the art of horse rearing and also horse riding.

Art an Architecture: Metallurgical works were carried on at a place called Tabal. They were able to manufacture implements which could be used for breaking the rocks and chiselling the rock blocks. Phrygians had produced beautiful architectural monuments. Such wonderful pieces could be seen in rock cut and hewn structures, sculptures and figures in temple facades. They had carved figures of beautiful proportions in wood also such wooden sculptures could be equated to those of Lycia. The ancient traditional mode of chiselling figure on the capitals of the Pillars was said to have been started only be these Phrygians.

Residential houses were unearthed in the city called Gordium. They all belonged to the 8th century B.C. Some of them were made of rock stones, bricks and some of them were built of timber. There is a gigantic city entrance along with its buildings. Fort walls of the city also have been excavated.

Sculptural monuments are meagre in Phrygia. Figures chiselled out of rock stones found at Bogazkoi are simply beautiful. The Goddess "Ma" was also called the "Mountain Goddess". It appears that the Goddess had worn a cloth in her head and two musicians standing on either side of the Goddess. One among them seem to play on Lyre and the other one playing with flute. Phrygians were much interested in music. It is said that Phrygians had invented the musical instruments like cymbals and flute.

Religion: They worshipped the Goddess 'Ma', the 'Great mother'. She was considered to be the "Mountain Goddess" and hence Phrygians worshipped the mountains themselves. This kind of mountain worship was passed on to Greece in the 5th Century B.C. and to Rome in 204

B.C. The statue for the great Goddess 'Ma' could be seen in places like Siphybes, Dindymus and Ida which were the seats of Goddess 'Ma'. Such Phrygians were converted to Christian religion by 2nd century A.D.

Alphabets and the Language of Phrygians: The alphabets of the Greeks and Phrygians were derived from the common Phoenician letters. Phrygians had invented the method of teaching moral lessons through animal characters. They are the animal fables which were later on developed as Aesop's fables. From this we can understand that Phrygians wanted to live with ideals and without vices. They must have considered righteousness and disciplined way of life as something more desirable.

8 (iii)

Lydia

Lydians were the most popular people in the 7th and 6th centuries B.C. of near Eastern regions. They were living in the areas of West Asia Minor. Sardis was their capital city. This city was situated at the source of the tributary called Pactolus of Hermus river. It was a fort city with an impregnable citadel.

Political History: We come to know about the Lydians for the first time from the clay tablets of Ashurbanipal of Assyria of 660 B.C. In the clay tablets, Ashurbanipal describes how Gugu the King of Lydia had accepted the supremacy of the Assyrians and how he was deported to Assyria. That King Gugu must be definitely the Gyges of Lydia. This was the king who had dilapidated Phrygian Kingdom of Midas. Only because of this great aggression the Lydians who were living on the South and Western regions of Phrygia came to limelight and had brought about a glorious civilisation. Both the great Greek historian Herodotus and the native historian of Lydia namely Xanthus, viewed that a dynasty called Heraclid had ruled Lydia. But no sources of genealogical history or archaeological excavation corroborate this view of Heraclid dynasty ruling the Lydian Kingdom.

Lydian Kingdom: Lydian Kingdom, which was quite well known to the Greeks was founded in the 7th century B.C. It was a period of political crisis in which Lydia emerged as a formidable power. It became a Kingdom which cultivated the cult of war and aggression under the leadership Mermnad King which meant "The House of the Hawk". The prophet Jeremiah of Hebrews called this dynasty as the mercenary army of Egyptians.

Lydia was a terror to the Ionians who were living on the sea coastal regions. The trading class Lydians though not sailors, had conquered not only the inland areas but also the ports of Ionians. The King Gyges with his strong cavalry had conquered the colophon soldiers. This information is provided in a Greek colophon by Mimnermus. Ardys, the son of Gyges had conquered a small region called Priene. Though Priene was defeated for a number of times, it could not be subjugated for it had a great commercial power. Hence, a pact was concluded between Lydia and Priene. It was the Lydian aggression upon the Ionians which caused the Ionian settlers to embark upon a greater area of maritime trade.

After, Sadyattas, the son of Ardys Alyattas ascended on the throne. He was the most successful of the five Mermnad Kings. He had driven away the Cimmerians to the eastern extreme and there by captured the city Smyrna. He did not solely rely upon his cavalry for this expedition but he followed another technique of besieging the enemy's forts. The huge heaps of stones used for the siege and the clay pots of 7th century B.C. helped a lot for the archaeologists of Turkey to fix up the chronology of the period.

Cyaxares, the King of Mede was jeopardising the Lydians on their eastern frontier. It was this king who had ruined Assyrians at the time of the rule of Alyattas. However, Alyattas after strenuous war against the Mede King had retained the independence and sovereignty of his country.

Alyattas was succeeded by his son Croesus. During his period of reign, Lydia had many memorable accomplishments. Economic prosperity, internal peace and above all, victories over neighbouring Kingdoms were the highlights of such accomplishments. He invaded Ionia and conquered Ephesus and other island cities. These victories could be considered as the apex of all other previous conquests of the Lydians.

In the meanwhile, Persians had established their paramountcy in Iran. Croesus had married his sister to the last ruler of the Kingdom of Medes. Croesus now formed in alliance with the rulers of Babylon, Egypt and Sparta against that of the Persia. But his attempt ended in fiasco. It was so because Cyrus the Great of Persia was a veteran in the strategies of the battles and hence he defeated Croesus very easily. Thus, the Lydians's power and authority were brought to an end by the Persians.

Culture of the Lydians: There are no proper and sufficient sources for studying about the culture and living habits of the Lydians. But we came to know a little through the archaeological surveys made by the Americans in the Lydian capital city Sardis. But to their surprise, the remains taken out from the excavations reflect the features of more and more of Graeco-Roman civilisation. But the huts with roofs filled up in the trading streets of the Lydians are found in less numbers. In short, we have to depend more upon Herodotus for a study about the Lydians. According to him, the Lydians living habits were more akin to that of the Greeks except prostitution found among the Lydian women.

The women of Lydia were permitted to carry on the prostitution business and to earn money for their marriage and money required for their dowry. It was also admitted by the religion of Lydians like that of the Babylonians. It was the Lydians who minted coins in gold and silver and also introduced the habit of circulating such coins for the first time in the world. Besides, these Lydians were the first to introduce shopping system with permanent trading centres and shops. Greeks had found the shops for the first time in their lives a place with a number of shops only at Sardis, the capital of Lydia.

Lydians acquired the knowledge of using the precious metals like gold and silver from their acquaintances made both in eastern ant the western directions. With this basic knowledge, they had evolved the method of utilising these metals for minting coins. Since it was in the beginning stage the coins were coarse and rough without any artistic execution. The invention of the coins after 150 years had revolutionised their commerce in Greece.

8 (iv)

Phoenicia

One of the most noteworthy civilisations that emerged on the western side of the Mesopotamian Fertile Crescent was the Phoenician civilisation. Their civilisation was more or less akin to those of the Greeks in their mode of life and other features. The present day world is indebted to these Phoenicians also in a number of ways. Let us examine these aspects which we can consider as their legacies.

The Land of the Phoenicians: Nothing is definitely known about their origin. Some scholars consider them as Semitic people and the natives of Tyre, one of the Phoenician cities. They might have come from the shores of the Red Sea and occupied a narrow strip of land between the Lebanon mountains and Mediterranean sea. The Greeks called them Phoenicians probably because of the purple dye their merchants sold, an extract from a tree that grew on the coast of Phoenicia. Their land was unsuitable for agriculture and hence they were forced to carry on trade for a living. The rugged coastline of Phoenicia furnished excellent harbours for their city Kingdoms. The Cedar forests of Lebanon provided them timber for the construction of vessels. From Tyre and Sidan, Phoenician sailors sailed throughout the Mediterranean, Black seas and perhaps beyond the Gates of Gibraltar into the Atlantic Ocean. They never attempted conquests but founded a number of cities.

Phoenician City States: The Phoenicians had a city State form of Government like those of the cities in the later Hellenistic civilisation. They established city colonies but there was no imperial administration. They stationed garrisons at strategic points along the Mediterranean coast and in course of time they developed into cities. Cadiz, Carthage, Marseilles, Malta, Sardinia, Corsica and Sidily saw the emergence of such cities. These city colonies acknowledge allegiances to the master city. The Governments of the individual cities varied greatly as each pursued its own course; but as a general rule they were very autocratic and despotic.

Trade Commodities: The trade of the Phoenicians was not limited to any one commodity or place. They mined gold, silver and tin in Spain and carried the metals to different parts of the known world. They excelled in metal casting. They manufactured glass by borrowing the technique from Egypt. They became famous for their stuffs dyed with Tyrian purple. These dyed stuffs along with imports of India wines, textiles and precious stones were sold to the wealthy peoples of eastern Mediterranean and exchanged for lead, gold and iron from the South states of the Black Sea, ivory from Africa, Silver from Spain. It was through this trade, they made known to Europe the lotus flowers, the sphinx and even the style of dress.

Pride of the Phoenicians in Trade: The Phoenicians were skilled craftsmen as well as traders. In their own cities they made beautiful pottery; they produced stuffs of gorgeous colours, they engraved metals; and they manufactured furniture. Homer referred to their beautiful tunics and their chains wrought of gold. Ezekiel mentions their carved ivories, and the Hebrew book of the chronicles describe their work in gold, silver, brass, iron and wood. Many powerful kingdoms depended upon the Phoenicians for the articles of luxury that they alone could produce or collect from distant places. Phoenician workmen were employed by Assyrian kings to make furniture for the royal palaces and by King Solomon to build the Temple at Jerusalem.

Nature of Their Trade: Phoenicians were very shrewd in their trade and always aimed at exorbitant profits. They made no difference between trade and treachery, commerce and robbery. They used to steal from the weak, cheat the stupid and appeared to be honest with the others. They committed highway piracy by capturing every ship they met. They used to attract the natives to visit their ships, captured them and then sold them into slavery. They fabricated stories like Seylla and Charybdis in order to frighten other people in their trade routes. Enraged Ezekiel had foretold the doom of Tyre and Sidon. They became quite unpopular in the eyes of Europe especially the Greeks.

Navigation of Phoenicians: They contributed much for the improvement of boats and ships. They introduced low and narrow galleys. They fixed a single rectangular sail to the keel for the slaves to row the ships. With this improvement in navigation, the Phoenicians sailed in the open sea with the guidance of the stars. They had also circumnavigated the continent of Africa. It was these people who first discovered the modern Cape of Good Hope. They occupied Rhodes, Cyprus and Milos and these became the centers of trade and places of refuge to the Phoenician sailors. With their trade they bound the East and West in a cultural union and save Europe from barbarism.

Economic Prosperity of the Phoenicians: The main source of their wealth was their trade. The aristocrats desisted from war and concentrated in enriching their cities and in controlling their administration. One among such cities was Sidan. It became a prosperous and wealthy city. It developed the technique of constructing ships especially war ships. It seems that the Phoenicians of Sidon had supplied best ships to the fleet of Xerxes when he invaded Greece. Another prosperous city was Tyre. It was their metropolis and the centre for the traders and slaves. It had become very prosperous under its ruler Hiram in the ninth century B.C. It had become the wealthiest city in the Mediterranean world at the time of Zecharia its ruler (520 B.C.). It possessed majestic buildings with several storeys.

Religion of the Phoenicians: Every Phoenician city had its patron deity. Baal was their God of fertility. People grew the wine, figs and flax through the blessings of this deity. Nelkarth was the God of strength for Tyre. This God was considered to be the cause for their martial marvels. Astarte was their Goddess of charity and also Goddess of physical love. Her women devotees had to offer their long plait of hair. Astarte was said to have loved Adoni who was murdered by a boar. Phoenicians used to mourn the death of Adoni by loud wailing and beating of breasts. Moloch was their most terrible God and hence they offered their children in sacrifice to propitiate it. Once at Carthage 200 boys of the best families were sacrificed to the God Moloch in 307 B.C. when that city was besieged by the Romans.

Their Alphabet and Other Contributions: Their greatest contribution to the modern world is their alphabet. They borrowed it partly from Sumeria and partly from Egypt and out of these they developed 22 signs. Each sign represented a single consonant and altogether all the 22 sign constituted the first real alphabet of true letters. The signs were arranged in a definite order so that they could be committed to memory was made by calling every sign an everyday word that began with it. The Greeks took their alpha and beta from the words representing a and b. All Western alphabets of the modern day were derived from the Phoenician source. It was these Phoenicians who introduced the pen, ink and paper for writing into Europe. They had very little literature. It was principally composed of business records. Of course these were religious records and treatise on farming.

9

Greek Civilisation

Introduction: Greece or Hellas is a Peninsula of about 25,000 square miles extending from the mainland of Europe into the Mediterranean sea. The Pindus mountains form the backbone of the Peninsula. It extends southward almost to the Gulf of Corinth. The Sea penetrates the coast line of Greece in many places forming excellent ports. This makes Greece an ideal place for its navigation of small ships. Wind was also favourable to their navigation. Besides, that soil was unsuitable for agriculture. The numerous inundations of the land caused by the sea and many mountain ridges influenced the establishment of their political organisations namely city states. There is a very desirable climate. The temperature is mild but not monotonous. It is not too hot in summer and too cold in winter so that the people enjoy long outdoor life. Under this climatic condition, the Greek had plenty of time to ponder on the higher things in life, and to pursue cultural heights.

Government: The Greeks had recorded little of their history during their migrations but they filled in the many gaps with a number of legends and mythologies. The Helen of Troy is a story about restoration of their Queen Helen of Sparta who was abducted by Paris a Trojan Prince. All the Kings of Greece formed a league and laid siege to the city of Troy where she was kept by Paris. This story abounds in imagination of the Greeks. The *Iliad* and *Odyssey*, the two great epics of Homer illustrate the heroic adventurous deeds of the Greeks. Homer mentions about the strong cities they built, the Council of Old men and the Assembly of the People. The city state was the outstanding political achievement of the classical Greeks. Each city had its own government, its own deity, its own religious ceremonies and its own individuality.

Many of the City States had representative governments, a form of council and a public meeting place. Decentralisation of powers was the most characteristic development in the Greek political system before

500 B.C. This kind of individualistic attitude was given up when the Persians invaded them and they aimed at unity and co-operation among themselves. They defeated the Persian at the battle of Marathon in 490 B.C. and at the battle of Salamis in 480 B.C. These events marked the beginning of a period of great activity among the Greek city States especially Athens. But at the same time, the struggle for supremacy in Greece arose among the city states. As a result the conflict between Athens and Sparta was not only a contest for supremacy but also a struggle between two ideals of culture. Sparata championed the cause of the privileged few, their rights and traditions whereas Athens advocated progress and the rights of people as a whole.

Sparta: It was a militaristic State. All the able bodied citizens were soldiers and devoted their time to military training. The males spent their time in fighting or living in a military camp. A boy of seven years was admitted in the military training where he had to spend 12 years in getting training. At nineteen he would become a member of the army. Spartans considered the death in the battle field a great honour than the survival after the defeat which the mothers could not forgive. The real pride of Sparta lay in the army, noted for its courage, discipline and skill.

Spartans did not have much industries and hence she did not possess a powerful trading class like that of the Athens. Every Spartan was expected to be good and brave. Hence, her cultural contributions compared with those of Athens were quite insignificant.

Athens: The Pride of Athens was furthered by their splendid victory over Persians. They visualized a great grand future for their City State and felt the urge to dominate the civilised world. They had a Council of Elders which had only very limited powers. But a more popular Council of Five Hundred was incharge of the political administration of the State. All citizens except labourers without property were given the right to hold office in the City State. They were generally chosen by the lot system. The military commander was elected. He soon became the most important official in the State with the support of the army.

Pericles (460 B.C.): Pericles was one of the greatest of the Greek leaders who came to power in this way. He was also one of the foremost patrons of art in Athens. Under Pericles, Athens reached the peak of her success. The government was efficient and reflected many of the most outstanding of Greek political ideals. The body of all the citizens formed the Government. It possessed the administrative, the legislative and the judicial functions. The popular assembly, formed by the citizens chose and removed the administrative officials and controlled the Judiciary.

But citizenship right was not given to all the inhabitants of Athens and hence it was not a democracy in the modern sense of the term.

The Greeks did not have the degree of social equality. There was constant struggle between the oppressors and the oppressed. Solon (600 B.C.) introduced the ideals of humanity in the laws of Greeks. He abolished birth privileges but regulated political rights according to wealth. Cleisthenes (509 B.C.) tried to break the power of the nobility in the assembly. While these two city states were flourishing, jealousy and hatred among them were increasmg mutually. Hence, they fought the first Peloponnesian war (431 B.C.). In the third Peloponnesian war (405 B.C.) the Spartans defeated Athenians completely. But the supremacy of Sparta was only short lived as she was in no way fitted to rule Greece. In the contest for the mastery over the Greece, Thebes finally won Sparta in the Battle of Leuctra (371 B.C.) and became the master over the other city States. Soon, the Macedonians under Philip invaded and formed the "Eternal Hellenic Confederacy" with Philip as protector in 337 B.C. He was assassinated while his plan was still in threshold. But his son Alexander the Great, desirous of materialising the dreams of his father, decided to form a great empire in the orient. He marched his army into the heart of the Persian empire and conquered. Finally, he led his victorious army to the Indus river, and after having conquered the whole of the civilised world known to him he died in 323 B.C. Alexander's career was decisive and brilliant. He was one of the greatest generals that the world has produced. His name is still remembered for his task of spreading Hellenic civilisation.

Social and Economic Features: The Greeks followed the footsteps of the Phoenicians and established colonies in the Black Sea, in Southern Asia Minor, and in Southern Italy and Sicily. The Athenian ships brought cattle and slaves from the Danube in exchange for pottery and wine. From Egypt and Mesopotamia, traders fetched carpets, rugs, precious stones, silk, frankincense and spices. The Western Mediterranean furnished grain, dairy products, woods, silver and gold. As a result of the conquests of Alexander, far reaching economic and social changes were introduced. A world market was formed. Which reached from Western Africa to Central Asia and India. Alexandria in Egypt, Antioch in Syria and Rhodes became great warehouses of the world trade. Goods arrived in Antioch from India, Central Asia and Iran while Rhodes served as a distribution point for Mediterranean ports. Alexandria was the center of much industrial activity. Roads were built and harbours were improved. Glass, textiles, perfumes and metals were built and harbours were improved.

Glass, textiles, perfumes and metals were produced and exported to foreign countries from Greece. Agriculture was also improved in keeping with the commercial activities.

The social inequality was conspicuous by the luxurious life of the upper strata of people whereas the poor people lived in suffering and privation. The creditors had the right to claim possession of debtors and hence every worker was always obsessed by the fear of debt and enslavement. Conscription was on the increase and hence revolution threatened constantly everywhere and ultimately it brought an end to its golden age.

Art of the Greeks: Greek art was built upon the firm foundation of the accomplishments of the Egyptians and the Aegeans. The Greeks possessed a specific track of taking some thing in the crude form and turning them out into a masterpiece. The development of the various forms of Greek art may be traced through three distinct periods — the archaic, the Hellenic and the Hellenistic. The archaic period was the formative period in the Greek art, the gradual emergence from barbarism and the infusion of ideas from other people. The Hellenic period was the culmination of the Greek ideal. The Hellenistic age was a mixture of Greek culture with that of the other peoples in the near East as a result of Alexander's victories.

Music: The Greeks developed music for the beauty and for its aesthetic qualities. Homer, the Great epic poet, composed and recited verses in hexameters. Terpander sang Homeric epic verses to the accompaniment of the cithara and started the practice of professional minstrels. They introduced the new style of marching songs and chants for marriages and funerals. Flute was a common musical instrument and by skilful manipulation beautiful music was produced. Lyre and cithara were very popular. Apollo's new-year celebration was presented solely with instrumental music. Pythagoras (570-500 B.C.) succeeded in developing musical sound scientifically, something that came close to being an opera in the modern sense of the word — "The Trojan Women" was presented in 415 B.C. Music in the Hellenistic period was accepted as an essential part of the culture.

Dancing was woven into a fine art with the choral singing. The Greeks saw its origin in the movements of the stars. Gradually dancing rivalled music in age and popularity. Socrates praised it as it made every part of human body healthy. There were folk dances for every major event in life and every season and festival.

Architecture: One of the features of pride of the Greeks was their contribution in architecture. Temples for the Gods of the city States were magnificent monuments. The Parthenon at Athens, built in 447-438 B.C. marked the zenith of the Greek Doric architecture. Today it has only a remainder of its ancient glory, but often in ruins it stands majestic, harmonious and beautiful. Another style of architecture was the Ionic order. It was characterised by the style of its columns. One of the best known examples of a building of the Ionic style in the Erechtheum, which stands near the Parthenon on the Acropolis. An admirable example of architecture, is the chargic monument of Lysicrates at Athens erected in 330 B.C.

The Hellenistic architects were concerned with secular buildings — They made innovations in the form of royal palaces, pavilions, country residences, libraries, museums end theaters. Cities were constructed with the greatest care. Alexandria bears witness to the glory of the city in the Hellenistic age. Corinthian columns were used extensively. The most characteristic features in this style is the capital of the column which carries elaborate decoration. The pavements were covered with beautiful mosaics and the walls were adorned with painted pictures.

Painting: Painting was done on vases in the early period. The ceramic art was known in Greece. The early vases bore geometrical designs showing charioteers and animals. Then came coloured vases. Some of the coloured vases were exquisite in design and execution. Painting reached its apex in Greece in the 5th century B.C. Polygnotus of Thrace, a contemporary of Phidias, portrayed distinctive characters in his works. Apollodorus introduced shading and painted on wood blocks instead of vases and walls. His masterpiece is "Priest in the Act of Devotion". In the Hellenistic period, painting became more worldly and more highly embellished. Apelles the court painter for Alexander the Great, and a great painter himself, founded a school of painting.

Sculpture: The sculpture of the Greeks is one of their greatest accomplishments. It provided a means of expressing their ideals and an outlet for the manifestation of their talents. In the field of sculpture, there was an evolution of development. The earliest Greek sculpture was crude and archaic. In the beginning of the archaic period, the sculptors used soft porous stones but they improved their technique. They began to use excellent marble stones which were available in abundance in Greece. The "Charioteer" at Delphic is one of the few originals remaining from that period.

In the Hellenic age, there were equally famous sculptors. Phidias of Athens (500-435 B.C.), friend and adviser of Pericles and the artist responsible for the sculpture on the Partheon was one of the most famous.

His "Theseus" is also one of the finest of the remaining fragments. Myron of Eleitherae achieved fame for his nature studies. His "Athena and Marsyas" was his master piece. Polycletus (480-420 B.C.) was the third great sculptor of this period. He was famous for his bronze statues of athletes.

During the Hellenistic period, there was a noticeable transformation. The sculptors of this period, introduced the naturalism of everyday life and extreme emotions. The Lao coon" statue was declared as a marvel of art by Michelangelo. It represents a priest of Apollo and his two sons, attacked by serpents. The sculpture had portrayed an organising death struggle by means of the grouping of the figures and of the impression of writing movements in the intertwined forms of human beings and serpents.

Religion of the Greeks: According to Greek conception of religion Gods were glorified men worldly, lustful and brawling. They were represented as immoral, living and acting much the same as men, except that they were endowed with immortality. The Gods were numerous that space does not permit even a complete enumeration of them. Zeus was the lord and master of all the Gods. There were countless local and house hold deities besides the universal divinities. Gods played a very important part in the cultural life of the Greeks and about them developed a vast amount of mythology. Greek mythology refect a clear view of the religious point of view. They explain the divine origin of man. Worship of Gods consumed a comparatively small amount of time and activity of the Greeks. They were too philosophical minded to subscribe to a formulated and routine worship. There were priests to perform religious ceremonies but Greece was never priest-ridden. Priesthood in Greece was not an exclusive profession. The father in each family was a priest, both in theory and in practice. The Delphic oracle of Apollo and the Olympian names held in honour of Zeus provided means of preserving unity of religious practices among the Greek City States.

Mysteries played an important part in the religion of the Greeks. These mysteries centered around the story of a God who died and was resurrected, an idea that appealed to many because it promised immortality. This cult became very powerful and it received the support of many of the Greeks especially those of the lower social order.

In Hellenistic times, morality and a future life were stressed more than in the earlier period. It was due to the influence of the religious of the orient and to the teachings of the philosophers. Alexander the Great himself asked his people to list him among the Gods and demanded honour to him as they would do to a God, by such acts as prostration on entering his presence. Besides this, rationalism and materialism, agnosticism and atheism were prevalent and gained considerable headway.

Philosophy: The early poets of Greece namely Homer and Hesiod wrote about cosmology. They tried to seek a natural and retional solution of how the material world came into being. Thales (624-548 B.C) the first nature philosopher, predicted the Sun's eclipse of 585 B.C. and held that the primal substance of all things was water. Pythagoras said that numbers were the basis of all principles and that life was regulated by music and mathematics. Democritus (460-370 B.C.) established an atomic theory which stated that particles varying in shape and in size arranged themselves into various combinations.

Sophists believed that the most important thing was to be able to persuade others, to better an adversary in argument, rather than to try to prove anything conclusively. The Sophists made a real contribution to learning. Their inquisitive and orderly approach to a subject encouraged scientific approach. They taught the youth of Greece to excel in politics, to take part in public affairs and to become intelligent citizens.

Socrates (470-399) is one of the best known and one of the most famous of the Greek Philosophers. He followed the Sophist method of question and answer, but he deplored mere pretense and rhetoric. He poses as a seeker of truth. He convinced the people of their ignorance and led them into right concepts. His philosophy was that everyman knew how to act rightly so as to bring true happiness. His teachings were considered immoral and corrupt by the officials of Athens. He was arrested on the charge of leading the youth of the native city astray and was killed by administering the hemlock poison. He become the supreme example of intellectual integrity for he would not retract what he believed to be truth.

Plato (427-347 B.C.) the most notable pupil of Socrates, founded an academy and taught his students through dialogue form in the most alluring way. His work was deductive and based on faith rather than on reason. He advocated an idea of immortality that conceived the preservation of works and ideas rather than the individual. His contribution to politics is beyond calculation. He formulated the first idealistic principles of a democratic state.

Aristotle (384-322 B.C.) a student under Plato, was the teacher of Alexander the Great. His "History of Animals" was the result of hard work and close observation. Several of his conclusions anticipated modern discoveries in the field of science. They dominated the intellectual world for nearly 2000 years.

In the Hellenistic age, the people were conscious of their wealth and wanted to get contentment, which they considered to be the secret of happiness. Two philosophers advocated happiness as the goal of life. They were Epicurus and Zeno. Epicurus (342-270 B.C.) was materialistic in his book and rejected the religions of his day. He advocated that man should enjoy himself and turn all his intellect in that direction. Zeno (350-260 B.C.) was an advocate of stoicism. He asked the people to endure sufferings without emotion. Cynicism was another philosophical approach to happiness. It was a form of social defeatism. The cynics ridiculed rulers and ignored social customs. Diogenes (412-323 B.C.) was one of the famous cynics.

Literature: Epic was one of the earliest form of Greek literature. Homer stands as a symbol of epic poetry. His two masterpieces *Iliad* and *Odyssey* are outstanding examples of epic literature. *Odyssey* is closely related to the *Iliad*. Hesiod (750 B.C.) is another reputed epic poet. His works "Works and Days" and "Descent of the God" are his splendid contributions. His works are more valuable as historical records than those of Homer's work.

Lyric poetry was written to be recited to the accompaniment of the lyre or flute. It was mere personal and emotional than the epic. Archilochus (7th century B.C.) invented the satirical verse so admired by the Latin poet Horace. Pindar was considered by his contemporaries to be the "God of Song" and a special favorite of Apollo. The lyrics of Hellenistic period do not have the beauty of style and expression as that of the Hellenic age.

Drama: It is the most familiar of the Greek forms of literature. Aeschylus (525-456 B.C.) was the greatest of the tragic poets. His two most famous plays are "Promethesus Unbound and Agamemnon". Sophocles (496-406 B.C.) represents the peak of Greek drama. His Antigene and Electra are well known to modern students of the theater. Euripides (480-406 B.C.) was the third of the great tragic poets. He was a spokesman for the poor and the oppressed. His best known work "The Trojan Woman" pictures the suffering of women during a war. Aristophanes (448-385 B.C.) was the greatest comic poet. Political satire reached high level in his writings. Drama became such an instrument for social criticism.

History: The inquisitive minds of the Greek enabled them to produce history. Herodotus (484 B.C.) has been given the title of the "Fatter of History". He glorified the history of Greece, especially the victory over Perisa to such an extent that much of his material is untrustworthy.

Thucydides (460-400 B.C.) wrote about his own times, the Peloponnesian war and his own travels. Xenophon (434-355 B.C.) continued the work of Thucydides, writing the "Anabasis" a history of a Greek expedition into Persia.

Oratory: It was considered to be indispensable. Oratory was resorted for the attainment of honour and prestige. Demosthenes (384-322 B.C.) the greatest of the Greek orators, used his talent in defence of Greek democracy. He made oratory a part of literature.

Learning: The aristocrats of the Pericles period were learned. Some of them were engaged in research also. The philosophers were responsible for Greek advancement in learning. The Sophists emphasised an oratory, grammar, dialectics, physical science, history and literature. In the Hellenistic period, public libraries were built, the most famous of which was the one at Alexandria. This mine of learning contained 500,000 works. Books were made accessible to the people. In some places, the State supported elementary schools. After completing the course in them, the sons of wealthy families were admitted in private schools. Professional courses in Engineering, Medicine, Astronomy and Geography were also run.

Science: It was the Greek Philosophers who offered the stimulus for the beginning of the study of Science. Aristotle laid the foundation for the study of natural science. His works on Fishes still hold good. His pupil Theophrastus established botany as a recognised science. Aristarchus (310-230 B.C) advanced the heliocentric theory of the Solar system, and made a computation of the size of the earth. Eratosthenes (276-196 B.C.) computed the circumference of the earth, drew a map of the world and suggested that it would be possible to reach India by sailing westward.

Mathematics: Geometry was the first science that the Greek pursued independent of philosophy. Pythagoras (570-500 B.C) made a practical use of numbers and proved mathematically that the earth was round. Euclid (300 B.C.) wrote geometry that is still accepted as authoritative. Archimedes (287-212 B.C.) discovered that a body immersed in a fluid loses weight equal to the amount of fluid displaced and invented the tubular screw.

Biology: Anaximander was one of the first Greeks to speculate in biological science. Empedocles contributed to the theory of evolution. Diogenes of Appollonia (500-430 B.C.) wrote the first anatomical treatise.

Medicine: Greeks made distinctive contributions in the field of medicine. Hippocrates (460-377 B.C.) "The father of Greek medicine" repudiated the belief that disease was the work of evil spirits. He relied more on diet and exercise that on drugs for his cures. The Hippocratic Oath placed the practice of medicine on an ethical basis with social responsibilities. Herophilsus (3rd century B.C.) is known as "the father of anatomy". He dissected the human body, and observed the functions of nerves and muscles. These men placed the practice of medicine on the dignified level of a profession.

Legacy of Greece

The culture and civilisation of Greeks had exerted deep impact upon the countries of Europe and near East. Rome especially absorbed the features of Greek civilisation to a greater extent. They were spread not only in Rome but also in all the countries that were conquered by Rome. They were carried to countries of Asian continent through Byzantine empire and also to countries like Arabia and Spain. The Muslim and Jewish scholars of Byzantine took the masterpieces of Greek literature to Italy and thereby caused the efflorescence of Renaissance.

The cultural heritage of the Greeks could be perceived in every aspect of the modern day life of this world.

Government: Democracy and dictatorship were their contributions in the various forms of Governments which they introduced to this world. The present day representative type of democracy, jury system, freedom of thought, speech, writing, assembly and freedom of worship were all the legacies of Greeks. Arts and crafts, mining industry, engineering industry, commerce and industrial systems were also the contributions of the Greeks to the present day world.

Education and Religion: Our schools and universities have their roots in Greek institutions for education. Gymnasium Stadiums, Games, Tournaments and Olympic Games were their contributions. The concepts of Eugenicmating, self-containment, self-control and natural method of maintaining the health and Pagan's ideal of shameless living were all evolved in Greece. The doctrines and practices of Christianity are indebted to the religions of Egypt and Greece, Ideas like, sacrifice of the life of the son of God, Resurrection, Proselytisation sermons, Holy sacrifices, Holy communion, Heaven and Hell, purgatory, creation, and final conflagration and superstitions were all taken away from the culture of the Greeks.

Literary Service: The modern literature also are a great deal to Greeks for its development. The alphabet came through Greece and Rome. The Greek words have brought forth a number of European languages. Technical terms in science used at international level are derived from

Greece. The grammar, rhetoric and even punctuation and paragraphing were Greek inventions. The classification of literature into lyrics, odes, idyls, the novel, easy oration, biography, history and above all the dramas are drawn from Greece. Their language and literature are still held as a model of perfection to the art of expression.

Art and Architecture: Their art presents a revelation of surpassing heavy and creative power. Today, broken specimens, statues without heads or arms, mere fragments of the originals are priceless possessions. The form and much of modern sculpture is Greek, for no other art had been influenced so much, until lately modern architecture is influenced by the Greek practices. The lesson of moderation, purity and harmony found in the sculpture and architecture is really a valuable gift to us. Modern music is partly indebted to Greece. The oratorio and the opera owe to Greek drama and the choral dance. The theory of music was first expounded by the Greeks. But in painting our debt is the least. But strain of Greek painting is visible in the mural painting of our own days.

Achievements in Science: A list of the scientists and their accomplishments is sufficient proof of progress in their sphere. However, the scientific facts that they established are not so noteworthy as are the scientific spirit and methods that they introduced. But anyhow the liberation of science from theology, the independent development of scientific research were the adventures of the Greek. They laid the foundation of Trigonometry and Calculus. They began and completed the study of conic sections and brought to some perfection the three dimensional Geometry. Democritus expounded the atomic theory, Archimedes produced new mechanisms. Aristarchus anticipated and perhaps inspired Copernicus. Hipparehus laid the foundation of astronomy. Eratosthenes measured the earth and mapped it. Anxagoras and Empedocles laid the foundation of the theory of evolution. Aristotle and Theophrates developed Botany, Zoology and Embryology and Meteorology. Hippocrates liberated medicine from superstition and philosophy and gave an ethical code. Herophilus and Erassitratus raised astronomy and physiology which but for Galen Europe would not have acquired until renaissance.

Philosophy: Even in Philosophy, Greek legacy is not small. No nation had treated nature so thoroughly and so affectionately and made the first discovery that it was a cosmos of order and hence could be studied. Homer and Hesiod wrote about cosmology. The philosophers went beyond a super natural and mythological explanation of the universe to seek a natural and rational solution of how the material world came into being. In philosophy they reigned supreme. Socrates, the dean of philosophers, and Plato and Aristotle, the other two members of the triumvirate, remain the most outstanding philosophers of all times. The Greek philosophers, in their philosophical quest explored every aspect of life — realism, nominalism, idealism and materialism, monotheism and pantheism and atheism and immoralism of Nietzche. There we can find synthesis of Spencer and psychoanalysis of Freud. Greek did not talk of philosophy but they lived it. The sage and not the saint or warrior was the pinnacle of ideal in Greece. This philosophy entered Rome, inspired Roman Emperors, Christian Fathers, Scholastic theologicians, Renaissance heretics, Cambridge platonists and the rebels of enlightenment.

Civilisations do not die. They migrate. The decay of one makes room for another. It merely sheds its old skin and surprises death by its new youth. Greek civilisation is alive. It moves on inspite of its defects. But those who cherish freedom, reason and beauty will forget these defects. The names of Solan, Socrates, Plato, Eurepides, Phedias of Epicurus and Archimedes will continue to remain as living personalities for centuries to come.

Last but not the least, the Greeks discovered the significance of the individual. Earlier civilisation, and same since, considered man as a mere creation of circumstance, a playing for Gods and rulers. The Greek's philosophy of a good life was developed on the basis of the individual. To them "man is the measure of all things" and "of all the wonders on earth, none is more wonderful than man". The Greeks succeeded in originating both the feeling for life and the understanding of it.

10

Roman Civilisation

Rome kept a rich legacy through her classical culture. In many respects, Roman civilisation belongs to the Hellenistic classification, a continuation of Greek culture with modifications typical of the Romans. The culture of the Romans represents the final stage of classical civilisation in Western Europe. The present day world is indebted in many ways to the legacies of the Roman civilisation. We may make here a brief review of the contributions of Rome in various fields.

Land and the People: Roman empire included the whole of the Mediterranean basin, the southern part of Europe, the northern fringe of Africa, and a considerable part of the Near East. Italy is a Peninsula about 650 miles long and 100 miles wide shaped like a huge boot extending into the Mediterranean Sea. There were traces of Paleolithic and Neolithic cultures in Italy. The Etruscans settled in Etruria, just north of the Tiber River, about 1000 B.C. The Italians who were racially related to the Greeks, invaded Italy about 1500 B.C. They were divided into four major groups: the Samnites, the Latins, the Umbrians and the Sabines. The Latins ultimately conquered the whole Peninsula and dominated the civilized Western World. The Greeks colonized the southern part of Italy in 800 B.C. and their cultural influence on the Romans is inestimable. The Gauls then settled in the Po River valley about 400 B.C. In short Roman civilisation and the Roman people as well, were a mixture of all these cultural and racial elements.

Political Contributions: Rome's greatest contribution was in the political field. Romans were not only great conquerors but also had a great genius to organise the conquered areas and provided them with good government. Rome gave to the diverse people of the great empire the much desired 'Pax Romana' (Roman peace) which lasted for many centuries.

Government: According to Roman mythology, Romulus and Remus were the founders of Rome. They united the early Latins into a compact political and social unit. Rome became a city kingdom under an Etruscan king about 750 B.C. About 500 B.C. the Romans succeeded in driving out the Etruscans. It was their first military accomplishment. Then Rome was brought under the rule of monarchs. It was followed by a republican form of government. This period was marked by a struggle between Plebians and Patricians for supremacy. The Plebians came out victorious by establishing the tribunes (471 B.C.).

Another series of wars for supremacy of the Western Mediterranean ensued between Rome and Carthage in the period between 264-146 B.C. They were called as Punic wars. Carthage was led by Hannibal. In the third Punic war, (146 B.C.), Carthage was destroyed and Rome became supreme in the West. Julius Caesar conquered Gaul, Britain and also overthrew his opponents in Asia Minor and thereby continued the extension of the empire. Under him the Roman empire attained its greatest extent about A.D. 113. He was followed by other famous rulers of the Roman empire namely Augustus Caesar, Constantine and Justinian. Justinian contributed to the culmination of Roman law.

Administration and Statesmanship: The medieval and modern world learnt invaluable lessons of imperial administration from Rome. The Republican constitution of Rome created the principle of checks and balances for the prevention of concentration of power. The Roman imperial machinery evolved wholesome principles in law, taxation and citizenship to bring out uniformity among different peoples. In the ancient world, Romans had no equals in administration and statesmanship.

One World Idea: Rome sowed seeds of one world idea of demonstrating the feasibility of enabling the people of different nations to live under Roman authority amicably. She evolved the fine principle of "Imperium et Liberata" empire and freedom. As per this principle, the diverse people subject to the authority of Rome, had local freedom as regards language, religion, customs and wages. Terms like 'Republic' and 'Liberty' are derived from Latin.

Roman Law: The most outstanding intellectual contribution of the Romans was the formation of a body of laws. It became an instrument of justice based upon reason. The early codified law in Rome was given in the Law of the Twelve Tables (449 B.C.) displayed in the Forum. Rome produced several geniuses in law. Roman jurists such as Paetus, Paulus, Ulpian and Papinian contributed much to the development of Roman law. By 176 B.C. a new praetorian law called the "hus gentium" or law for non citizens was evolved. Hadrian appointed a corps of Jurists led by Salvius Julianus. They produced the code known as pretorial perpetual Edict. In their attempt at codification, they borrowed many legal principles from the just natural (Natural law) and humanised the law. The Theodosian code (438) was an attempt to incorporate into Roman law the ideas of Christianity and some of the German concepts. The development of Roman law culminated in the "Corpus Juris Civilis" of Justinian. He has been called as the 'Law Giver of the Civilisation' It furnished a fine source for the study of Roman law and served as a model for later civil and canon law of the world even today. Even the conception of popular sovereignty could be traced in the Roman law which has become the basis of modern representative government.

Public Works: Julius Caesar, Augustus Caesar and other rulers built cities and towns. When a major part of the city of Rome was destroyed by fire in 64 A.D. Nero reconstructed it and made it look better with its well paved straight and broad streets. A typical Roman city had all facilities like public libraries, temples, churches, stadia and good water supply system.

Romans had laid well paved roads connecting the distant parts of the empire. These facilitated the movement of the armies, the postal system, trade and commerce. Italy had 372 main roads. In the beginning all roads were built from Rome, and Rome was linked with the other parts of the countiy. Hence, the familiar saying "All roads lead to Rome". The Roman government employed Roman, Greek and Syrian engineers for building roads, bridges, ships, harbours and docks.

Romans had a very well organised system of drainage and water supply. They drained the marshes and the waste of the metropolis with the assistance of workers, legionaries and slaves. The water supply scheme was both massive and efficient. Fourteen aqueduct with a total length of 1,300 miles conveyed to Rome daily three hundred million gallons of water.

Economic Contributions: The basic occupation of the Romans was agriculture and they made few contributions to agricultural methods. They used crude ploughs, harvested with sickles and trampled out grain threshing on floors. They grew barley, beans, millet and wheat. They kept orchards and grew grapes, figs and olives. Much wine was produced and exported.

Agricultural economy was supplemented by a score of industries developed everywhere. Different craftsmen like butchers, bakers, smiths, tanners, dyers, masons, musicians and barbers were common in the

Roman empire. At Pampey the archaeologists found forty bakeries. Craft associations like guilds were organised. The 'Collegia' were made up of men working at the same trade.

Factories produced tiles, pottery, bricks, glass, paper and other products. The Romans developed mining and metallurgy on a large scale. Gold, Silver, Lead, Tin, Coal, Iron and other metals were extracted.

Trade by land and sea was organised. Italians exported glazed pottery, metals, wine, olive oil, and lumber. They imported commodities like dye, glassware, pearls, grain, tapestries and cosmetics from the Black Sea, Anatolia, Arabia, Syria, Egypt and India. In order to facilitate the flow of merchandise, the part of Ostia, at the mouth of the Tiber River was improved.

Art and Architecture: Romans had built awe inspiring palaces, baths, theatres, Amphitheatres and stadia. But the Roman art shows distinctly Greek influence. The chief of the architects of Rome is Marcus Vitruviers Pollio, whose book "On Architecture" is still regarded as a masterpiece in the field. Beautiful temples for the Gods like Jupiter, Juno and Saturn were constructed. Augustus Caesar also built several temples. One among them was dedicated to Apollo. It was completely made of marbles. One of the best preserved and most famous of Roman buildings is the Pantheon built in 124. Vespasian built the Colosseum. It is a combination of the arch and lintel systems, the arch being the vital part of the construction, with columns and platforms serving only for decoration. This combination gives structural solidarity, impressive dignity and elegant magnificence.

The triumphal arch of Titus, one of the most beautiful of many similar memorials, was the most lavish of Roman constructions. The bas-reliefs on that arch are the best examples of Roman historic relief scupture. Architect Apollodorus built the first-hot-spring bath in Rome and a bridge over the Danube, which was considered a miracle of architectural skill.

Sculpture: In relief work and sculpture, the skilful artists of Rome reached great heights of excellence. "The head of a Roman youth" (ca 100) is a good example of Roman sculpture at its best. Victorious generals raised triumphal arches with superb reliefs. Arch of Titus constructed to commemorate the capture of Jerusalem in 70 A.D. is the greatest. The Romans distinguished themselves in portrait sculpture. Roman scuptures are depicted with realism and vigour. Roman sculptors carved real living men and women. Pasiteles, a Greek lived for about 60 years in Rome produced excellent carvings in gold, ivory and silver. He was not only the greatest sculptor but also wrote five volumes on the history of art.

Rome was full of portrait busts of great generals and emperors carved in bronze and marble. The greatest portrait bust is the so called "Head of Caesar" of black basalt in Berlin. Besides the bust and images of Pompey, Augustus Caesar and Cicero still speak about sculptural perfection of the Romans.

Painting: Romans lacked originality in painting. They depended on the Greek themes, traditions and, methods. Painters restricted themselves to fresco and tempera. Portrait painters were favoured much. The best of the surviving mural paintings are found in Pompey. Some 3500 frescoes were found there. Those paintings that deal with mythological subjects show a Greek influence, but the nature studies appear to be original. The emperors, the nobles and the rich in Rome spent lavishly on their passion for painting.

Literature and Learning: Romans developed Latin as a great language and it reached the classical level. In the Golden Age of Augustus, great Latin writers made their rich contributions. The king and the nobles encouraged the production of first rate literature.

Poetry: The Roman poets raised the prestige of the Latin language. Catullus (87-54 B.C.) was a romantic and nature poet. He immortalised himself in his poem 'Lesbia' dedicated to the lady he loved. Virgil (70-19 B.C.) was the greatest Latin poet. His poems "Ecologues" dealing with rural life brought him great fame. His most beautiful poems "Georgies" (Labour of the land) glorified agriculture as the noblest of the arts. The English poet Dryden praised it as "the best poem of the best poet." Another great contribution of Virgil the "Aeneid" is an epic on the foundation of Rome. He assumed the highest place among the poets of the Golden Age of Augustus.

Horace (65-8 B.C.) was another great poet of Rome. The 'Odes' formed his greatest work, which Augustus himself said was immortal. Ovid (43 B.C.-17 A.D.) was also another great poet. His greatest work was "Metamorphoses". His "Art of Love" appealed to the romantic but caused a stir in Rome.

Prose and History: Great Roman historians had produced excellent prose works. Cato the Elder (230-149 B.C.) was the earliest writer of good Latin prose. He was an orator who published his own speeches. His greatest work "Origines" deals with the histoiy of Italy. Julius Caesar (100-44 B.C.) not only made history but also wrote it in excellent prose. His "Commentaries" was about his Gallic campaigns. Polybius (204-122 B.C.) wrote on the history of Rome and praised its constitution. He wrote a "Universal History" of 40 books. Cicero (102-43 B.C.) was not only an author and statesman, but also an excellent writer of Latin prose. His "Republic" and "Laws" offer his ideas on Government.

Livy spent four decades (23 B.C.-17 A.D.) in writing a history of Rome in 142 'books'. His history is full of defects. He does not rely on original sources and draws no distinction between fact and fiction. Tacitus was the greatest historian of Rome and one of its greatest historians of the world. His most famous work is the 'Annals' dealing with the history of Roman emperors like Tiberius and Nero. Juvenal (ca 60-140) wrote a series of satires. His works have historical values. Plutarch (46-126 A.D.) wrote in Greek many biographies called parallel lines of prominent Greeks and Romans

Drama: We can see the profound influence of the Greece in the Roman dramas too. Seneca wrote tragedies which form the model for the 16th century dramas. Plautus (250-184 B.C.) wrote comedies. He was an admirer of the Greek poet Menander, his dramas were all adaptations from Greek literature. Terence (190-159 B.C.) was another writer of comic drama. His dramas were more refined than those of Plautus.

Philosophy: The Romans made few contributions in philosophy; but they were students and interpreters of Greek philosophy. Cato (234-149 B.C.) sometimes called Socrates of the West opposed the Roman subjection to Greek culture and advocated the retention of Roman culture. Like Socrates he was a devotee of reason, enlightenment and moral discipline. Panaetius of Rhodes (180-110 B.C.) brought stoicism to Rome and condemned myths and advocated monotheism. Lucretius (95-55 B.C.) sponsored Epicureanism in Rome. He ridiculed superstitions, the worship of gods and the fear of death. Cicero compiled a philosophical encyclopedia. Seneca (4 B.C.-65 A.D.) was one of the greatest of the Roman philosophers. He was a stoic, a believer in Rome's destiny. All men in his estimation were naturally equals; rich and poor must fight, the fight that is called life. Marcus Aurelius Antoninus (121-180 A.D.) the philosopher emperor answered to the description of Seneca's dream. He interpreted stoic philosophy in his small book "Meditations".

Science: Roman contribution in science were very limited. Pliny the Elder (A.D. 23-79) wrote a "Natural History" which he described as a systematic view of nature. It was written in 37 volumes summarising the science and errors of his age. Ptolemy, a native of Alexandria developed spherical trigonometry and computed the value of as 3.1416. He believed that the earth was a fixed sphere with a circumference of about 18,000 miles. Reform of calender on the basis of astronomical learning was a Roman contribution. The solar year of 365 days, with an extra day added every four years was instituted in 45 B.C.

Medicine: The Roman government accepted the responsibility for public health and sanitation. All towns had public physicians who gave free medicine to the poor. They were paid from state exchequer. The army had its own hospitals and doctors.

Galen (130-200 A.D.) the greatest physician of Rome was a Greek born at Pergamum in Asia Minor. He was a surgeon in the gladiatorial school at Pergamum. He gave scientific explanations about the respiratory system, the spinal cord, the heart, and muscles. His physioligical theory was an outstanding accomplishment in the history of medicine.

Engineering and Technology: Aqueducts, roads, bridges and other colossal buildings are surviving monuments of the practical skill of the Romans. Scientific knowledge for the construction of cranes, mortars, windmills, and heating units for buildings were available in Rome. Frantinus (40-103 A.D.) wrote a pioneer work on engineering.

Religion: Among the primitive Italian tribes family duties were most conspicuous. Every home had its guardian spirit called Janus: the hearth was guarded by Vesta; Genius the god of man's virility and Juno controlled women's power to conceive. A special ritual was employed for the worship of each. Worships with simple ceremonies were presided over by the father of the family.

The development of city-states led to the worship of gods to protect them. Mars, the god of war and Jupiter were considered to be important for a long time. When the Etruscans invaded Rome, they introduced gods like Minerva and Diana. Temples were built and images were placed in them. Mysticism played an important part in Roman religion. One of the most important of the mysteries introduced from the east was the cult of Cybele, "the great mother of god". Mithraism, an offshoot of Zoroastrianism gradually superceded the cults mentioned above. The naming of the days of the week after planets and the celebration of December 25 as birth day of the Saviour God were derived from practices adopted from Mithraism. Gnosticism was another religion that reached peak in the 2nd century of Christian era. The attainment of salvation could be made only through performing rituals and practicing magic. The Gnosticists bitterly attacked Christianity. One group even denounced Christ as a devil.

Augustus Caesar borrowed from the East the idea of a ruler posing as a god. This imperial cult was a form of patriotism and religious festivals were held in honour of the emperor, and imperial god to whom all were to pay homage. Diocletian posed himself as a Sun — God.

Christianity in the Roman Empire: Christianity possessed the dynamics of a religion of salvation and hence the Romans at once embraced this religion. Jesus as a boy had experienced the unsettled conditions and hardships of his people. He was greatly influenced by John the Baptist who taught the need for repentance, spiritual cleanliness and the promise of a great leader to inspire the world. The execution of John the Baptist inspired Jesus to continue his work. He preached to all sects of people and his disciples especially Peter soon recognised him as "Messiah". But he was denounced as a "false prophet" by pharisees and scribes. Hence, he was arrested and crucified but died only to come to life again. Jesus brought a message of brotherly love to the inhabitants of a cruel world. He taught that man should serve one another and that by so doing, they would serve god.

The Apostles of Jesus especially Peter and Paul rendered commendable service to the spread of Christianity. Paul of Tarsus was largely responsible for the admission of Gentiles into Christian ranks. Paul established churches at Antioch, Ephesus, Corinth, Athens and Philippi. He wrote letters explaining the doctrine of this religion and preached the universality of Christianity. The teachings, of Christianity had a tremendous appeal to the disillusioned, the weak, and the suppressed.

The simple sermon "come unto Me all Ye that labour and are heavy laden" were strongly appealing. The early Christians were not only converts to the religion but also convinced of a mission to carry the gospel to all men. The most despised classes of the Roman empire embraced this religion. In the beginning the new religion was accepted as one among many religions of the Roman empire. But the inauguration of emperor worship changed the attitude of the government. The Christians refused to bow before the emperor as a god and thus became revolutionaries. Hence, Trojon made the refusal to pay homage to the emperor a criminal offence punishable with death. Marcus Aurelius ordered Christians to be persecuted. Diocletion ordered the burning of Christian churches and the prohibition of the freeing of Christian slaves. But Christianity could not be exterminated through persecutions. They gained in numbers and many Romans in the upper social order were converted. The Roman Empire began to decline. Emperor Galerius issued the Edict of Toleration (311 A.D.), Constantine issued the Edict of Milan (313 A.D.) through which the Christians were granted the liberty of worship, removal of legal disabilities and the restitution of property. Under Theodosius I (A.D. 379-395) Christianity became the only religion recognised by the State.

11

Asian Civilisations

(I) ARYAN CIVILISATION

(A) Early Vedic Civilisation

The civilisation of India after the Sindhu (Indus) civilisation is known to us through the Rig Veda. It is the first literary source for the history of ancient India. From the contents of the Rig Veda, it is proved that the Aryan people were of the Indo European race. Some other scholars feel that the Aryan people came to India from some outside territory namely Central Asia. There are other historians who regard that the Aryans were of Indian territory. This is advocated by A.C. Doss. Though there is a controversy about the origin of the Aryans, all the scholars agree the fact that the Aryans replaced the political power of the people of the Sindhu civilisation in India in about 2500 B.C.

Reg Veda: Since Rig Veda is the earliest of the four Vedas, which are the sacred literary sources of Hinduism, the historians also call the civilisation depicted in it as the early Vedic civilisation. The Rig Veda had in it 1,017 hymns and they are arranged into ten Mandalas. Those hymns supply valuable historical data pertaining to the social, economic, political and religious life of the Aryan people in the early Vedic or the Rig Vedic Age.

POLITICAL CONDITIONS

Political Units: During the Rig Vedic period the Aryans lived in small villages. The basis of their political and social organisation was the family or 'Kula'. Father was the head of the family. He kept all the members in the family in perfect discipline. Many families formed a 'Grama' or village headed by a 'Gramini'. Many villages used to form a 'Visya' whose head was called a 'Visyapathi'. Many Visyas collectively called 'Jana'. Every Jana was ruled by a king called 'Rajan'.

Kingship: During this period there were very many tribal principalities. There are references in Rig Veda about subduing one king by the other. The king occupied a highly dignified and supreme position.

The form of government was monarchy. The King had limited powers. In some tribes monarchy was elective, in some, monarchical power was exercised by all the members of the royal family; and only in a few tribes it showed a tendency to become hereditary.

The king was expected to be a 'Mitra' in kindness 'Varuna' in virtues and 'Indra' in valour. He was responsible for the safety and security of his subjects. He was also to look after the material welfare and spiritual advancement of his subjects. He was the fountain of justice. He was the supreme commander of the army.

The people paid him voluntary taxes. Taxation was not a stable source of income. So the king resorted to plunder and pillage. Above all very often he offered sacrifices to gods expressing his gratitude for success over the Dasyus. In short the king was expected to rule according to the customary laws of the land.

Officials: Many officials assisted the king during this period. The chief among them were (1) Purohita (2) Senani (3) Gramini. Purohita was the temporal Guru of the king. He also accompanied the king in wars and prayed to God for his success. Senarni was the commander in chief of the king. Gramini was no less influential than Purohita.

Sabha and Samiti: Two assemblies, called the Sabha and Samiti formed an essential feature of the government. They were popular institutions. Sabha was a small institution which dealt with the local problems whereas Samiti discussed national problems. Members of the Sabha were the learned and the rich people of the state. The Samiti had, as its members, the common men of the state and its meetings were presided oyer by the king or the elected chief. Both, the Sabha and the Samiti, had considerable powers in political matters and they exercised considerable checks on the head the state.

Warfare: The Aryans had a high code of warfare. They were brave and courageous. The army at that time consisted of infantry, cavalry and chariots. The king and his chiefs made use of chariots drawn by horses in battle field. The rank and file fought on foot. Arms were not used against women, children and the old.

Law and Crimes: customs and traditions were taken as laws of the land. The king could not violate them. Punishments were very severe. Ordeal by fire and water was practised in certain cases.

SOCIAL CONDITIONS

Family: The unity of society was patriarchal family. The father was the head of the family. He wielded considerable authority over the children and other members. The Aryans followed the Joint family system in which all the members of the family lived in co-operation and affection with each other.

Position of Women: Women enjoyed equality with men in every walk of life. Domestic religious ceremonies were to be performed by the husband and wife together. No restrictions were placed on the education of women during this period. They participated in philosophical debate like men with men. They also practised penances. Visva Vara, Ghosa, Apala and Lopamudra were well versed in the sacred texts. The last one was an expert in music and dancing.

Marriage: Girls were married long after they attained the age of puberty. Freedom was given to them in choosing their life partners. Consent of the parents was essential for their marriage. System of infant marriage did not exist in the early Vedic society. Monogamy was the order of the day, Polygamy existed but only amongst the kings and the chiefs. Widow marriage was also allowed. Sati was unknown.

The foremost aim of the marriage was to increase the progeny. Prayers were offered by women folk for male children. The women were under the protection of their father until marriage, of their husbands after marriage, and of their brothers if not married.

Food and Drink: The early Aryans consumed milk and its products like butter, ghee etc. Grains like wheat, barley were used by them. Cakes were baked from the wheat or barley flour. They also took fruits and vegetables. They also consumed meat occasionally. Certain intoxicating drinks made from plant and grain called the 'Soma' and 'Sura' were on use. The former was drunk during sacrifices and considered religious.

Dress and Ornaments: Their clothes were made of cotton, wool and skin of the animals, Their dress consisted of two garments. The lower garments was called 'Vasa' and the upper 'adhivasa'. The garments were embroidered with gold. Both ladies and gents used ornaments. The ear ornament was called 'Karnasobhans'. Armlets, anklets, and necklaces were also used by the ladies. They used precious stones for their ornaments.

Games and Amusements: Both men and women were fond of music and dancing. The drum, the lute and the flute were also used by the ladies. Hunting, horse and chariot racing and dicing were the pastime of the gentry. Gambling was another favourite entertainment of the people.

Education: It was offered through oral method. First of all the teacher recited the Veda mantras which was then followed by the students. The aim of education was the sharpening of the intellect and developing the character. Sometimes education was imparted by the father to his son. They did not know the art of writing.

Medicine: The Vedic Aryans were acquainted with medicine. Surgery was known to the Vedic Aryans. Medicines were made with the help of herbs and plants. Blindness was cured during their period.

Caste System: In the early Vedic civilisation, the Aryans did not have caste system based on the birth of a person in a particular family which followed a specific occupation. Caste system based on the birth developed in the later Vedic period. In the early Vedic period, member of a family followed different occupations according to their skill and aptitude. Practice of the occupation was not hereditary. Members of the society worked in government, military and trade without consideration of their birth.

There existed in the early Vedic society, the people who were known as the 'dasyu' or 'dasa'. They were members of the aborigin tribes in India who were conquered in warfare by the Aryans. The dasyus or dasas served as slaves of the Aryans or in royal household.

Economic Conditions: The Aryans were essentially rural people and they lived in villages. Their society was self sufficient.

Agriculture: It is seen from the Rig Veda that agriculture was their main occupation. Tilling the soil, cutting of furrows, sowing the seeds, the cutting of corn with the help of sickle were known to them. Irrigation was also known to them. They did not cultivate rice. They used manure for their crops. Meadows and pasture were left for the animals to graze.

Cattle Breeding: Their most valued possession were cows and bullocks. Cow became a sacred animal in due course of time. Cowdung was used as manure. It was also used as medium of exchange. Aryans domesticated other animals like buffalo, goat, sheep, horse, camel and elephants.

Trade and Commerce: From the Vedic hymns we come to know that the Aryans had maintained excellent trade and commerce during this period. There was inland and foreign trade. Bargaining was there in the market. Barter system of exchange was chiefly in vogue. The gold coin used by them was known as "Niksha'. The chief items of commerce were cloth and goods made of leather. Goods were transported by means of chariots, horse and bullock carts. From Rig Veda we learn that trade was controlled by a particular section called 'pani'.

Occupation and Industries: There were carpenters, goldsmiths, bronze-smiths, and weavers among the skilled artisans. Gold, Silver, Copper and Bronze were used to make ornaments, weapons and utensils. There were some cottage industries like sewing, weaving and painting of mats from grass or reeds. Hunting was known to them. Bows and arrows were used to kill the birds and animals. Butcher profession was also known and practised during this period.

Religious Conditions: The religion of the Rig Vedic Aryans was one of Nature worship. The Aryans at first feared nature, then admired nature and finally worshipped nature. The powers of the nature were personified and worshipped.

Agni was their fire god. The first hymn in the Rig Veda is addressed to him. Surya was their Sun god. The most sacred hymn in the Rig Veda known as the Gayatri is addressed to the Rising Sun. Indra was the God of war. Varuna was their rain God. Usha was the goddess of Dawn and supposed to be the consort of Sun. Rudra was the fierce storm God. Soma, Agni and Vayu were deified and worshipped.

Elaborate sacrifices were made for the propitiation of these gods, for whom there was neither temples nor images. Offerings like ghee, grain and flesh of sheep were made to Agni who represented the other gods. 'Adityas' the 'Asvins' and the 'Vasus' were minor deities. The idea of one supreme god was a later development.

(B) Later Vedic Civilisation

The later Vedic age is the period of the later Vedas namely, Yajur, Sama and Atharva Veda and Brahmanas. It was also the period of the Epics and hence it is known as the 'Heroic Age' The Brahmanas are prose explanations relating to Brahmana, prayer and sacrificial ceremony. The Aranyakes have a special importance since they contain the celebrated philosophical speculations of Ancient India, known as Upanishads. The two great epics, the 'Ramayana' and the 'Mahabharatha' are regarded as semi-historical documents. From there we can draw a picture of the Epic or Heroic Age in a detailed manner.

Political Conditions: Monarchy was the popular form of government during the later Vedic Age. The Aryans who moved eastward came right up to Bengal. Kingdoms became large in size and were ruled over by more powerful kings than in the Rig Vedic period.

From the Jumna the Aryans moved south down the Chambal and settled first in Malwa and later reached the Narmada. Kings patronised hermits. Philosophers and men of letters exercised supreme judicial powers. To assert their supremacy the most powerful among them performed elaborate sacrifices, the 'Rajasuya' the 'Vajapeya' and the 'Asvamedha' which are not mentioned in the Rig Veda. The Raja suya was the sacrifice performed on the occasion of royal coronation. The Vajapeya was a sort of rejunevation ceremony of a middle aged king which raised him from the status of a simple 'raja' to that of 'samrat'. The Asvamedha commemorated the successful challenge thrown by a king at his neighbour through a horse sacrifice.

The kings were engaged in constant war with one another. In the age of the Mahabharatha, there were according to tradition 56 kingdoms in north and central India, and all the kings are said to have taken part in the battle of Kurukshetra fought about 900 B.C.

The old tribal assemblies *viz.* Sabha and Samiti had definitely lost then power and to that extent royal power had increased. It was limited only by custom, tradition and the power of the pursuit. The kings retinue included besides the purohit and senapati, the chamberlain, the charioteer and a host of palace servants.

The king was allowed to enjoy the taxes, presents and benevolences offered to him by the people. Fines and toll tax also formed the source of income for the king.

SOCIAL CONDITIONS

Family: The family was an important institution during this period. Each Kula or family consisted of several members. There also existed joint family system. The head of the family was called Kulapati usually either the father or the eldest brother.

Stages of Life: The Ashram system developed during this period. Literally an Ashram is a halting or resting place. The word, therefore, signifies a halt in the journey of life; just for the sake of rest, in a sense to prepare oneself for further Journey. It was presumed that every individual must live for a period of 100 years at least. Each ashram was, therefore, for a period of 25 years. They were (1) Brahmacharya (a religious student); (2) Grihastha (house holder); (3) Vanaprastha (one who has retired from active life and (4) Sanyasa (mendicant).

The Brahmins denied the right of becoming Vanaprasthas and Sanyasa to other castes and it was this Brahmin exclusiveness that led the other castes to find out other methods of obtaining Moksha.

The Caste System: The difference in colour between the Aryans and non-Aryans was regarded as the basis of caste system. It is called the Varna theory Varna literally means colour.

There were four castes during this period. They were : (1) Brahmanas; (2) Kshatriyas; (3) Vaishyas and (4) Sudras.

The Brahmanas enjoyed the highest status in the society. Purohita came from this caste. There also existed another class of Brahmana called 'Pujaris'. They lived in village temples.

Next to the Brahmana were Kshatriyas. They were the ruling community. The kings and officers belonged to the Kshatriya class. They had to maintain peace and order. Their primary duty was to protect the country from foreign invaders and impart justice.

The Vaishyas were next to Kshatriyas. But their position was on the decline during this period. It was due to their contact with the Sudras. Trade and commerce, industry and agriculture were also their mainstay.

The Sudras were in the lowest strata of the society. Frankly speaking they had no recognition. They were not even provided with the basic facilities. They were not eligible for education. They were ill treated by the higher classes. The Sudras had no rights to property. The condition of Sudras was really pathetic and pitiable.

The prohibition of inter caste marriage was not rigid and cases of ascent to the highest social status are on record. Valmiki, the author of Ramayana was a hunter. Two changes came in the caste system later on. One was that while the caste arose as a result of the functional division of society, gradually it came to be based upon birth. Another change was that the caste system became rigid, and inter-dining and inter marriage were forbidden.

Position of Women: Considerable deterioration took place in the position of women during this period. In the society monogamy was the rule. Polygamy was confined to the kings. Child marriage was unknown and post-puberty marriage were normal. Besides, there were eight types of marriage during this period.

The sale of a daughter was known, but viewed with disfavour. The birth of a daughter was not regarded as a sign of good omen. The Aitareya Brahmana describes that a daughter is a source of misery and a son alone can be the saviour of the family. Inspite of all this sati system and purdah system did not develop during this period. Widow remarriage was allowed.

The education of women in the Rig Vedic and Epic periods was of a high standard. In the Upanishads Yajnavalkya is questioned by his wife Maitreyi and challenged by Gorgi though that sage met the challenge successfully. There were women teachers. Though women's status was inferior to men, her equality with man in religious ritual was substantial. It was the intellectual starvation of women in later age that led to their inferiority complex and subordinate position.

General Education: There was a well planned system of education. A boy was admitted to the Gurukula after the upanayana ceremony. The student lived with his Guru in his ashrama. He was to study there and serve his Guru. The Vedas, the Puranas, the Upanishads, astrology, astronomy, mathematics, military education and other subjects were taught to the students. After the completion of education he paid dakshina to the teacher.

Food and Drink: The people used milk and milk products. The Atharva Veda mentions 'A pupa' a cake made of rice. Barley and ghee-rice cooked with milk and with beans is mentioned in Satapatha Brahmana. Meat eating was fairly common. Sura was also used by them.

Amusements: During the later Vedic period the Aryans played both indoor and outdoor games. Gambling and dicing were very common. People were interested in chariot racing and horse racing. Music, both vocal and instrumental and dancing continued to be among the chief amusements of this age. The women generally taught music and dance. They used drums, flutes and lutes of various types and the harp or lyre with a hundred strings. It is interesting to note that a 'pole dancer' or 'acrobat' has been mentioned in the Yajur Veda.

Dress and Ornaments: Generally the wool of sheep or the goat was used. Besides woollen, cotton clothes were also used. The dress in this period consisted of three garments. They were (1) Nivi; (2) Vasa and (3) Adhivasa. The turban was worn both by men and women. Skin was also used as clothing. The 'Sandal' or 'Shoe' was made of bear skin.

Many ornaments like armlets, finger rings, ear rings and nishka were used by them. The pearls, jewels and rubies stung on a thread were worn round the neck.

Medicine: The profession of the physician was well established during this period. The Atharva Veda enumerates a large number of diseases such as consumption, dysentery, boils, swellings, convulsions, ulcers, rheumatism and so on. Medicines were administered with the recitation of hymns to the sick.

ECONOMIC CONDITIONS

Agriculture: It was the main occupation of the Aryans during this period. According to various sources, it is seen that six, eight, twelve and even twenty four oxen were used to drag the plough. Manure was used. Rise came to be grown.

Cattle Breeding: It received an impetus during this period. Cow was regarded sacred during this period. In Atharva Veda death penalty was prescribed for cow slaughter. Wars between rival kings were fought on account of cattle lifting. 'Virataparva' in 'Mahabharatha' refers to the cattle lifting by Duryodhana and Arjuna's recovery of the Viratanagar cattle.

Trade and Commerce: Money lending was a flourishing business during this period. The internal trade was carried on both by land and water routes. The profession of the merchants was hereditary. The 'Satamana' a piece of gold was used as coin. Barter system was in existence. 'Nishka' was also used by them as unit of value. The chief articles of trade and commerce were garments, coverlets and goat skins.

Occupation and Industry: During this period the Brahmanas were assigned the profession of teaching and they also served as priests at sacrifices. The Kshatriyas looked after the task of fighting and safe guarding the country. Agriculture, trade and commerce were mainly the monopoly of the Vaishyas and all the menial jobs fell to the lot of Sudras. Besides, many occupations, arts, crafts and industries are mentioned in the Taittireya Brahmana.

Means of Transport: From the Atharva Veda we learn that there existed some sort of roads. Bullock carts were used for transports. Ships and boats were also a popular mode of transport. Sometimes elephants and horses were also employed for transporting goods.

Religious Conditions: Religious beliefs underwent a great change. The old nature gods gradually gave place to the celestial trinity, Brahma, Vishnu, and Siva, conceived as the creator, preserver and destroyer. The worship of Krishna and Narayana was coming in vogue.

Sacrifices and domestic rituals became more elaborate. Some of the sacrifices required the attention of 16 or 17 priests. Domestic rituals were succinctly described in the Grihya Sutras which were special editions of the Dharmasastras for the edification of the householder.

The Upanishadic teachings encouraged metaphysical speculation. The ascetics and sages were taken up with the study of the soul, the relation between the individual soul and the universal soul or Brahman the transmigration of the soul, karma and rebirth etc. Matter was regarded as illusory (Maya) Moksha or escape from rebirth and the identification of the individual soul with the divine came to be the end and aim of life.

(II) BUDDHISM

Early Life of Buddha: Gautama Siddhartha or Buddha was the founder of Buddhism. He is called the 'Enlightened one', 'Tathagata' (one who has attained the truth) and the Sage of Sakyas. His father Suddhodana was the ruler of Kapilavastu. His mother was Mayadevi Gautama was born in the Lumbini garden near Kapilavastu (Nepal) in 567 B.C. Mayadevi passed away seven days after the birth of Gautama and he was brought up by his aunt named Mahaprajapati Gautami, who gave him milk and fed him from her own breast.

The child called Siddhartha was brought up in great luxury. In course of time he married his beautiful cousin, Yasodhara or Gopa or Peinda and they lived a happy life for 10 years. At the age of 29, a son was born to him and he was named Rahula.

Four Great Signs: The sights of an old man, a diseased man, a dead man and a Saint had profound impact on Siddhartha and turned his attention to the troubles and bondage of human life.

Renunciation: Obsessed by those sights, Siddhartha wanted to find out a solution for all the sorrows of hyman beings. Hence, he decided to renounce the worldly life immediately. He left his wife and child sleeping and went away accompanied by Chhana, the charioteer.

Enlightenment: Siddhartha wandered for a long time here and there in search of truth. Then he went to Rajagriha and studied philosophy under two vedic scholars. Finding no solace he wandered over jungles and performed terrible penance for six years. He went to Gaya and meditated under fig tree (Pipal tree) or Bodhi or Bo tree for 7 years. He took the following vow, "I will not leave this place till I attain that peace of mind which I have been trying for all these years". Ultimately he got enlightenment and came to be known as the "Buddha" or "The Enlightened one". This happened when he was 35.

As a Preacher: He realised that he had discovered a new way to attain 'Nirvana', freedom from births and deaths. He went first to Benaras and delivered his first sermon at the Deer Park at Saranath. Buddha travelled in various parts of the country. Within a few months he gathered a large number of followers. Bimbisara, the King of Magadha and Presenajit, King of Kosala accepted Buddhism. His religion of love attracted the high and the low. People of all castes became his followers. In short, he taught his creed for 45 years through conversation, lectures and parables. Finally, the Buddha or the Enlightened passed away at the advanced age of 80 in the village of Kusinagara in 487 B.C.

Doctrines of Buddhism: Buddha gave a simple practical moral code, free of all mysticism for the common people to follow. In his sermons he preached the "Four Great Truths", "the Noble Eightfold Path" and the "Ten Commandments".

Four Great Truths: (1) Life is full of sorrow or pain. (2) Desire is the cause of pain, and unfulfilled desires lead to rebirth. (3) Cessation of suffering i.e., When desire ceases, rebirth ceases and that is Nirvana or liberation. (4) The path or the way to end sufferings *i.e.*, Desire is to over come by following the 'Right path".

Eight Fold Path: Right path was a middle path between the extreme of asceticism and sensuality. It was the Noble eight fold path consisting of the followings : (i) Right Belief; (ii) Right Thought; (iii) Right Speech; (iv) Right Action; (v) Right Living; (vi) Right Effort; (vii) Right Mindfulness and (viii) Right Meditation.

Ten Commandments: Buddha laid down the following 10 commandments :

(1) Speak the Truth; (2) Not to steal or commit adultery; (3) To follow Brahmacharya; (4) Not to covet anything; (5) To practise Ahimsa; (6) Not to use flowers and scents; (7) Not to sing and dance; (8) Not to associate with women; (9) Not to eat at forbidden times and (10) Not to sleep on soft beds.

The first five were for the house holders but a monk was to follow and practise all the ten commandments.

Gautama vehemently criticised caste system. According to him none is high or low by birth. It is his Karma which make low and high. All are equal in this world. He told them that irrespective of birth and position one could obtain Nirvana by pursuing the eight fold path or Ashtasila. He condemned violence and considered non-violence an integral part of life. He had no faith in dogmatic religions.

The Sangha and the Vihara: The five ascetic companions of Gautama before his Enlightenment and to whom the Buddha preached his first sermon at Saranath were duly ordained the first members of the Buddhist order or Sangha. Among the early converts the most famous were Sariputta, Mohallana, Ananda, Upali and Kasyapa. In course of time, the Buddhist holy palaces came to be known as Chaityas. Many of the holy places developed into great centres of Buddhist order. These were called the Sangha and the Vihara. While the Sangha was an association of Buddhist monks, organised for preaching and propaganda, the Vihara was a monastery given to education and organisation of worship.

Admission into Buddhist Sangha or Vihara was not restricted by caste or sex but warriors, debaters, bondsmen and minors were not admitted. Twenty was the minimum age for membership.

The nuns dwelt in separate establishments but had to undergo the same discipline as the monks. The rites of admission included a ceremonial tonsure of the whole head, wearing three yellow robes and pronouncing the three jewels and the ten commandments or precepts. The three Jewels were : (1) Buddham charnam gacchami (I go for refuge to Buddha); (2) Dharmam charnam gacchami (I go for refuge to Doctrine) and (3) Sangam charnam gacchami (I go for refuge to order).

The Sanghas and Viharas did not follow any common rales nor obey common authority. Each monastery framed its own rale in the light of the teaching of the Buddha within the monastery. The monks enjoyed much freedom. The chief monk was often elected by the monks of the monastery. The daily life of the monk was spent in work, study and meditation.

Buddhist Literature: The early religious books of Buddhists constitute to Tripitaka — the sutha pitaka, the vinaya pitaka and the Abhi damma pitaka. The pitakas were written in pali. The first contain the sermons of the Buddha and his chief disciples. The second is concerned with monastic discipline and the rule intended for the observance and guidance of monks and nuns. The last and the third is a detailed and highly technical exposition of the Dhamma.

Besides, there are some sacred books like Dhammapada, the Theragatha and the Jataka tales. The Dhammapada is a collection of select ethical precepts. The Theragatha reveal the personal experience of monks and nuns respectively. The Jataka tales describe the innumerable previous lives of the Buddha. These are called the Buddhist canonical literature. Some informations about Buddhism are available from the Dipavamsa and Mahavamsa, the Ceylonese Chronicle, of the 4th and 6th centuries A.D.

Causes for the Spread of Buddhism: The religion of the Buddha founded in one comer of India spread not only in India but also made its way to Ceylon, Burma, Tibet, Jawa, Sumatra, Bomeo, Champa, China, Siam and Central Asia. This phenomenal growth of Buddhism was due to many causes.

(1) The first and foremost cause for the spread of Buddhism was the simplicity of the teachings of Buddha. His Philosophy was very simple. It did not require any employment of priests and the expenditure of money.

(2) The language employed by Buddha was also very simple. It was very familiar to the people. He gave his lectures in Pali language which could be understood by the people.

(3) Buddhism did not believe in any caste system and so it opened its door for all races. Many people came forward to follow Buddhism.

(4) Another cause for the spread of Buddhism was that the practice of Hinduism has been made very expensive by the Brahmanas. A lot of money was required to perform many sacrifices in the life of a man. In the case of Buddhism it was not so. He could attain Nirvana by regulating the life.

(5) The personality of Buddha was also responsible for the spread of Buddhism. He devoted his life for the sake of spread of Buddhism in nook and corner of India. He possessed a magnetic personality so as to attract all sorts of people.

(6) The Buddhist Sangha was also responsible for the spread of Buddhism. Both the monks and the nuns played a dominant role in promoting the cause of Buddhism. They worked from morning till night preaching the gospel of Buddha which alone was the object of their life. The Buddhist monasteries or Viharas became great centres of education. Many people came forward to learn things about Buddha from the Bhikshus.

(7) Great Kings like Ashoka, Kanishka and Harsha patronised Buddhism. The only object of Asoka was to spread the law of piety or piety of Dharma. He took series of measures to carve out the Buddhistic principles on pillars and rocks throughout the length and breadth of this country.

(8) Since there was no rival to Buddhism it flourished successfully in the land.

Causes for the Decline: Many causes were responsible for the gradual decline and fall of Buddhism in the land of its birth although it continued to flourish in countries beyond India for centuries. Even today it has a large number of followers all over the world. However it has practically disappeared from India.

(1) The decline of the Buddhist Sangha was one of the important causes for the decline of Buddhism with the passage of time, the Sangha became the hot bed of instrigues and corruption. The monks and the nuns began to lead a life of pleasure and ease.

(2) The revival of Brahmanical Hinduism also gave a set back to the cause of Buddhism. The Gupta rulers were great patrons of Hinduism. No king gave support to Buddhism after Harsha. No wonder, many people gave up their faith in Buddhism.

(3) From the 8th century to the 12th century most of the northern India was governed by the Rajput princes who took pleasure in fighting and blood shed. They did not attach importance on the principle of Ahimsa. So it declined gradually in the land of its origin.

(4) The Muslim conquests of India gave a death blow to Buddhism in the country. They slaughtered many Buddhists and the remaining were converted to Islam. They plundered and pillaged the viharas.

(5) The decline of intellectual activity paved the way for the decline of Buddhism. The people lost their faith in this religion and so it declined rapidly.

(III) JAINISM

Previous History: The 6th Century B.C. was a great age of religious ferment. From the time of Rig Veda people began to follow many rituals and ceremonies. They became tired of those things. Hence, they wanted to have simple and straight faith instead of their good old mantras and tantras. Under the circumstances two great prophets Mahavira and Buddha appeared in the scene to answer their call. They propagated new great religions of Jainism and Buddhism respectively.

The Sacred Books of Jains tell us that real founder of Jainism was Rishabha who was succeeded by 23 Tirthankaras. According to the orthodox view Rishaba was the father of King Bharata, the first Chakravartin, King of India. According to Prof. Jacobi, Parsvanath was the real founder of Jainism.

Birth: Mahavira was the last Tirthankara or Prophet. According to tradition he was born in 599 B.C. at Vaisali in a Kshatriya family. He was the second son of Siddharatha, a Chieftain of Kundagama near Vaisali (Magadha). His mother was Trishala, sister of Chetaka who was the ruler of Vaisali.

According to Kalpasutra, the father of Vardhana celebrated the occasion of the birth of his son on a large scale. Many concessions were given and great and small fines were remitted. The astrologers made a forecast at the time of his birth that either he will be a great King or a great Saint. There is a lot of controversy regarding the date of birth of Mahavira.

Early Life: Mahavira spent his early life in royal luxuries. He was married to a beautiful princess named Yasodhara. A daughter was born to Mahavira. Her name was Anoja. The parents of Mahavira were the followers of Parsvanath which also affected the life of Mahavira. At the age of 30, his parents died and with the permission of his elder brother and authorities of the town he renounced the world and turned an ascetic.

As An Ascetic: For twelve years he led the life of a wandering mendicant subjecting himself to all kinds of penances and austerities. In the first year he wore a single garment and later even that was discarded. According to Acharanya Sutra "He wandered naked and homeless people mocked at him — set dogs on him — beat him with sticks and with their feet and threw fruits. But like a hero in the forefront of the battle, Mahavira withstood it all. He never cared about his wounds, bath and cleaning of his teeth. Often he drank no water for months". In the 13th year of his penance he attained enlightenment under a Sal tree and was recognised as 'Jina' (conqueror) and 'Arhat' (great). Very soon he became a reputed leader of a land of ascetics and preached for 30 years in Magadha and adjacent Gangetic area. He was patronised by Kings. In 527 B.C. at the age of 72 he died as a result of self-imposed starvation at Pava near Rajagriha.

His Teachings: Mahavira rejected the theory of divine creation of the universe and held that the world is eternal. It goes through an indefinite number of ages and in each age there are periods of progress and decline. The universe is filled with souls or 'Jivas' (lives). Originally a soul is an infinitely small object naturally bright, pure blissful and all knowing. Due to adherence of 'Karma' or action, the soul becomes clouded, heavy and unfree.

First it gets spiritual and then a material body. The adherence of more and more Karmic matter makes the soul pass through several births. If a soul wants to free itself from rebirth and attain Salvation or 'Nirvana' (a state of action free eternal bliss) it should attain 'Kevala Jnana' or Supreme knowledge. This could be attained only by the practice of strict 'ahimsa' or non injury to a living being, renunciation of all worldly interests, charity, chastity, truth speaking and honourable conduct.

Tri Ratna: Jainism emphasises the following three Jewels or Tri Ratna (three principles) to its followers in order to annihilate the influx of bad Karmas and to save oneself from the effects of present Karmas.

(1) Right faith; (2) Right knowledge and (3) Right conduct.

Right faith is a firm belief in the omniscience and infallibility of Mahavira and 23 predecessors or Tirthankaras and in their capacity to save them from the ocean of misery and enable them to attain salvation.

Right knowledge is the belief that the world is not created by any supreme. Being that all animate and inanimate things have souls that the soul migrates from body to body in obedience to the Law of Karma and that it can obtain Moksha only after the exhaustion of Karma.

Right conduct include the methods to be adopted for the destruction of Karma and the attainment of Salvation.

Jain monks are required not to injure life, not to speak lies, not to steal, not to perform the sexual act and not to be selfish. Monks had to carry brooms with them for sweeping the floor lest they should cause harm and destruction to any crawling creature, to cover the mouth with a veil lest they should take in any living organism and to carry a staining cloth to stain the water they drank.

Austerities of a severe kind were prescribed by Mahavira to ascetics with a view to discipline their mind and body. They were required to pluck out their hair and end their lives by starvation.

Mahavira did not believe in the existence of God, the creator of the world, According to him, not only human beings but also inanimate things like plants and stones had soul. Hence, no injury should be done to animals, birds, plants etc. According to him a person could be released from the cycle of rebirths only after attaining the 'Siddha Sila'.

After Mahavira: The above teachings of Mahavira have still remained the cardinal doctrinces of Jainism. Though Jainism did not spread beyond India, it has stayed in the country. It claim about two million followers many of whom are rich merchants. From its original home, *viz.*, the Gangetic valley, where it left no trace. Jainism spread to western India and the south. In the South its influence gradually diminished with the rise of the new devotional sects of Saivism and Vaishnavism.

The Great Split: In the first century A.D. (about 80 A.D.) a schism arose within the Jain community on the question of wearing clothes. Those who wore cloths were known as Svetambaras (white robed) and those discarded them were called Digambaras (sky clad). There were however, no great differences in doctrine between them. In course of time the Digambara too began to wear clothes.

Jain Literature: The Jain cannon was for a long time unwritten. About the 5th century A.D. the Digambars and the Svethambars formulated their own texts which were supposed to be authorised versions of the original canon. In the middle ages there appeared several commentaries on the texts and secular works too. Mallinatha, the famous commentator of Kalidasa's work was a Jain monk. Nayachandra, a Sanskrit poet of the 14th century was a Jain monk.

In Tamil literature, Jain poets had a high place for centuries. The 'Jivaka Chintamani' which is perhaps the finest of all Tamil Poems is a jain work. The Kural of Tiruvalluvar was also a Jain. There are some Kannada literature written by Jain poets and scholars. Hemachandra was probably the greatest of all Jain writers. He did a lot to the Jain literature. His period was 1088 A.D.

It is to be observed that a lot of work has been done on Jainism by Prof. Buhler, Prof. Jacobi, Dr. Hoernle, Dr. Banarsidas Jain, Mrs. Sinclair, Mr. Stevenson and Mr. Shah.

Jain Monachism: Jain Monachism or monasticism was well known for its rigorous discipline. It was recognised that full salvation was not possible for the lay man. If one wanted to attain 'Nirvana' he should enter the order of monks and drive out all Karma by study, meditation, penance, fasting and self mortification. One should lead pure life to attain Nirvana. Otherwise, it was inaccessible to him. He should take the following five vows abjuring : (1) Killing; (2) Stealing; (3) Lying; (4) Sexual activity and (5) Possession of property besides meditation and penance.

12

East Asian Civilisations

(I) CHINESE CIVILISATION

Chinese civilisation occupies a unique place in the cultural development of the Far East. Diderot admits that the Chinese were superior to all Asiatics and even surpass Europeans in the fields like intellect, art, philosophy and wisdom. The Chinese claim that they were the most refined and civilised people of all times. Europeans and Americans were second at as if they were barbarians. Let us see how far the ancient Chinese had developed such an enviable civilisation.

Land: China is surrounded by Pacific on the East and South, Tibetan Plateau on the West, Plateau of Mongalia on the North and thus enjoy a certain degree of natural isolation. This gave her a security and aloofiness and hence developed a civilisation without any outside obstructions. China has many contrasting topographical features. There are barren deserts, rugged mountains and their peaks, broad upland plateaus, and wide fertile river valleys. The ancient Chinese civilisation developed along the two great rivers-Yangtse-Kiang (son of the Ocean) and Hwang-Ho (yellow river) and along the major streams of the country. They developed their prosperous civilisation in 5000 B.C. by slowly clearing the forests, draining the marshes, eradicating the deadly insects and fighting out the barbarians in these river valleys.

People: China is the place of human habitation since the remote past of mankind in the world. Neolithic remains have been discovered in Northern China. Because of the natural barriers there has been less racial mixing in this country. The Chinese belong mostly to the Mongolian race. Tribal people from Russia, Mesopotamia and Central Asia also got merged with them. There were many types of Chinese and so there were many cultures.

The Early Rulers: Chinese mythology records names of rulers as far back as 3000 B.C. Fu Hsi (2852 B.C) was the first civilised ruler according to legends. He taught his people marriage, writing, fishing, music and so on. His successor, Shen Nung introduced agriculture, commerce, and the Science of Medicine. He was followed by Huang Ti. Huang Ti taught the people the crafts and form of civilisation. He was followed by four rulers Chuan, Hsia Ku, Yao and Shun. Yao was one of the greatest rulers of ancient China. Confucius had paid glorious tributes to him.

After Shun, Yu founded the Hsia dynasty. It was followed by Shang dynasty and was superseded by Wu, the founder of Chou dynasty (1122-225 B.C.). In this period, China made notable progress. The Chou ruler was both King and priest functioning equally as priest and as secular ruler.

Feudal Age: During the closing years of the Chou period the empire disintegrated into a number of small feudal states. The ruler was reduced to a puppet. Confucius gives an excellent description of the State of 'Lu' one of the many feudal organisations, in his "Spring and Autumn Annals". Countless petty wars, treacheries, social and economic conditions are depicted in it. War Lords waged war on each other, entered into alliances against a powerful Lord to destroy him, and then fought among themselves over the spoils. Finally, there arose the province of Chin under the leadership of Shih — Huang Ti (246-210 B.C.) who founded Chin dynasty.

Chin Dynasty (221-207 B.C.). Shih Huang-Ti sometimes called the first emperor, was one of China's greatest rulers. The name China came from Chin, the province over which he ruled. It was he who built the Great Wall of China, one of the wonders of the world.

Chaos followed for a short time after the death of Shih Huang-Ti, but order was restored under the Han dynasty. Han dynasty (202 B.C.-220 A.D) was founded by Liu-Hang an ordinary farmer. This dynasty maintained peace and prosperity for four centuries in greater part of China. Wu Ti (140-87 B.C.) was the most important ruler of this dynasty. The period of Han dynasty was one of the richest and most inspiring periods in China's long history. The Chinese accept this period as their Golden Age. Wang Mang was another noteworthy ruler of this dynasty who introduced economic and social reforms. Barbarian invasion ended this dynasty by 221 A.D. Then political anarchy prevailed in China during 221-618 A.D. It was called a Dark age. This came to an end when Tei Tsu (618-626 A.D) found Tang dynasty. He was succeeded by Tai Tsung (627-649 A.D) whose period of reign is regarded as glorious in the history of China. In the period of Tang dynasty, architecture and sculpture attained new peaks of excellence. It was a great age of Chinese poets. Block printing was invented in this period. After a short period of political confusion due to the Tatar invasion, Sung dynasty (960-1279) came to the power. After three centuries of Sung rule China came under the Mongols.

Mongol Rule: The Mongol invasion forms an important part in the annals of Chinese history. Mongols entered under Temujin followed by Chengizkhan and Kubla Khan. Peking was made their eastern winter capital in 1264. To put an end to all the miseries of Chinese from the Mongol tyrants, Chu-Yuan Sang founded the last native Chinese dynasty called Ming dynasty (1368-1644). Finally, came the last ruling dynasty of china namely Manchu dynasty which wielded the authority from 1644 to 1911. Kang Hsi, Chien Lung and Shien Feng were the remarkable rulers of this dynasty.

Thinkers and Philosophers: Sixth century B.C. in China was a period of enlightenment. A number of philosophers and religionists emerged and guided the people. Confucius Lao Tze, Mo-Ti, Yang Chu and Mencius were the outstanding philosophers of China. Lao-Tze's book Tao-Te-Ching or the "Books of the way and virtue" is considered to be the Bible of Taoism. The Books of Confucius namely "The Book of History", "The Book of Poetry" and "Record of Rights" contain principles of ideal human life and morality. He emphasised virtuous conduct both in private and public life. He advocated ethics as basic to good government. In his view, the ruler must not only set an example, but by his action serve as a positive force for the moral regeneration of the society.

Mo-Ti, the altruist advocated universal love as the panacea for the social evils. Mo-Ti was an idealist. Another school of philosophy of egoists was led by Yang Chu who advocated epicureanism. But these philosophers were condemned by Mencius who was mainly concerned with the organisation of State and Society. Obedience was the basis of his organisation. Monarchy was an ideal form of Government for him. He advocated war, not against other countries but against poverty and ignorance within the country, for they were the causes of the crime.

Hsun Tse, was a realist. He advocated self denial for ending the evils in the society. Chuang-Tse echoed the philosophy of Lao Tize. He preached a return to nature. We can perceive the ideas of Buddhism and Upanishads in his philosophy.

Thus, Philosophy forms an important contribution of China to the modern world.

Poetry: Chinese poetry is known for its brevity. Poetry for the Chinese was a moments ecstasy and its expression in a few words. It lends itself freely to picture writing. It appeals to mature minds.

Li-Po (705-762) was one of the greatest poets of China. He was said to have mastered all the works of Confucius and began writing poetry even at the young age of 10. His lyric to "The Maid of Wu" is a typical example of his love of nature and human sympathy. Tu Fu (712-770) was the "Keats of China". He was a personal friend but professional enemy of Li Po. He entered the service of the Ming emperor and won a reputation for poetry. He concentrated on sadder themes such as trying to console mothers whose sons had been called to war.

Po-Chou was another Chinese Poet who rose to eminence in the State and even became the governor of the city of Hang Chow.

Prose: Prose writing was not regarded as an important contribution in the field of literature. Historic fiction formed a part of literature in China. They portray vividly the past of China. Liae Chai-Chih I or Short stories are famous for their beauty. They are written in 24 volumes. History was the most appreciated literature in China. The history of 214 dynasties of China runs through 291 large volumes. Szuma was the greatest historian of this period. Han-Yeu was a great essayist.

Chinese Drama became popular in the time of Kubla Khan. The drama was mixture of history, poetry and music. Every drama inculcated a moral. The dramas inculcated Confucian virtues especially filial loyalty.

Music was largely used in religion and on the drama stage. It was not considered an art by itself. Music with the Chinese was a nectar in life.

Learning: Confucius was the "uncrowned King" in Chinese learning. His ideas on teaching methods were followed by several cultural Chinese. According to him education should be independent of state control. Theoretically any man could become a State official if he could pass the examination.

People's Features: Chinese were a vigorous people known for their physical stamina and courage. The peasant women were as strong as man themselves. The women of upper classes were beautiful, applied powders on their face, coloured their lips and eyes. Men usually wore caps. Women used both silk and cotton cloths. Short feet were considered to be a sign of beauty.

Art of Writing in Ancient China: People had invented and developed their own art of writing. It was pictographic script. There were nearly 40,000 pictographs. Out of these 600 pictographs were of basic nature in the Chinese script.

Their language was free from grammar. It consisted of 400 to 800 word sounds and various thoughts were expressed by combination of them.

In the beginning Chinese people wrote on chips of wood with a bamboo pen. Then they used silk cloth and linen paper. When paper was invented by the Chinese scientists in 1st century A.D., they began to use it as writing material.

Economic Conditions: Chinese people lived in communities in villages surrounded by walls. They went to the fields together. Without rotation of crops or use of manures, they raised two or three crops in a year. Rice, macaroni, vermicelli, vegetables and fish formed the food of the average Chinese. A rich man's menu included atleast 40 items and the meal took 3 to 4 hours where as poor people suffered from starvation.

There were several industries. Textile and Silk industries formed the major part. Most of the industries were organised into guilds. Even barbers and cooks had their own guilds.

Men formed the main means of transport. Sedan chairs were used to carry men and materials. They were good traders. They exported silk, tea porcelain, paper, glass, tobacco and opium. They used leather currency which became the fore-runner of papper currency.

Science: (1) Gun powder was invented during the Tang period. (2) They were the first to use coal as a fuel. (3) They produced excellent books on agriculture and sericulture. (4) They wrote books on geography. (5) They developed Algebra and Geometry where a negative quantity was used for the first time. (6) They adopted a lunar calendar. (7) They became well versed in medicines. (8) Plenty of drugs and a kind of anaesthesia were produced.

Art and Architecture: The ancient Chinese architects constructed the Pagodas and the Great wall or China. The Pagodas were used as temples in their different cities and towns. The structure of the Pagoda was of the number of uneven storeys with peculiarly shaped roofs. The Great wall of China is one of the most impressive of Chinese architectural accomplishments. This was regarded as one of the wonders of the ancient world. It was constructed by Shih Hwang Ti (221-212 B.C.). It was from the sea shore near Peking to the desert of Gobi. At regular distances, the Great Wall had vaulted gates and strong square towers.

Sculpture: The Chinese sculptures prepared several bronze works which were decorated with the figures of animals monsters, lines and different designs. Sculpture worthy of particular note are figures of a female deity called Bodhisatva Avalokiteshvara. These figures belong to the period of Tang dynasty.

Painting: Since Chinese held the view that a cultured person should possess a skill in the art of painting. This art flourished in ancient China. They produced landscape paintings, scenes of historical events, portraits etc. They were highly imaginative and thought provoking. Wang Wei (699-759) was a great landscape painter and teacher of art. His manual on landscape work was a standard one for centuries together.

Porcelain: Porcelain, one of the greatest of their arts reached its zenith in the Sung dynasty. Innumerable articles were made : plates, cups, bowls, beakers, vases and so on. The most famous are the Jade green pieces (celadon) which cannot be reproduced.

Religion: The Chinese Society was built on a mixture of religion, moral and philosophy. Both Confucianism and Taoism are philosophies, but out of them a nature religion sprang. Buddhism was accepted by many Chinese and has played an important part in their history.

Confucianism: The Philosophy of Confucius developed into a religion called as Confucianism in China by 206 B.C. It was the State religion of China during 206 B.C. to 1912 A.D. and it guided the activity of the Chinese government on proper lines. It instilled the Chinese people a love for higher learning. It prompted many of them to undertake an activity to become persons of higher merit.

Taoism: The teachings of Lao Tze became a religion Taoism in China. Tao's was an appeal to return to the primitive simplicity of the past, when men followed and accepted the way of nature. It was combination of a pantheistic conception of absolute being with the superstitions of the people. It was a eclipsed by Buddhism which was introduced into china from India in the 1st century of the Christian era.

Buddhism: Emperor Ming Ti, the first convert to Buddhism sent a mission to India to visit the holy places connected with the life of Buddha and collect the sacred books. The mission returned with large collection of books and two reputed Buddhist Saints — Kashyapa Matang and Dharmaraksha. At Loyang a monastery was built to translate those collections into Chinese. In 381 A.D. Emperor Hein Wu built the first Buddhist temple at Nanking. Chinese pilgrims like Hiuen Tsang, Fahien, Itsing and others visited India.

The chief centres of Buddhist art in China were Tunhuang, Yun-Kang, Long-meng where grottos and Buddhist sculpture are found in large numbers.

They remind us the technique of Saranath and Ajanta schools. The storeys of pagodas, the extended brackets with hanging bells, the golden pinnacles and engraved pillars in the temples show Indian influence.

Thus, the Ancient Chinese civilisation has contributed much to the development of world culture.

(II) JAPANESE CIVILISATION

Land and the People: The Japanese legends say that the Gods commanded Izanami, two of the deities to create Japan and the Japanese race. They were brother and sister. Japan is situated on the East of China. Chinese considered that the Sun rises from that country and hence called Japan as the land of rising Sun.

Today Japan consists of 4223 Islands of which 600 are inhabited and four of which are of considerable size. They are Hokkaido, Honshu, Shikoku and Kyushu. Honshu, the largest is about 81,000 sq. milles in area. Those islands were the result of earthquakes that were common in that part of the world. These earthquakes have claimed several lives and villages. Inspite of the great sufferings and losses caused to them by those earth quakes, the people have never thought of abandoning the land but endured them patiently and have developed their own culture.

The origin of the Japanese is not yet unravelled. It is shrouded in mystery. The earliest settlers were Ainus, a white race, who came from the Amur river region. In about the Seventh Century B.C. people of Mongol origin entered the country from the Korean region. Then came a brown-black people from Malaya and Indonesia. After hundred years of assimilation came the present Japanese race.

Primitive Civilisation: From early times, Japan absorbed Chinese learning its art and philosophy. Izumo, and Yamoto were the two centres of ancient Japanese civilisation. The present 'Mikado' traces the origin of his dynasty to Jimmu Tenno who is said to have ascended to throne in 660 B.C. The descendants of Jimmu Tenno had since been enthroned as rulers of Japan. No single dynasty had ruled for so long a period in the history. The theory of divinity ascribed to Mikado, the ruler of Japan still holds good. In 522 A.D. Mahayana form of Buddhism entered Japan through China. In those days Daimyos the land lords dominated the political authority. In 645 A.D. the theory of absolute monarchy was proclaimed. In the following years, principles of administration were enunciated and all important posts were monopolised by the members of the Fujiwara family. Although the Emperor remained the fountain head of all powers, the real authority came to be exercised for 400 years by the

Fujiwara family. Finally, the emerging mutual rivalries among the jealous nobles resulted in chaos and confusion. Yoritoma rose up as the most powerful person out of this chaos. He was given the coveted title of "Sei-i-tai-Shogun".

Shoguns: Yoritomo was the first Shogun. He exercised the real authority of Mikado and administered the country efficiently. His period of defacto rule extended from 1192 to 1198. Samurai were feudal soldiers who assisted the Shoguns in their administration. Ashikaga Takauja established his Shogunate after Hojos and Tojos. Shogunates revived the power of Mikado. But the credit of established peace and order goes to three personalities. Oda Nobunaga, Toyotomi Hideyoshi and Tokugawa Ieyasu were those three who dominated Japan in the 16th Century. Ieyasu became the undisputed master of Japan and assumed the Shogunate in 1603 called the Tokugawa Shogunate. The Tokugawa Shogunate was the happiest and the most prosperous period in the history of Japan. People enjoyed a long period of peace under a military regime which patronised art and architecture in its own way.

Religion: Animism, ancestor worship and sex worship were the religions of the people. They believed in innumerable spirits that lived everywhere — in plants and stars, on trees, plain and mountain tops. Out of ancestor worship developed Japan's oldest religion Shintoism. It did not have either creed or a priesthood or a code of morals or a ritual. It did not speak of heaven or immortality. It only behoves every one to make an occasional pilgrimage to a Shinto centre and reverence for one's ancestors, the emperor and the past.

In 552 A.D. Mahayana Buddhism entered Nippon through China. It became the popular religion of the masses. Amitaba and Kwannan were the two important Bodhisatvas. It advocated virtues of piety, peace and obedience. Prince Shoku Taishi (592-621 A.D.) is considered to be the Asoka of Japan because he aided the Buddhists to build temples, encouraged and supported Buddhist clergy and enacted Buddhist dharma into laws. He built the oldest Buddhist temple of Haruji.

Society's Divisions: The ancient society of Japan consisted of three classes. They were Samurai, Traders and Slaves. Besides these three, there were soldiers, artisans and others like scavengers and tanners. Every class of people had their own particular form of dress and ornaments. They adhered to specific regulations exclusively meant for themselves alone. They had organised certain festivals. People from distant areas came to visit their beautiful gardens and flower shows at places like Kyoto.

Society's Conditions: There were many number of fiefs based upon feudal principles. The feudal lords ruled their areas according to their whims and fancies. However, they acknowledged the overlordship of the ruler.

The Ashikaga Shoguns encouraged arts and letters. The Tokugawa Shogunate under Iyeyasu organised a perfect system of feudal government. He introduced a common religion by mixing Shintoism and Buddhism to his people. The Tokugawas patronised literature and painting of Kano and Tosa schools. Trade and commerce developed in this period. Rich people raised beautiful constructions. But there was disparity among the rich and the poor. The rich became richer and poor poorer. Kyoto was their capital city.

Samurai or sword bearing guardsman formed the bottom of the society. Every noble had a large number of Samurai who were ready to die for their masters.

Law of Japan: Like religion and culture, Chinese law influenced Japanese legal system. Tenchi Tenno started codifying the law which was completed and promulgated in the reign of Emperor Mommu in 702 A.D. Until 1721, the law recognised family responsibility for the good behaviour of its members. Ordeal was permitted and torture was used to face confession of crime. Emperor Yoshimura became popular by his prison reforms. He formulated the first Japanese feudal code in 1721.

Philosophy: Philosophy too entered Japan from China. In the middle of the 16th Century, Fujiwara Seigwa went to China to study neo-Confucianism and returned with some books on philosophy. Soon he became famous and youths were attracted towards him. His disciple Hayashi Razan excelled his master in making new Confucianism very popular. Another Philosopher Muro Kyuso said that one should seek God not outside but within his own heart for the heart is the abode of God. Kaibara Ekken, another neo-confucianist made character the foundation of his philosophy. He was said to have written hundred books on his philosophy. Nakaye Toju (1608-1648) observed that man's mind is the mind of the world. He had guided the people to reach eternity. But in course of time Japanese philosophy turned to original teachings of Confucius and thus appeared the classical school of Ito Jinsai and Ogyu Sorai. Ogyu Sorai was the greatest of the later confuciantists who criticised all philosophers past and present.

Language and Writing: The Japanese language clearly displays the impact of Mongolian and Chinese language. There are 47 letters in the Japanese alphabet. In the early days writing was the luxury of rich. Only by 19th century second half, it spread among the masses. At Kyoto, the rich organised schools for their own children. Emperors Tenchi and Mommu established the first Japanese University at Kyoto in the 8th century. In 1630, a training school in Public administration was opened at Yedo which later developed into the University of Tokyo.

Poetry: The earliest form of literature of the Japanese was poetry. The "Manyoshu" a collection of 4500 poems was the earliest poetical work. Another important work was "Kokinshu" an anthology of poems brought together under Emperor Daigo. We can not find an heroic or epic strain or lyric of light in their short poems included in their anthologies.

Prose: Japanese novels ran into several volumes. 'Genji Monogatari' was said to have been written by Lady Murasaki Noshikibu in 1001 A.D. It run into 54 volumes covering 4234 pages. The author was a widow who lost her husband after four years of married life and she consoled herself by writing elaborately such a voluminous work. Kyokutei Bakin (1767-1848) was a romantic writer of history whose work could be compared to those of Sir Walter Scot and Dumas.

History: 'Kojiki' is a historical work with more legendary nature. Arai Kakuseki was a great scholar and the greatest Japanese Historian. His 'Hankampu' in 30 volumes was masterpiece in Japanese history. He lived in Yedo and through his eloquent speeches, he won over the Shoguns of his age. Lady Shri Shonagon was an essayist. Another equally prolific writer was Kamono-Chomei.

Drama: The Shinto dumb-shows were the beginning of their dramas. But 14th Century they added choral songs and then individual characters. Thus, their drama was born. Actors included such eminent men as Nobunaga, Hideyoshi and Iyeyasu and several others. Each actor wore a mask. The well human figure in Japanese drama was Chikamatsu who is compared to Shakespeare by some writers.

Arts: Japanese life is an art by itself. The King of Korea was said to have sent 80 musicians to perform ceremonies when the emperor Inkyo died. These musicians taught the people to play various musical instruments. Dance became a popular art in Japan. Doning clothes became an art. Everything that they carried with them was artistic. Hidari Jingaro, the greatest Japanese Sculptor was well known for his fine carvings on wood, ivory and other things. He had carved the elephants and the sleeping cat at the tomb of Iyeyasu at Nikko and in a temple at Kyoto.

Architecture: Architecture accompanied Buddhism from China. Emperor Suiko ordered for the construction of Buddhist temples which work was entrusted to Prince Shotoku. He imported all the technicians from China and began his work. The Golden Hall of the Todaiji temple at Nara is the most beautiful of those ancient structures. Yoshimitsu an Ashikaga Shogunate beautified Kyoto with temples and places. He built a pagoda of 360 feet. The Japanese rivalled the metal workers of Damascus. Beautiful bells like the 49-ton bell at Nara produced sweeter melodies than the bells of the west. Pottery was made with Japanese delicacy and fineness. The introduction of tea drinking increased the demand for Chinese tea-cups of the Sung design. Painting came to Japan from Korea and then from China. Buddhism stimulated the art and Buddha became its object. From 1150 A.D, onwards, a purely Japanese art dealing with Japanese flowers and landscapes grew up under the patronage of the Emperor and the nobility of Kyoto. But the art by which Japan came to be known in Europe was engraving. Preparing blocks and taking prints out of them were invented in Japan. Printing in general made rapid progress. Prints of various colours were made. The greatest of these print-makers were Hokusai and Hiroshigi.

Thus, Japan until 1853 remained a land of beauty in all its forms. Their greatest contribution is the creation of beauty rather than pursuit of truth.

13

Civilisations in America

(I) MAYA

Early History: Very recently the people of United States have begun to realise the many rare qualities of the lands to the South of their own country. American Indians had established a civilisation in the regions comprising of the peninsula of Yucatan, Mexico, Guatemala and Peru. But the racial origin of man in the Americas has not been determined. The theory generally subscribed to that the ancestors of the American Indians were Proto Mongolians who crossed the Behring Straits into Alaska. Another theory is that they were the immigrants from Europe who came by way of Greenland. Some others say that they were the descendants of the inhabitants of America itself.

Very little is known about the civilisation of Mayas because most of their achievements were destroyed by the Spanish conquerors. The only available remains of their civilisation could be seen in Dresden and Paris museums.

Mayan Government: The capital of Mayas was Chichen Itza. Their kings had both spiritual and temporal powers, the first being dominant. Yet the provincial cities were provided with autonomous powers. They had a flourishing trade. There were cities which specialised their products of commerce. Copan in Honduras for sculptures, Tikal for wood carving and Palenque for mouldings were such popular centres of trade.

The year 613 B.C. is considered by the Mayas as their Zero year. Their first empire was founded in Gautemala in the 1st century of the Christian era but the zenith of their accomplishments was reached in 5th and 6th centuries. They settled in the Yucatan peninsula by the 7th century.

In the 12th century, the Mayas were conquered by the Toltecs — a war like people who subjected most of the Maya cities and forced the inhabitants to pay tribute. Quetzacotal (1207) of Toltecs was not only an able ruler but an artist, scientist, and humanist philosopher as well. By 1220, the Aztecs overran the territory.

Art and Architecture:

(1) Mayas rank very high in the field of architecture. Temples, palaces, and fine buildings were produced in abundance. There were huge pyramids on which were temples, monasteries for the priesthood, palaces for the rulers, astronomical Observatories, courts for athletics and vapor baths.

(2) Mayas did not use the true arch in their buildings. They used Cantilinear arches for roofs.

(3) The temple of the warriors at Chichen Itza was upon a pyramid built on another pyramid and was approached by winding stairs. The buildings were ornamented with bas-relief paintings.

(4) The Mayans used sculpture in the service of religion. They were efficient in making human figures. The Serpent motive dominated their sculptures. Their gods were half human and half animal. The serpent symbolism indicates the true emotional nature of the Mayans sculpture.

(5) Their painting was moderate. Their codices, wall frescoes, and ceramics were the only examples that have survived. Their codices or ancient books were in pictographic writing. In making figures they used a subtle way of blending various colours, which give the paintings a beauty and an artistic effect.

(6) The Mayans, like the Aztecs and Incas, were artistic craftsmen and made fine pottery. Their woven cloth and feather work became an art with them. Wood carving, bell making, gold ornaments and ornaments in jade and other precious stones of Mayas are also discovered in the excavations.

Religion: All their religious practices were based upon the earthly matters since their main stay was agriculture. Many of the numerous Gods were earth Gods associated with the direction East, West and so on. There were Gods of forests, rain, plains fertility and animals. Prayers and ceremonies were performed before cutting a tree, or before sowing the seeds or launching on a hunting.

Their rain-gods were called Chacs. Itzamua was an important God of the skies. Their Sun-God was Kinichahau Kulkulkan, the feathered serpent was the patron deity of Chichen Itza.

Ceremonies and Sacrifices: Mayans religion was associated with the months of the year. The festivals were kept up with elaborate ceremonies. The new year began with pop and the festival was celebrated on a grand scale after a long fasting lasting two or three months. The month of Zip was devoted for the Gods of the hunt. It was an elaborate ceremony and on that occasion human sacrifices were offered. Children, virgins and young men were offered for sacrifices and among them children seem to be the chief. The priest chief of whom was Ah Kin Mai, were in charge of these sacrifices. They played an important role in Mayans Government and the society.

Literature and Learning: The Mayans and Aztecs used complicated hieroglyphics for writing. Both of them wanted to preserve their history, mythology and literature in sculpture and architecture. The whole system of written expression is most perplexing. No personal or place name has been definitely recognised and translated, although great quantities of material have been found. But much of their literature, sculpture and architectures had been destroyed by the Spanish invaders.

Science: (1) Calendar is the greatest scientific achievement of the Mayas. It was based on mathematical and astronomical observations. (2) The year consisting of 365 days, was divided into 18 months of 20 days each. The five remaining days were considered unlucky, but were added to complete the year. (3) One of the main uses of the Calendar was to be a guide for the farmers. The lucky days were marked on the calendar for cultivation and harvesting the crops. (4) The Mayan mathematical system had the zero. (5) But instead of a decimal system, they used the vigesimal system in which 20 was represented by 19 days and a zero. (6) All the fundamentals of modern arithmetic were known to them even 2000 years ago, at least 5 centuries before the Indians developed the fundamentals of arithmetic.

(II) AZTEC

Land and the People: Aztecs developed a rich civilisation in the most fertile land of Mexico in America in the ancient period. It can be equalled to those of Egyptian and Indian civilisation. The valley of Mexico was occupied by various tribes. The earliest of them were Toltecs, the ancestors of Aztecs. They established their capital at Tula, north of the Mexican Valley and we could find the ruins of their buildings in that city.

Later they occupied the South western border of the great lake where they built their capital city Mexico, called after their war-God Mexitle. As a result of their military discipline they became powerful and won a reputation for courage. By the middle of the 15th century the Aztec power spread beyond the Mexican Valley.

The Government: Aztec and their allies called Tezcucans were ruled by despotic Kings. The ruler was elected from among the brothers of the diseased ruler by a council. The chosen ruler was installed after a religious ceremony but before that he should have led a successful campaign, brought home enough prisoners to grace his entry into the capital. The nobility held large estates and were usually governors of provinces and cities.

The legislative power was vested in the emperor and royal despotism was checked by independent tribunals which dealt with civil and criminal cases. Over each district, there was a supreme judge with original and appellate jurisdiction. These judges held office during their life time. Below the Supreme judge there was a court in each province.

The Aztecs showed a high regard for right to property and life. Bribery or collusion with the suitors was punishable with death. Judges were paid by alloting a part of the produce of royal domain. Law of the land was registered and published in hieroglyphic writing. All crimes against society — murder, theft, adultery, removal of boundary stones were severely punished. It is really surprising that a primitive people like Aztecs had a high sense of equity in the application of law.

Marriage was celebrated with great formality and separate court was instituted to deal with cases arising from it. Divorce could be granted only by that court and that, after hearing both the parties.

Slavery was an important institution among the Aztecs and they were also entitled to enjoy certain number of rights.

Taxes: The revenue came chiefly from the royal domains. The tax was generally in kind. Certain taxes were collected from manufacturers like cotton dresses, feather work, ornamented armour and so on. Garrisons were stationed in important cities particularly the newly conquered to maintain law and order. Defaulters were liable to be sold as slaves. Huge granaries and store houses were maintained at the capital under a Receiver-General who became a great functionary. Any misappropriation of revenue was severely punished.

Communications: Courier service was maintained to pass on communications to the distant parts of the country. Post houses were stationed at regular intervals. Messengers by a relay system conveyed the message to the Emperor.

The Army: The soldiers in Mexico were held in high esteem. Military expeditions were undertaken chiefly to secure prisoners for sacrifice to the God of War. They believed that those who died in war entered the regions of the Sun God.

Their art of war was not scientific in any sense of the term. They advanced singing their martial songs. There were brisk encounters and sudden retreats. Hospitals were built for the sick and the wounded and the paid surgeons carried out their day to day duties.

Religion: Aztec life was bound up with religion. There was the supreme creator and the Lord of Universe and one God. Since they found it difficult to grasp this idea of unity, they resort to a Pantheon. Of these there were 13 chief deities and about 200 of inferior status. Each of them had a special day and a special ritual. At the head of the Pantheon stood Huitzilopochtli the war God and the patron deity of the nation. Another interesting deity was the God of the air. The priest was the embodiment of everything in science and of knowledge of the community. The priests were powerful, and were incharge of choirs arranged festivals, according to the calendar, and looked to the education of the youth. Human sacrifices began in the 14th century.

Writing: The development of the arts was one of the brighter aspects of Aztecs culture. They used the hieroglyphics system for writing. Cotton cloth, or skins nicely prepared were used as writing material. But for the most part they used a material made of leaves of aloe. This material retained its freshness and the paintings on it retained their brilliancy of colours. But such manuscripts which could have enlightened us had been destroyed as a result of Christian fanaticism.

Science: The Aztecs used certain form of rotation in arithmetic. Numbers 1 to 19 were represented by as many dots. 20 had a hieroglyphic sign of a flag. The Aztec year was divided into 18 months of 20 days each and 5 days were added to the last month and these days were very inauspicious to the people. The month was divided into 4 weeks each of 5 days and the 5th day of the week was the market day. Astrology had always exercised a great influence on man.

Agriculture: Agriculture was fairly well developed with the help of irrigation. When the land was exhausted it was allowed to remain fallow. Their main crop was maize and got their sugar from its stalk. They also cultivated bananas and cocoa — They used aloe leaves for several purposes. These leaves were used for thatching their houses. They also cultivated many medicinal plants some of which had been introduced into Europe. As Mexico includes regions of different climates, it became a garden of different flowers. It was indeed the land of flowers.

Industry: The Aztecs exploited the mineral wealth of their country. They got their silver, lead, and tin from the mines of Tasco and their copper from the mountains of Zacotolan. They cast the gold into bars or converted them into dust. Iron was unknown to them. But brass served the purpose of iron. They also cast vessels of gold and silver and carved them in a delicate manner. The entrance and angles of their buildings were richly ornamented with images of their fantastic Gods and frequently of animals. Large number of sculptured images were scattered all over the country. The most remarkable of their sculptured art is indicated by their calendar stone of dark porphyry weighing nearly 50 tons.

Social Life: There was no caste system among the Aztecs. The son usually followed the profession of his father. Various trades were organised into guilds. The profession most respected in Mexico was that of the merchant. Slave trade was also carried on. The merchant community enjoyed a special status in society. They were allowed to have their own insignia, law courts and they formed councils of finance. They were consulted by the rulers and some of them were closely associated with him.

The discipline of the children especially at schools was very severe. Polygamy was practised by the rich. The obligations of the marriage life was impressed upon the couple when a religious ceremony was administered during the marriage. The womenfolk were respected by their husbands. The women took active part in festivities and banquets. People applied perfumes, Tobacco was also used by the people. Meats of all kinds especially of game, of which turkey was important were served at the table. Then followed fruits and vegetables of all kinds and then confectioneries and pastry. On religious occasions meat of man was served as a special dish.

When the banquet was over the young danced to the accompaniment of music while the elderly continued sipping the drinks. Intoxication was condemned among the young.

This was the civilisation of the people of Mexico.

(III) INCAS

Land and the People: The Incas had developed a rich civilisation in an area covering the modern countries of Ecuador, Peru and Bolivia. Cuzco, the capital of Incas was situated on the banks of the lake Titica, The land around Lake Titica, about 40 miles wide and 120 miles long and more than 12,500 feet above sea level was one of the most famous centre of these people. In this stimulating climate, the natives were able to grow crops, raise Lamas for meat and wool, and use the copper that existed in abundance.

The ruins found around the lake indicate that it must have been originally the home of a highly advanced people. But we cannot say who these people were and when they came. It is possible that the new invaders, the Incas, might have made them accept their supremacy. Before the middle of the 15th century A.D. Topa Inca Yupanqui occupied the southern region of Chile and established the Inca empire. The Incas had evolved a rich civilisation in Peru.

The Government: Heriditary principle was followed for the succession to the throne. The heir was the son of the Coya or the legal wife who was distinguished from concubines.

The heir chosen to the throne was entrusted to the care of the wisemen who instructed him in such elements of knowledge as they possessed. He was also trained in every art of war. At the age of 16, he passed through a test of strength, dexterity and skill conducted by some of the oldest members of the Incas. Wrestling, boxing, running long distances and living under the most trying conditions were the chief exercises. When the prince had thus qualified himself he was allowed to take part with councils of his father and was appointed to offices of trust at home.

The Inca government was a despotism of a mild character. As representative of the Sun, the Inca was the head of the priesthood and presided at the most important of their festivals. His dress was made of the finest vicuna wool.

Royal palaces noted for their solidity and strength and built of stones were scattered all over the country. Its interior walls were studded with Gold and Silver ornaments.

The favorite residence of Incas was at Yucay, some four leagues away from Cuzca. They lived in enormous affluence. When the Inca died, all his palaces except one were closed and all the wealth he had amassed was locked up; for it was believed that soul of the departed Inca would return to animate his body and he needed all those. The body was embalmed and was taken to the temple of the Sun at Cuzco.

The Nobles: The Peruvian nobles were divided into Incas and Curacas. The former claimed descent from the Sun God like the King. They held the key positions of the State. They led the armies, and were governors of the provinces and commandants of garrisons stationed in various strategic posts.

The Curacas consisted of the caciques of the conquered people or their descendants. They were required to educate their children at the court as a mark of their loyalty. They did not possess high positions in the state.

The strength of the Peruvian monarchy lay in the Inca nobility. They formed the royal bodyguard. They were the foundation of the peculiar civilisation and polity of the Incas.

Administration: The Kingdom was divided into four parts or provinces each occupied by the conquered people. Each of the provinces was under a viceroy who carried on the administration with the aid of one or more councils.

The whole empire was divided into departments each containing 10,000 inhabitants and under a governor who exercised jurisdiction over the Curacas and other officers below him.

There were magistrates in towns or in small communities. They dealt with petty cases. Serious cases were decided by the higher courts under District officers or provincial governors. Every case had to be disposed off within five days. There was no appeal from one tribunal to another.

The laws were severe and penalties were cruel. Theft and adultery were punished with death. A liar had his tongue nailed to a board for the third offence.

The Peruvian regulations regarding property were remarkable. The land in every province was divided into three parts — one for the Sun, the second for the Inca and the third for the people. The agrarian law of the Incas was better than any other country's law.

There were a number of Industries and some regulations existed in industries also. The Peruvian sheep belonged exclusively to the Sun and Incas. The sheep were reared at the appointed time and the raw wool was stocked in royal magazines. There were a number of mines from which minerals were extracted. The workers were provided with the tools they needed.

Their economic system was peculiar. The members of the royal family, the nobility, various priesthoods and officers were exempted from taxation and naturally the burden of taxation fell heavily on the common man. No man could change his social status. "As he was born, so he had to die" was their dictum.

Public Works: The Incas were much interested in the public works. The ruins of their palaces, temples, fortresses, aqueducts speak of their faded fame. The roads, bridges and precipices were all built with utmost efficiency. The roads were flanked with shade giving trees. The traveller could enjoy the perfume and taste of the delicious fruits from the trees grown on the sides of the roads. Caravansarais were erected at every 10 or 12 miles perhaps intended for the travellers.

Postal System: The system of communication was improved by post houses found along all the main roads leading to the capital. Special runners, chosen for their speed and honesty waited there to carry the messages. It was really creditable that a postal system existed in America much earlier than it appeared in the West. The great capitals, Cusco and Quito were kept in immediate correspondence.

The Army: They professed peace at home but they were always at war with the neighbouring tribes. Often religion gave them a pretext for bellicose activities. The enemies were given an option of either surrendering to Sun God or war. Compulsory military training was given to people. Great attention was paid to the health of the soldiers. Incas settled down in the conquered territories. Temples to Inca Gods were built and numerous priests instructed the people in the religion of the conquerors.

Religion: Religion was the basis of their polity and of their social existence. It was in all its essence a theocracy. Their most popular God was the Sun for whom temples were built everywhere. The Incas also worshipped other Gods also. Moon and Venus were such Gods. They dedicated temples to Thunder Lightning and Rainbow also. The most ancient temple of the Sun was on the island of Titicaca. There was another renowned temple at Cuzco which had grown into palace of Gold. Besides these, there were several other temples numbering more than 40. There were not less than 4000 priests with a high priest. The priests attended to the ceremonies and were expected to be well acquainted with rituals of different festivals. The greatest festival was Rayami held in honour of the Sun God. The virgins of the Sun formed a novel institution. Their number at Cuzco was about 1500, all selected from the noble families of Incas. Though these virgins were employed in the service of the Sun, they were the brides of the Incas.

Nobles followed polygamy whereas the common man adopted monogamy. Equality before the law and of opportunity was recognised and made real.

Education: It was the sole monopoly of the nobility as they were the sole administrators. The children of the nobility were trained in their duties and responsibilities of the respective positions they might be called upon to occupy. They learned to speak their language correctly and use Quipu which was a mean of communicating ideas. But those, who were to become priests, were given religious instructions.

Agriculture: Their method of Agriculture was certainly scientific. They had a good system of irrigation. The technique of constructing canals through rocky mountains deserves high praise. The Incas planted new colonies in the desert areas after providing irrigation facilities. Fairs were organised in populous areas to help the people to exchange their agricultural produce. The method of exchange was exclusively by barter.

The fleece collected from Lama and the hindered sheep was used for the manufacture of woollens. The Peruvians had regulated hunting. In Peru, law protected both man and the beast. Peru was rich in gold. The remains collected show a curious and elaborate workmanship. The Peruvians had excelled in architecture too. They produced monuments of architectural taste and magnificence.

Thus, the Incas had evolved a peculiar kind of civilisation in Peru.

MEDIEVAL PERIOD

14

Legacies of Christian Religion

Christianity is regarded as one of the great religions of the world. Most of the people in the world are Christians. It was established in Palestine. In other words it was established in West Asia spread in Europe and now it had turned as a world religion.

Birth of Jesus: The founder of Christianity Jesus Christ was born at Bethlehem in Palestine. He was a Jew by birth. His parents were Joseph and Mary. He should have born some 5 or 6 years before the actual commencement of the Christian era.

Early Life: Jesus lived in Nazareth for about thirty years. During his stay at Nazareth, his occupation was of a carpenter, the profession of his father. John the Baptist was a notable preacher of that time. Jesus was attracted by his preaching. After getting baptism from his hands on the banks of the river Jordan, Jesus also began to preach. He visited many places including Judea and Galilee. He taught as he travelled and attracted increasing number of followers. His ideas spread nook and corner of Palestine. When he reached Jerusalem, thousands flocked to see and hear him.

Teachings: (1) There is only one God according to Jesus. (2) God is the loving Father of all that lives and that all men are brothers. (3) Jesus compared God to a king, but the kingdom of god, he said, is not like a worldly kingdom. (4) 'Do unto others as you would like them to do to you'. (5) Ceremonies, rules and regulations were of little importance in comparison to brotherly behaviour. (6) 'Love your enemies, Do good to them that hate you'. (7) 'Turn the other when some one slaps one of your cheeks'. (8) Jesus preferred the humble and the poor to the rich. (9) Blessed are you who are poor in spirit for the kingdom of God is yours. (10) His teachings about the law, anger, adultery, divorce, owes, revenge, and love for enemies and about charity, prayer and fasting are considered as gems and the corner stone of the Bible.

The Sermon on the Mount occupied a prominent place in his teachings. Jesus saw the crowd and went up the hill, where he sat down. His disciples gathered round him and he befgan to teach the above things.

The teachings of Jesus are recorded in the first four books of the New Testament of the Bible. These books are called 'the Gospels' (Good News) according to St. Mathew, St. Mark, St. Luke and St. John who were the followers of Jesus.

Jesus led a simple life and loved the poor. He realised that service to the people is the service to God. He preached through parables or stories and his teachings appealed to the masses.

Reaction Among the Jews: Though the Jews accepted the teachings of Jews in the beginning, they developed their hatred towards him and later on due to the increasing popularity of Jesus. Some of his teachings opposed the commands of the Jewish law. The idea of 'kingdom of God' was opposed by the Jews. They considered themselves to be 'God's chosen people' and looked down upon all non-Jews.

At the same time Jewish prophet had prophesied that a Messiah would be born who would become king, rescue them from their subjection to the Romans and lead them to their glorious destiny as the chosen people of God. The followers of Jesus claimed that Jesus was the Messiah and regarded him as the Christ. The word 'Christ' means the 'anointed one' in Greek language, the word 'Messiah' means same in Hebrew language. Hence, the orthodox Jews hated him like anything. They became furious and wanted to put a end to him.

End to Jesus Christ: During this time Palestine was under Roman rule. The Roman procurator (Resident) was Pontius Pilate. He was a stern man who opposed any rebellion or serious disturbances in the country. The furious Jews put pressure on the procurator and conveniently convinced him that Jesus was a disturber of peace. As a result Jesus was arrested and sentenced to be crucified. Jesus was nailed on a wooden cross. This memorable event happened probably in the year 30 A.D. during the time of the Roman Emperor Tiberius. After three days, Jesus resurrected with his body and went to heaven.

Contributions of Christianity: The Apostles of Jesus took series of successful steps to spread Christianity in Asia Minor. Greece, Gaul and Spain. Later on it spread to other parts of the world.

The Apostolic Christianity was open to all, to kings and nobles, the peoples of the middle classes, the Jews and the gentiles. It held out great hopes to the poor and the downtrodden and it was readily embraced by them. The common people were impressed by the feeling of equality and a deep sense of humanity.

The Roman emperors Nero and Diocletion presecuted the Christians. But emperors like Constantine Justinian, Theodosius and Charlemagne did a great service to Christianity. Thereby this religion became a world religion and made wonderful contributions.

(1) The first and foremost contribution of Christianity was that it saved the ancient civilisation and culture of Rome. The invasions of Huns destroyed Roman empire to a great extent. After that the churches played a significant role in protecting the culture and civilisation by its efficient organisational set up in the land.

(2) Secondly, the churches rendered remarkable service. A rich theology and philosophy developed by Christianity attracted all races in the world. In the reign of Theodosius Christianity has made the state religion. The church offered seven sacraments to every Christian and they were considered essential for the purification of the soul so as to enable every one to reach the abode of God. Priests and Bishops were empowered to administer those sacraments and hence they also assumed importance among the people. People began to think that they could not live outside the church.

(3) The churches and church officials were responsible for the development of education in Europe and also in the other parts of the world. The monks maintained several schools. Educated men made copies of Latin literature for future generations. Among the monasteries the Benedictines order did a wonderful service to education. The Benedictines had an enormous impact on the world they renounced. Their schools produced the vast majority of literate Europeans during early middle ages. From the monastery many Bishops, Archbishops and the Priests came to the forefront. Twenty four Popes are claimed to have been chosen from the Benedictines order to occupy the exalted office of the Roman Catholic church. Moreover, there were more than 5000 Archbishops of the Benedictine order. The Benedictines served as a cultural bridge transcribing and preserving the writings of anitiquity.

(5) The people began to learn poverty, obedience and chastity in their life. They followed those three principles in their life through the monks. Those people were respected in the society.

(6) The church people gave great impetus for the development of agriculture. They realised that agriculture was the back bone of the

Empire. They cultivated the lands, raised all kinds of crops in the days of feudalism. Marshy lands were converted into arable lands. Forests were cleared for agriculture. They did all these things for economic developments of the empire.

(7) Christianity was responsible for paving the way for the disciplined life among the people in the world. Parents and elders were given respect and honour in society. The children of the family showed respect to their parents. Family was raised to the level of the centre of religious life. The kings, popes, the bishops and the archbishops set an example in this regard.

(8) Religion assumed importance in the moral life of the people. The Kings, Popes, the Bishops and Archbishops led a highly disciplined life and thus set a model to the people. Virtues began to be fostered among the human beings and thus enabled the people to live in an atmosphere of amity and peace.

(9) The Christian religion had contributed much towards the enrichment of literature also. Eusephus wrote a beautiful history of the church in Greek language. Chrysostorn John had written a very fine collection of religious sermons in the same Greek language. Ambrose the bishop of Milan had composed sweet hymns in Latin language. St. Augustine Bishop of Hippo in North Africa wrote two famous books, "The City of God" and the 'Confessions'. Bible was officially translated from the Greek version into Latin by Jerome. Later on it was translated into all languages of the world.

(10) The church sponsored art as a means of proclaiming the glory of God. Cathedrals, monasteries were raised with architectural beauty. Various styles of architecture like Romanasque, Gothic, Byzanitine were patronized. Church of St. Trophime in France, Church of San Ambrogio in Milan, Notre Dame Church at Paris and church of St. Sophia at Constantinople are a few specimens of architectural excellence. Sculptures were also encouraged and cathedrals became centres of sculptural development. Paintings of Michael Angelo, Raphael and Leonardo da Vinci are marvels of painting art. Decoration by means of coloured glass is also considered one of the greatest artistic accomplishments helped by the church. In church service, extensive use was made of music, and musical notation was introduced by a monk, Guido of Arezzo in the 10th century. The Christians revolutionised the musical instruments. Organs, guitar, violin, piano were introduced by them.

Thus, Christianity rendered a remarkable service to the humanity.

15

Byzantine Civilisation

Although the city of Byzantium was renamed Constanitnople when, in 330, Constantine made it the capital of the Roman empire. The terms Byzantium and Byzantine are still used to designate the Eastern culture. The Roman empire in the west had vanished in 476 A.D. But the Eastern emperors, with their capital at Constantinople retained control of an immense realm girdling the Eastern Mediterranean from the Balkans through Asia Minor, Syria and Palestine to Egypt. It continued to exist for a thousand years after the fall of Rome or until 1453.

In the meantime, the Greek ousted the Latin language and there developed an entirely new type of civilisation. The new name for the empire in the East was 'Greek Empire' or the Byzantine Empire. The word Byzantine was derived from the Greek name Constanitnople (Byzantium). It cannot be denied that the Byzantine monarchy was a direct continuation of the Roman empire on a reduced scale. Constantinople became the New Rome or Second Rome.

Political Evolution: The emperor Justinian (527-565) was the greatest of the Byzantine rulers. His ambition was to reconquer the countries possessed by the ancient Romans. He was determined to restore the empire, to regain its lost territories and to rebuild its cities. He reunited the East and the West under a government that was essentially an oriental despotism.

Justinian was a great conqueror. He was supported by a large fleet and a standing army. He had efficient generals like Belisavius and Narses. He crushed Vandals; destroyed Goths and brought the Franks under his control. The tide of reconquest even reached far off Spain where Justinian seized a ship of south eastern coast with very little difficulty. Besides, Justinian was able to conquer Persians and the Slavonics.

Justinian was not only a great conqueror but also great administrator. He rendered remarkable service in the economic and religious fields.

His contribution to art and letters cannot be under estimated. Of all the contributions, the contribution to law is immensely great. Hence, it is said 'Justinian' real conquest of the west came many years after his death not through his armies but through his law.

Trade and Industry of the Byzantine: The great wealth of the Byzantine Empire was the result of commerce, industry and agriculture. Species, drugs, perfumes, precious stones and valuable woods from the orient passed through Byzantine cities to markets farther west. Cities like Constanitnople, Antioch, Damascus, Beirut were prosperous. Industry ranked second in importance as a source of wealth. There were numerous textile mills in Constanitnople. Silk also became a major article of commerce. They attained self-sufficiency in agricultural produce. The mosaic works were made prominent by the Byzantine Empire. It was considered as a real contribution to world civilisation. The enamels, and ivories of that period were very popular during middle ages. Besides these the pearl and gold works and its paintings were eagerly coveted and zealously guarded in the western treasuries.

Administration: In the field of administration the Byzatine did a lot. The Arabs who conquered Syria and Egypt in the 8th century took over much of the administrative system and many of intellectual traditions of the old Eastern Empire. The bureaucracy set up by the Byzantine rulers was followed later on in many European countries.

By lasting contribution to the European History lies above all in its "conversion of Russia and Balkans".

Law: Under Justinian rule. Roman law reached its fine shape. Many efforts had been made since the days of the Antonine to codify Roman law, that is to summarise it in, a logical and complete form; and these efforts culminated at last in the great 'codix Justinianus'.

Prior to his reign the records of the laws and the judges' decisions were in thousands of volumes. In short 'Roman law became so vast and bulk'. The lawyers and magistrates found it impossible to establish what in fact was 'good' law. Justinian, therefore, resolved to recodify the law in such a way that reference to it should be peaceful and convenient. Within a year he completed this great work under the guidance of a famous lawyer called Tribonian.

Tribonian published those books in a collective form. It was called 'Corpus Juris Civilis'. They were divided into four units. They were 'Digest', 'Code', 'Institutes' and 'Novels'.

Justinian's work was considered as a treasure beyond price. Roman law thus presented was destined to have an immense influence of the development of European politics and thought during the later middle ages.

So Justinian's real conquest of the west came many years after his death not through his armies, but through his law.

Social Conditions: The Society of the Byzantine was an urban one based on Hellenistic society. Constanitnople constituted an industrialised community. The upper class of people like nobles, wealthy officials and large land holders lived in luxury but at the same time they were cultivated and talented people. The middle class of people like merchants and manufactures lived well but were conservative in out look. The lot of the peasant was miserable and towards the end of the Byzantine rule, many of them were reduced to slavery.

Religion and Philosophy: Though Christianity was in the ascendancy in the Eastern Roman empire, they never accepted the ideologies of the Roman Catholics. A controversy between the Greek and Roman point of view in religion was always prevalent. Roman catholics advocated the Trinity of god. But the Arians disputed this concept; the Jacobites accepted only two characteristics namely the Divine word and the man Jesus. Hence, the Roman Catholic Church condemned them as heretics. The patriarch of Constanitnople did not recognise the supremacy of the Pope in Rome. The iconoclastic issue resulted in a final break. In 1054 the Pope excommunicated the patriarch of Constanitnople and till now no reconciliation was ever effected.

Art and Architecture: In the field of art and architecture the contribution of Byzantine Empire was immensely masterpieces. Many majestic churches were built by the ruler of the Empire. The best example of such a type of church is St. Sophia at Constanitnople. Moreover, St. Vitale in Ravenna and St. Marks in Venice are enduring masterpieces of those.

During the time of Justinian many marvellous buildings were erected. The buildings of St. Sophia was his successful achievement. The dome is its central feature. The effect of the dome when seen from within is awe-inspiring. One feels lost in its vastness.

Justinian's most famous buildings are found in Italy, in the places of Ravenna and Classe. Their mosaics were made of thousands of glass cubes which reflect light in different directions and bathe whole church in coloured light. The buildings created by Justinian were of high artistic quality and inaugurated the golden age of Byzantine art.

Thus, Justinian's magnificent buildings influenced both the eastern and western Mediterranean world for centuries after his death.

The Byzantine painting influenced profoundly the beginnings of painting in Italy. Many painters were patronised by the Byzantine rulers. The artists not only made decorations for their own churches but also sold much of their work in the west for the decoration of Roman catholic churches. The Sarcophagus, which represents the chief work in sculpture, is elaborately decorated with sacred monograms, peacocks, and fruited vines. Jeweled ornaments, fine silks, and chalices were produced in abundance. Byzantine art, taken collectively lacked naturalness, imagination and spontaneity. Those defects were due primarily to the religious restrictions.

Saviour of Ancient Culture: The cultural contribution of Byzantine Empire was far reaching and tremendous. As a custodian of Greco — Roman culture, the Eastern empire provided an invaluable service to the emerging civilisation of western Europe. It preserved the cultural traditions of Greece and the political techniques of the old Roman empire. The learning and literature of ancient Greece was also praised by the Empire. Manuscripts of Greek philosophy and letters were studied at Constanitnople. Many Byzantine scholars complied encyclopedia and lexicons. Historical writings were studied well. Saints' lives were vindicated to the people. Besides, many medical works, legal treatises and technological ideas were compiled during this time. In short, it made a significant impact on the Italian Renaissance.

16

Rise of Islam

In the 6th century A.D. a new religion was founded by Mohammed which was known as Mohammedanism. It is otherwise called Islam. Islam is an Arabic word meaning 'submission to the will of God'. Those who follow the religion of Islam are called Muslims. Muslim is also an Arabic word meaning 'one who submits to the will of God'.

Early Life: Mohammed was born in Mecca about 570 A.D. and his family was one of importance there. Mecca is in Arabia. We know little about his early years except that he was a poor orphan. He did not get proper education. Naturally he turned out to be a shepherd. As a shepherd boy he earned very little. Then he became a camel driver. He was a hard worker. He earned his livelihood by his hard work. Then he entered into the service of a rich widow Khadija. At the age of 25 he married his employer Khadija. Thus, he became the master of her house. So he was respected in the city of Mecca.

During Mohammed's journeys in Arabia and Syria he came into contact with Jews and Christians. He had discussions with them about religion. This made him think deeply on the subject of God.

Condition of the Country: The religion of the country at his birth place was a strange mixture of ancient heathen rites of Judaism, and of Christianity, and in Mecca, worship was paid to a great stone, the famous Kaaba stone, which still remains there, a strange survival amidst the rites of Mohammedanism, Westward in Egypt and Northward in Syria the Christians were bitterly divided by disputes on matters of doctrine.

Mohammed began to see that one of the chief causes of the backwardness and disunity of his Arab fellow-countrymen, was their division into many small sects. Each sect worshipped its own tribal God. He envied at the well ordered religion with a cohesive society of the Jews.

Message from God: At this juncture he used to sit in meditation in a nearby mountain. He began to think about new religion. As a result of his deep thinking, the believed that he had messages from God (Allah) calling him to teach his people. Guided by the messages and meditations he was inspired to create a new religion. From the ideas he had obtained from the Christians, Jews and from the Pagan nomads, he worked out a synthetic religion. At the age of 40 he began to preach at first privately to his wife, his children and few friends.

Teachings:

(i) Mohammed preached one God with many prophets, of whom Moses, Christ and Mohammed were three, but Mohammed was the chief. He preached monotheism *i.e.* only one 'God-Allah'. He is all knowing, all powerful and invisible. There is no God but Allah and Mohammed is the Prophet of Allah.

(ii) The worship of any other god in any form whatever is idolatry and abomination.

(iii) Mohammed considered him not as a God, but as a Prophet only.

(iv) Mohammed preached the doctrine of fate or predestination.

(v) He preached, too, a higher personal and social morality. Theft, intemperance, slavery, polygamy were all attacked or regulated by his movement.

(vi) Mohammed taught that there would be a 'judgement day' and a resurrection from the dead. God had predetermined the course of human affairs and we must obey him. The good, who obeyed the will of God would go to heaven and those who refused to accept his teachings would go to Hell.

(vii) Mohammed asked his followers to be free from greed, falsehood, drunkenness and gambling.

(viii) He asked his followers to be liberal, patient and humane.

(ix) He insisted that slaves be treated generously.

(x) He gave his followers the assurance of eternal salvation if they led upright, sober lives and followed the precepts of Islam.

(xi) He preached brotherhood of man. Islam commands all Muslims to treat one another as brothers and to act in a kind and brotherly way to all fellow Muslims whatever their rank or wealth.

(xii) All faithful Mohammedans were to worship five times a day, give money to the poor, engage in fasting in the month of Ramzan, go on a pilgrimage to Mecca at least once in their life time.

After the death of Mohammed the followers collected the teachings and oral instructions of Mohammed and wrote them down in a book (in Arabic) which came to be known as the 'Koran'. It is considered as the Bible of the Muslims.

Reaction of his Teachings: In the beginning there was no enthusiasm for the message of Mohammed. It was unnoticed and uncared. His wife, his adopted son, cousin and one friend were his followers. In Mecca the people opposed his teachings vehemently. There was growing public disapproval to Mohammed's new faith'. He was practically boycotted for years. But the people of Yathrib (Medina, 'the city of the Prophet') were willing to accept Mohammed and his teachings. As his life was in danger at Mecca, Mohammed fled to Medina in the year 622 A.D. It was a turning point in his career. This event is called as 'Hejira' (Hegira). This is the Flight, the Hegira, from which all Mohammedans reckon their years.

After this event Mohammedans' rise to power began. He quickly won the hearts of the inhabitants of Medina, to his faith and became the city's political chief as well as its religious leader.

Spread of Islam: Mohammedanism spread rapidly through Arabia. Millions of poor and oppressed people welcomed the teachings of Mohammed. No other world religion at the time offered such advantages as Islam did. It spread from Arabia to Syria. From Syria it went to Mesopotamia and from their to Persia. The Arab attempted to spread Islam to West also. There it spread to Asia Minor and Roman Empire. Apart from this they could not get much success. So from Arabia they went to North Africa, Egypt and Spain. In Spain the Muslims were called Moors.

Caliphs: After the death of Mohammed Prophet in 632 A.D. the ruler of Islam was the Caliph. Caliph or Kalipha means deputy or representative of the Prophet. In other words they were called as Moslem Pope and emperor combined. Truly speaking they were his successors.

The first Caliph was Abu Baker. He was very interested in spreading the religion in the length and breadth of the country. His successor was Omar. Under the two Caliphs the Arabs united together to go on to spread their faith. Their seat of government was Medina. They made greatest conquests.

In 636 A.D. the Muslim forces utterly defeated the Byzantine Emperor. The lands along the Eastern Mediterranean, Syria, Palestine, Crete, Cyprus and Egypt were taken from the weak Eastern Roman Empire.

Umayyads: In 661 A.D. the Umayyad Caliphs became powerful and they transferred the capital to the Islamic Empire from Medina to Damascus. Their rule lasted from 661 to 750 A.D. During this period the political interests of the Arabs were given precedence over the religious interests of Islam.

Between 670 and 680 Constanitnople repulsed a series of powerful Muslim attacks. The Arabs pushed across North Africa into Spain and even across the Pyrennes into France. Spain became a Muslim Kingdom in 711 A.D. But in France the Arabs were checked by Franks. In 732 A.D. Charles Martel led the Franks in turning back the Arabs at the battle of Tours in Central France. Hence, the Arab invaders were gradually pushed south of the Pyrennes into Spain.

Then the Arabs diverted their attention in the eastern side. They took Persia and captured the old cities of Bokharo and Samarkhand under Mohammed Bin-Kasim. They conquered the Valley of Indus river in India.

Abbasids: In 750 A.D. the Arabs moved their capital to Baghdad. It was the seat of Abbasid Caliphate. Their rule lasted from 750 to 1258 A.D.

During the period of Abbasid Caliphate Baghdad reached its climax in all fields. Particularly during the time of Harunal-Rashid Baghdad became the centre of learning and education. Art and architecture reached its apex of glory. Many beautiful buildings were constructed by the Abbasids.

After Abbasids: After that the Islamic Empire began to disintegrate — Persia, Spain, Morocco and Egypt were independent states, each had its own Caliph who claimed that he alone was rightful successor of the Prophet.

In the later 10th and 11th centuries, the Fatimid Caliphate of Cairo rose to prominence. The Seljuk Turks became powerful in Asia Minor in the 12th century. The Seljuk power declined in the 12th century.

The Europeans were engaged in the crusading movement from the end of 11th century to the end of 13th century. In 1085 Jolda, a Muslim city in Spain was captured by Christians. After the victory of the Christians at the battle of 'Las Navas de Tolosa' in 1212 A.D., the Moorish power in Spain was crippled. By the later 13th century the moors were confined to the small southern kingdom of Granada where they remained until 1492 A.D.

Mediterranean: After capturing some lands along the eastern Mediterranean, the Muslims captured Corsica, Sardinia, Crete, Malta and Sicily. In 841 they took Bari the main Byzantine base in south eastern Italy. In 846 A.D. 1100 Muslims landed at Ostia marched upto the walls of Rome, freely plundered the suburbs and churches of St. Peter and St. Paul. Pope Leo IV took steps to prevent they enemy. The Saracens made another attempt to seize to the citadel of western Christianity. The united Italian fleet blessed by the pope, gave them battle and routed them. In 884 they burned the great monastery of Monte Cassino to the ground. Finally, in the year 916 A.D. the combined forces of the Pope defeated them on the Garigliano. Thus, a tragic century of invasion came to an end.

Spain was occupied by Muslims in 711 A.D. It remained under the domination of Ummayyad rulers for many centuries. The Arabians who settled in Spain were called Moors. They developed a culture of their own. This civilisation was spread westward through North Africa and into Spain. So Spanish or Moorish civilisation was much more advanced than that of the Germanic people who were occupying the rest of western Europe.

Contributions of Islam to World Civilisation

Many contributions were made by Islam to Europe. They are immensely valuable. They are :

(i) Education: In the field of education Islam made wonderful contributions. At first religious schools attached to mosques were established. Great Muslim universities at Baghdad, Cairo and Cardova developed during this time. The Cardova University was established in Spain. The students of Cardova universities carried culture and learning into the countries from which they came. These Universities exercised tremendous influence upon the Universities of Paris and Oxford. One of the most famous of the Christian students at the University of Cardova was Gerbert, afterwards Pope Silvestar II.

Gerbert did much to introduce the science of mathematics into Europe.

Thus, 'Spain under the Moors surpassed all the western Europe in learning'.

(ii) Arabian Numerals: The Arabs introduced their numerals into Spain. They are called 'Arabian Numerals'. They are 1. 2. 3. 4. 5. 6. 7. 8. 9 and 0. They borrowed this system from India. These Arabic numerals were easier to read and write than Roman numerals.

(iii) Algeba: It is an Arabic word. It was the creation of Arab mathematicians.

(iv) Science: In the field of science the Arabs did a lot. The Muslim scholars at Cardova made remarkable contributions to chemistry, medicine and surgery. In addition to this they developed the science of optics and astronomy. Nitric Acid, Alcohol and Silver Nitrate were known to them.

(v) Medicine: In medicine they made very remarkable progress. They performed some of the most difficult operations known. They knew how to use anesthetics. Some of their methods of treating patients are still in use today.

(vi) Art and Architecture: The architects of the Moors showed the influence of the Byzantine architecture of the East. They built beautiful mosques in many places. The splendid mosques like those of Cardova and Seville and fine palaces like Alhambra have given inspiration to architects through succeeding generations.

Cardova was a famous city in those days. It was a wonderful city. 10,000 men worked for 40 years to construct the new city. It was a wonderful town of amazing workmanship. Marble, iron, ivory and ebony were as lavishly used as stone and brick.

(vii) Literature: The Arabians made important contributions in Literature. They read Greek Philosophy and science and translated the works of Aristotle and others. Through these translations the Westerners familiarised themselves with Greek thought. It is beautifully remarked that 'without the effort of Arabs, Hindu and Greek wisdom would not have reached the west'.

(viii) Poetry: The Arabs took great interest in poetry. They had a special fondness for poetry but their most enduring production is the 'Thousand and One Nights'.

(ix) Trade: Arabians had close trade relations among the different parts of the Muslim world. Ships from the eastern Mediterranean were seen in the ports of Italy and Spain.

(x) Paper: Another important contribution of the Arabs was the manufacture of paper. They introduced the art of manufacturing paper to Europe. The Arabs probably learnt it from the Chinese but they were undoubtedly the means of its introduction into Europe.

(xi) Trees and Plants: The Arabs introduced many plants and trees. They planted and protected many kinds of plants and flowers. Grafting was known to them. They were able to produce some new varieties of fruits and vegetables.

(xii) Agriculture: Agriculture was known to them. The Arabs possessed good knowledge in agriculture. They knew the value and the way of using manure. Fertilisers were also used by them for the purpose of making the soil rich. Irrigational methods were known to them. Many canals were constructed by them. They knew the use of windmill. Thus, in the field of agriculture they made excellent contributions.

(xiii) Other Contributions:

(a) The Arabs made glass and pottery of the finest quality.

(b) The Arabs were expert in dyeing.

(c) The Arabs made tincture, essence and syrups.

(d) The Muslims excelled in horticulture.

(e) They were the first to make sugar out of sugarcane.

(f) The Arabs used glassware, muslin, polished steel and introduced them in the west.

(g) The Arabs taught to the west the method of converting iron into steel.

(h) They produced attar from roses.

(xiv) Mariners' Compass: The most notable contribution of the Arabs is the invention of Mariners' Compass. It was then very worthy contribution. Later on it was very useful to know the direction during the sea voyages.

17(a)

Feudalism

Origin: In the 9th and 10th centuries there were fresh barbarian invasions on Europe. The barbarians attacked the cities and destroyed most of them. The people of Europe were thus under the mercy of the brabarian invaders. The Government of the day was not strong enough to protect the people from the hands of the barbarians. The people, therefore, thought of getting protection from some strongmen other than the king. So the weak surrendered themselves with their lands to some strongmen like the Dukes, the Nobles or the Princes. Those strongmen promised to give protection to their life and property. Moreover, they allowed the people to occupy and cultivate their former lands as tenants. Thus, a new kind of society came into existence consisting of the lords and their tenants. The tenants were considered as their vassals. The relationship between the lord and the vassal was based on holding of lands. In other words it was a method of holding land by giving services to the owner during the Middle Ages in Europe. The word 'feudalism' is derived from the Latin word 'feudurn' which means a fief or piece of land held by a vassal. From this word the feudal was derived. The society consisting of the feudal lords and the feudal vassals came to be called as the feudal society. The conditions and contracts on which the feudal society was based came to be known as feudalism.

Features:

(i) The king was regarded as the holder of all the lands in the country.

(ii) The king parcelled out his kingdom into fiefs which were held from his chief vassals or their great lords.

(iii) Their fiefs were sub-divided into smaller fiefs and the same was given to the lesser vassals.

(iv) The lowest unit of fief was held by the knight. It was indivisible.
(v) The king was the lord of the chief vassals.
(vi) The chief vassals became lords of the lesser vassals.
(vii) In the feudal hierarchy everyone was linked with land whether he was a king or a serf.

The Duties of a Vassal

(i) The primary duty of a vassal was to fight for his lord.
(ii) The vassal must attend the court of his lord if requested to do so and assist in the administration of justice.
(iii) He must pay three aids. An aid was a sum of money paid when the lord's eldest son was knighted, when his eldest daughter was married, or if the lord was held for ransom.
(iv) Another payment of money was called 'relief' or inheritance tax.
(v) The vassal had to entertain the lord and his whole escort during then visit to his fief.

Responsibilities of Lords

(i) The lord had the right to take the lands of the vassals on their death.
(ii) If there was no heir to succeed them, the lord could take their lands. This right of the lord was called the 'escheat'.
(iii) The lord could seize the land he had granted to the vassal if he proved to be unfaithful. It was called 'forfeiture'.
(iv) The vassals were expected to give the requirements like food, shelter etc. when the lord camped in his locality. In this way the lord had the right to get their obedience. In return he had to protect them.

Ceremony

The ceremony of becoming a vassal was usually an impressive one. The man wanted to become the vassal of the lord had to appear before the lord and his court. There in the presence of the vassals of the lord he had to kneel before him, placed his hands in the hands of the lord and declared himself the 'Lord's man' for a certain fief. This act on the part of the vassal was known as 'homage'. Then the lord raised the man to his feet and gave him the kiss of peace, and with his hand on the Bible or on the sacred relic took an oath of fealty to the lord. Finally, the lord invested the man with a fief. Moreover, the lord invested the vassals with either a ring or a staff or some symbol of his. This corresponding act of the lord was known as investiture.

Advantages

(i) Feudalism was needful and also useful at a time when there was none to protect the life and property of the people. Feudalism offered protection. As a result the danger from new barbarian invasions were lessened. This was an important service rendered by Feudalism.

(ii) Feudalism provided for good government at a time when kings were unable to rule. It was a barbarian and disorderly age and under the auspices of feudalism some order came out of anarchy.

(iii) Feudalism arrested slavery in Europe. The feudal society was based on mutual contract and in such a society slavery could not thrive.

(iv) Feudalism saved the civilisation of Europe during the 9th and 10th centuries from the hands of barbarians. It cherished and nourished a great civilisation that contained many of the seeds of modern principles of liberty and modern democratic institutions.

(v) Feudalism was responsible for social harmony in the society. The feudal society was bound by mutual obligations, loyalty and service.

(vi) Under the auspices of feudalism some justice came out of force, some law out of custom. The feudal courts of the lords developed trial by jury and some fundamental concepts of common law.

(vii) Another contribution of feudalism was the manor. The manor was the economic unit of the feudal society.

(viii) Feudalism provided agricultural production and solved economic problems.

(ix) Christianity was saved by feudalism.

Disadvantages

(i) Feudalism divided the country into small principalities. Naturally feudalism paved the way for the decline of national and patriotic spirit of the people.

(ii) Feudalism was highly responsible for the petty wars and disturbances in the country. There was unbridled and continuous war among the nobles. Brother frequently fought against brother and sons against their father. Thus, feudal wars sowed the seeds of civil wars.

(iii) Feudalism stood as a stumbling block in the way of the development of democratic institutions. In the feudal society the wealthy alone had political power. Naturally such a society would not help the development of democracy.

(iv) Feudalism was responsible for the long drawn struggle between the empire and the papacy.

(v) Under feudal system the nobles or lords governed more or less in the same way in which a king ruled a country. The nobles had large armies and they became the real rulers of the country. The sovereign power was fragmented and the authority of the king became weak. The king's place was now replaced by innumerable local governments. As a result the monarchy was destroyed.

(vi) National unification was hampered due to feudalism.

(vii) The estates of the lords were tilled by peasants generally serfs who did not own their own lands. The condition of the common people and the serfs under feudalism was miserable. They were powerless and thrown to the tender mercies of the lords. The common people suffered at the hands of the nobles in peace as well as in war.

(viii) There was poor progress during the time of feudalism. The nobles were not interested in promoting the welfare of the people. They spent much of their time in war and had no time to plan for the progress of society. People did not know anything that happened beyond their manor. 'Feudalism made society stagnant instead of progressive and dynamic'.

Decline and Disappearance

The feudal society began to decline in the 13th century. It was due to the following causes :

(i) In Europe, many nobles from various Christian countries went to the East to take part in the crusades. They lost heavily in the crusades in terms of men and money. The crusades thus weakened the nobles.

(ii) The rise of middle class also weakened the feudal structure. The middle class people were against the exploiting feudal nobles and they were ready to help the king in crushing the power of the nobles.

(iii) Another reason for the decline of feudalism was the rise of strong monarchies. Strong kings like Henry VII in England seriously planned to put down the nobles.

(iv) The rise of towns was a blow to feudalism. Many towns were able to have their freedom from baronial control by paying a large sum of money and securing charters of right. By escaping to the towns and evading detection, many serfs earned their freedom.

(v) Feudalism was needful and also useful at a time when there was none to protect the life and property of the people. But in the later centuries of Middle Ages such protection was no longer needed. As feudalism had outlived its purpose it had to go.

However feudalism lingered till the 18th century in Europe. The French Revolution that occurred at the end of the 18th century completely destroyed feudalism in Europe.

17 (b)

Manorialism

The lord lived in the centre of his estate. The house of the lord was known as 'Manor'. The manor was surrounded by some plots of land which were cultivated for the lord by his vassals. It was primarily a agricultural estate. It consisted of a village. But a large manor consisted of more than one village. The manorial village was the local unit of feudal government. In short 'manorialism was the characteristic of medieval system of cultivating the soil by the labour of a village community'.

From the political and economic point of view manorialism is definitely a part of feudalism.

Features

(1) Freemen and serfs occupied an important place in the manorial system. In the manorial system nobles, clergy and people followed different vocations. Traders, artisans and farmers owning land were freemen.

(2) Free holders were minority in number and they were free to live on the manor or go away if they liked.

(3) The serfs were the tenants of the nobles' lands. They cultivated the lands owned by a noble or a baron. They could own no property. They were forbidden to leave one manor for another of his own accord or to move to a town.

(4) The serfs were expected to serve under their master even after the selling of lands *i.e.* a serf was not free to leave his manor.

(5) The lord reserved for his own use a part of the arable land of the manor. This was his 'demesne,' The rest of the land he allotted to the peasants who were his tenants.

(6) Apart from this a manor contained the lord's castle, manorial court, mill, baron and worker's quarters.
(7) The manor house was the centre for the local administration of the manor.
(8) The manorial court disposed all law suits arising between villagers.
(9) The manor contained one church and priest.
(10) The lord had officers called bailiffs and stuarts to supervise the work of manors.

Condition of Peasants: During the middle ages the condition of peasants was not satisfactory. The medieval peasant was ordinarily a serf. He seldom owned land or any property. He was the tenant of his lord's land. Annual rent was paid by him in terms of goods, labour or money.

The peasant paid three kinds of taxes. They were : (i) head tax, (ii) rent and (iii) arbitrary charges.

Besides the peasant gave the lord one-tenth of his crops and livestock. The peasant paid corvee (road tax) and inheritance tax also.

The peasant was expected to pay tithes to the church.

The peasant had to work three days of free labour to the lord's demesne. He had to do extra work for the lord in times of sowing and reaping.

The peasants lived in huts. They worked from sunrise to sunset in the manor. In the manor the lord had his bakery, a flour mill and the wine press. The peasants were expected to prepare their bread in their lord's oven, grind the corns in the lord's mill and press their grapes in the lord's wine press. The lord had a share in all these things.

Further the roads, the river and ponds, the forests and meadows were considered as the lord's personal property. So the peasants had to pay a fixed sum of money for using the roads, for fishing in the river and ponds, for cutting firewood in the forests and for grazing their cattles on the meadows.

To marry, a serf (peasant) had to get his lord's authorisation. He could not give his daughter without the consent of the lord. He could not send his son off to be educated or to town to learn a trade without getting the lord's consent or paying a fee. In short, the nobles considered the peasants as untouchables. If the lords happened to be quarrelsome, the peasant's lands were destroyed in fighting. To put it in a nutshell their condition was indeed miserable.

Significance of Manorial Life

(1) The first and foremost virtue of the manor was that it was largely self-sufficient. People received everything they needed by this manorial system. Many economic problems were solved by this system.

(2) The life of the peasant was pathetic and pitiable, but he was at least protected from the misery of unemployment.

(3) Another virtue of this system was the invention of three field system. This method showed to the world that more land could be cultivated with less ploughing.

(4) Serfdom was vigorously developed by manorial system. It began to decline in the late Middle Ages due to urbanisation, decline of feudalism and other factors.

(5) The serfs were confined to the lands they tilled. Hence, they had no idea of a Nation.

18

Holy Roman Empire

Origin

On the debris of the German tribal kingdom, the Frankish kingdom came to prominence during the 6th century A.D. Frankish king founded Carolingian empire and also made an attempt to revive the old Roman Empire. This empire lasted for only one century when it was assaulted by Northman and the feudal lords contributed to their own way in throwing away the empire. One of the most important kings of the Franks was Charlemagne, grandson of Charles Martel and son of Pepin.

Charles Martel had earned fame by defeating the Muslims at the Battle of Tours, where as Pepin got back from Lombards territories in central state and give them back to Bishop of Rome. Those territories were called as Papal states. Pepin protected Papal authority and this policy was also followed by his son, Charlemagne. He also signed with Pope a treaty of eternal friendship and in turn Pope recognised him as Emperor. He was also crowned by Pope Leo III. It was this union of Roman Emperor with the Pope that began to be called as Holy Roman Empire in the 12th century. Thereafter, it became essential that every Roman Emperor must be recognised by Pope.

Old and New Roman Empires

In the old Roman Empire there was practically no place for the Christianity. In fact Christians were considered as mischief mongers and motives of seditions were attributed to them. On the other hand in the New Empire Christianity was a recognised religion. There was close co-operation between the king and the Pope. Similarly one finds that in the old Empire, Rome was the real centre of power and authority. It was from here that directives were issued and appointments were made in so far as Provincial Governments were concerned. On the other hand in the new empire, Rome was only nominal centre of authority. A new emperor will only come to crown himself in Rome, and thereafter he will leave for his capital. Thus, whereas in the old Empire Rome enjoyed a prestigious position, in the new Empire it did not enjoy any such position. The old empire was Italian in its outlook and approach whereas the new one was German in nature and character. Thus, one finds that there were some basic differences between the old and new Empires. In brief, one can say that whereas old Roman Empire was really Roman, the new Roman Empire was in no way Roman.

Basis of Holy Roman Empire: Let us see the need and necessity of having a Holy Roman Empire.

The main idea of the creation of such an empire was to bring all the Christian states together in a fraternity. There is also no doubt that to some extent this idea also got maturity, and at one time the Empire included in its jurisdiction Germany, Netherlands, Czechoslovakia, Austria, Switzerland and large parts of Italy. In the Empire the Emperor was required to be crowned by the Pope.

The Emperor possessed more powers. In the Empire Northern Italy and Balitic enjoyed considerable autonomy and were practically independent. But in Germany there were many knights who did not care much for the authority of the Emperor. In the Empire there was no perfect peace and order and conditions in this regard were rather unsatisfactory.

Papacy and Emperor

In the Holy Roman Empire, as we shall subsequently see, there were frequent quarrels and disputes between the Emperors and Popes. Both wanted to have supremacy over each other. Whereas Emperor wanted that the Pope should be under his control, the Pope felt that he belonged to the other world and had superior position over the emperor, who belonged to this world. Similarly Pope also felt that whereas king had control over one kingdom, the Pope exercised his control and authority over all Christian kingdoms. The conflict for supremacy and authority continued for centuries together not only in the Holy Roman Empire, but all over Europe.

Services

The Holy Roman Empire rendered many significant services to the world civilisation.

(i) The greatest service of the Empire was that whole of European continent which was divided into small units, and united into one Empire due to the efforts of both the Pope and the Emperor.

(ii) It greatly checked the civil designs of the feudal lords.

(iii) It was due to this Empire that Germany was, united.

(iv) It paved the way for the rise of National states like England, France and Spain.

(v) Another effect was that under the systems German Emperors managed to get their sons elected to the throne.

(vi) It strengthened the hereditary system of Europe and weakened the republican system.

In short, the Roman Empire thus contributed a lot by way of crushing feudal lords and feudalistic tendencies.

Importance

The Holy Roman Empire occupies a very prominent place in the history of Europe. 'It is the designation commonly given to the lands ruled over first by the Frankish then by the German kings, for the countries from the coronation of Charlemagne in 800 A.D. until its dissolution in 1846'.

Voltaire, a famous French philosopher lived during the time of French Revolution had beautifully expressed that it was 'neither holy, nor Roman, nor empire'. If the question 'was the empire Roman' is asked, it had to be answered negatively. Because the rulers of the so called Floly Roman Empire were not 'Romans'. It was ruled first by Frankish and then by German Kings. The empire contained much land that had never been in the old Roman Empire and the largest part of the old Roman Empire was not included in it.

Otto I made Rome the seat of the empire. The other ruler concentrated their attention north of the Alps. Hence, it is better and fitter to call the 'Holy Roman Empire' as the 'Medieval German Empire'.

The next question is 'was the Empire holy'. Here the word 'holy' might have been used to distinguish and differentiate this Christian empire from the earlier Roman Empire. The Church conferred the emperorship to the first king and later on it continued. In other words it was Pope who crowned a king. But the emperors were Christian rulers. The earlier rulers were intimately associated with the protection of the Roman Church and Papacy. Apart from this the empire had no holy purpose.

During the time of the struggle between the empire and the papacy, the German emperors (especially Henry IV) had wasted much of their time and resources against the papacy. Pope Gregory VII was responsible for it. In 1085 the sack of Rome was brought by him. 'No Goth or Vandal has brought such destruction upon the city of St. Peter as this Priest (Gregory VII)'.

Germany and Italy was fragmented due to the conflict between Pope and the emperor. The two countries experienced untold sorrows and sufferings during the conflict. The Popes involved themselves in power politics and their spiritual role was more and more observed. From these things we can come to the conclusion that the empire was not holy.

In 1268 A.D. the empire came to an end, but it continued for centuries to exist in theory. At last it became a mere laughing stock: 'neither holy, nor Roman, nor empire' in Voltarire's famous epigram.

'With Charlemagne, it has been said, the destruction of the ancient world ends with Charlemagne the building up of the modern world begins'.

Charlemagne

Charlemagne or Charles the Great, the eldest son of Pepin and the grandson of Charles Martel was by far the most important of all Frankish kings. He was the most outstanding ruler in Europe during the entire period of Early Middle Ages. His reign lasted from 768 to 814 A.D. His long reign marked an epoch in the history of Europe.

His Character

Charlemagne was of pure German origin, spoke German tongue and usually resided in German lands. He was himself tall, strong and agile beyond the average of mankind. There was in his character a religious and exalted strain, which gifted him art of sensuality and grossness of the tune and made the man worthy of the work which he accomplished. Above all he was a great administrator, conqueror and promoter of education and a patron of arts and architecture.

His Policies

(i) Charlemagne's first and foremost policy was the expansion of his empire. His ambition was to include all the Germans in Europe.

(ii) Secondly, his policy was co-operation and alliance with the Papacy. It paved the way for the re-establishment of the Roman Empire.

(iii) Finally, his desire was to protect the Christians from foreign invasions.

His Conquests

Charlemagne was constantly engaged in wars during the whole of his reign, and though he does not seem to have shown any great genius in the conduct of his operations, his energy and organisation brought them all in the end to success.

(i) Lombards: During his early period the Lombards seized several Papal cities and despatched an army against Rome. The then Pope Hadrian I appealed to Charlemagne for help. Immediately Charles crossed the Alps with an army and laid siege to Pavia into which the Lombards had retreated. At the same time he visited Rome. Upon the collapse of the Lombard resistance he deposed the Lombard king and made himself king of the Lombards. Thus, Lombardy was made a province of the Franks.

(ii) Saxony: His campaign against the Saxons were far more prolonged and more important. The Saxons of those days lived on the low-lying lands round the mouths of the Ems, the Weser and the Elbe, a land of heath and marsh and forest. They themselves were fierce and warlike, attached to their own religion, and inspite of the work of Boniface, bitterly opposed to the Christian missionaries.

The war between the Franks and the Saxons was an extremely fierce one. The war had to be done over and over again for the Saxons again and again repudiated the submission they had made. On both sides there were cruelty and massacre, and when Charles conquered he always imposed Christianity as a sign and test of submission. At last the Saxon champion Widukind was forced to surrender and forced to accept baptism.

Monasteries were planted in the conquered country, and the new faith and the new government sank deep into the life of the people.

(iii) Spain: For the men of Middle Ages, the most famous of Charles' military exploits was his Spanish war. All Spain, as we have seen, was in the hands of the Saracens (Muslims). The wars were first effective counter offensive against Islam, a prototype of the crusades. The Franks under Charles fought on behalf of Christendom. Though Charles' first campaign ended in disaster, he was able to establish a Spanish march in 795 A.D. Thus, Charlemagne is reckoned the founder of modern Spain.

(iv) Bavaria: Bavaria was a German territory. Charles directed his attention towards Bavaria. He invaded and conquered Bavaria and incorporated it with the Frankish territory.

(v) Hungary: Charles fought, too, against the Avars of modern Hungary, penetrated their huge fortifications, and forced their ruler to accept baptism.

(vi) Other Victories: Charles struck, too, against the Slavonic peoples that lay to the east of the Elbe, the Abotrites, Slavs and Serbs, and forced them to recognise the supremacy of the Frankish power.

Charles Becomes Emperor: The culmination of Charlemagne's career was his coronation by Pope in 800 A.D. On December 25 (Christmas Day) in 800, Charlemagne was in Rome. While he was praying before St. Peter's altar at the solemn mass, Pope Leo III surprised him by placing a crown on his head. Immediately the crowd in the church proclaimed him 'Emperor of the Romans'.

Thus, was received the imperial title in Western Europe, and the title did not disappear for the next thousand years. The change was in truth a change only in name. Charles had been quite as powerful as king as he was as emperor. The new title was merely the recognition of the position that Charles had actually secured by his condition of the position that Charles had actually secured by his conquests and his organisation. But words are sometimes in themselves a power, and this new word 'emperor' applied to the Frankish kings was destined to exercise a vast influence over all the Middle Ages.

The coronation thus established the Holy Roman Empire and Charlemagne became the first emperor of the Holy Roman Empire.

Byzantium

Charlemagne conceived the project of marrying Jerene (the ruler of Eastern Empire-Byzantium) and thus uniting the eastern and western provinces. She was willing but her deposition and exile in 802 A.D. prevented the realisation of these plans. By 812 A.D. Charlemagne was recognised as emperor by the Byzan-tine Emperor Michael I.

Administration

Charles showed himself far in advance of his age in his organisation and government of his vast dominions. He was not only a great conqueror but also an efficient administrator, He was also a far-sighted statesman. The-conquered countries of Charlesmagne were consolidated and brought under good and stable rule. Aachen (Aix-la-Chapelle) was Charlemagne's famous capital. It was the 'New Rome' of the empire.

(i) Counties: The vast empire of Charlemagne was divided into districts each consisting of a number of counties. The 'county' was the essential unit of government under Charlemagne. A county was headed by a count. The King's chief problem was to keep his counts under control.

A special feature of Charles' government was the creation of certain officers called 'Missi Dominici' — royal agents. A 'Missi' usually consisted of two laymen and a bishop or an abbot. They acted as link between emperor and the local governments. They submitted regular reports to the emperor.

The counts and other officials were really carrying out the will of their master.

The counts ordinarily held office for life. There were assistants to the counts in the administration. They were called 'vice counts' and 'Hundredman' or 'Vicars'.

The counties were sub-divided into hundreds or 'vicariates'. The King Charlemagne continued to be represented throughout the realm by his personal appointees, the counts.

Thus, the government of Charlemagne was based on the principle of personal rule.

(ii) Capitularies: The legislation of Charlemagne was also remarkable. He held general assemblies or Diets consisting of nobles and bishops and with their approval issued special decrees of laws called capitualries. A series of laws (capitularies) were enacted dealing with every part of the social and religious life of the state.

Charlemagne showed special concern for the poor and made provisions for poor relief.

(iii) Church: The church administration was controlled by Charlemagne. The appointment of bishops and abbots were made by him. He supervised their spiritual and secular duties. He also enforced the Benediction rule to the monks of his Kingdom.

Charlemagne was the 'representative of God' and legislated on every possible ecclesiastical subjects. The council meetings were presided over by him. He told the priests what to preach in congregation and what to sing. In short, his power over the Papacy was unrivalled and the Popes were too weak to oppose him seriously.

(iv) Intellectual Revival: In the reign of Charles, there arose a real thought, short lived revival of literature and education. His foremost duty was to educate his subjects in the country. His 'Palace School' at Duchess was the leading school in Christendom. One of his capitularies called upon the clergy to take interest in learning. Every Cathedral and monastery was to establish schools for the benefit of the clergy and laymen. In short, he improved the quantity and quality of the schooling in his empire. A number of learned men were gathered at the court of Charles, of whom Alcuin of York was the chief. Literature was patronised, the services and the music of the church received careful attention. He established a library in his capital at Aachen.

(v) **Art and Architecture:** Charlemagne built a great palace at Aachen on the model of the palace at Constantinople. He also built many churches and cathedrals. In addition to this he built monastic schools and bridges and developed Romanesque architecture. Palaces were built for the Emperor at Ingelheim and Nijimagen. The structures in architecture borne the influence of Byzantine and Syrian style.

Estimate: Charlernagne was a great administrator. He was a great general. He was a great conqueror. He founded the medieval empire. He broke the darkness and ignorance of the early Middle Ages by stimulating literature and education. His work at each point was not transitory, but permanent. He co-operated with the forces of the time and the very foundations of our present European life are stamped with his name. He protected the Christians from the attacks of the Huns Saracens, Saxons and the Slavs. He claimed to have revived the Roman Empire. He was the greatest of Medieval Kings. Thus, Charlemagne's long reign marked an epoch in the history of Europe. He died in 814 A.D. After his death his son Louis became the ruler of the empire.

19

Contribution of Papacy to World Civilisation

Struggle

During the time of the High Middle Ages *i.e.*, from 1050 to 1300 A.D. the Popes in general devoted and dedicated their life for reform and the spiritual regeneration of Christian society. At the same time the reform of Papacy became involved in a bitter struggle with the Holy Roman Empire. It was really a tragic conflict which dominated European politics for more than two centuries. It was due to the following causes :

(i) Church offices were sold to persons who gave the highest amount of money. It was the order of the day during the time of Middle Ages. This practice of selling church offices by the rulers of the respective countries was hated by the Popes.

(ii) The Bishop and the Abbot were to be elected by the people of the locality in those days according to the laws of church. It was not followed by the empire. Hence, it created a sort of misunderstanding between the empire and the papacy.

(iii) The rulers had supreme control over the Bishops and the Abbots. But the popes had no such control over them. It was a great disappointment to them. Therefore, the popes hated the rulers.

(iv) The popes desired to get the control over the Bishops and Abbots by abolishing the selling of church offices (simony). This brought the conflict between the pope and the emperor during the Middle Ages.

(v) Most of the Bishops and Abbots were leading married life. But according to the rulers of the church the regular clergy like the Bishops and Abbots were expected to lead unmarried life. The

Pope who wanted to improve the morality of the clergy took steps to suppress the practice of marriage among the clergymen. Since the clergymen were not appointed by the Popes, they were not controlled by them. Hence, the struggle between the empire and the Papacy began so as to improve the morals of the clergymen.

(vi) In those days the rulers invested religious authority to the clergymen and not the other powers. The rulers gave the ring and the staff which were the symbols of religious authority on their appointment to the clergymen (Bishop and Abbots). This practice was known as lay investiture. The Pope realised that religious authority should be invested only by themselves and so they wanted to prevent the rulers who had no connection with religious matters. This led to the struggle between the Empire and the papacy.

(vii) The Popes in the Middle Ages were not only the heads of the church but also the rulers of the territory between Rome and Ravenna in Italy. Italy was the part of the empire and so the emperors were considered as the Lords of the Italians and the Italian territories. In other words the Popes were considered as the feudal vassals of the emperors. They were expected to show obedience to the emperor and pay the feudal dues. The Popes did not like this subjection. They were very anxious to free themselves from the control of the emperors. This desire also led to the struggle between the emperors and the Popes.

(viii) The emperors as feudal lords of Italy collected taxes and tolls from the Italian cities. Further they appointed their officials to supervise the municipal administration of the cities. The Italian cities did not like the control of the officers over their government. They also refused the payment of taxes and tolls. The cities were waiting for an opportunity to free themselves from the control of the emperors joined with the cities in the revolt against the emperors. The support given by the popes to the Italian cities was also a cause for the struggle between the popes and the emperors.

Thus, the two organisations, inevitably came into collision. Underlying all technical details there was the question, 'who is the master; Pope or Emperor'. The question was most urgent on German soil as indicated above.

First Stage or Phase

Henry IV and the Investiture Contest: The struggle between the empire and the papacy started in the reign of Henry IV. He had succeeded to the imperial throne in 1056 A.D. at the age of six. In 1075 Gregory VII the then Pope issued a papal decree against 'lay investitures'. All churchmen were the servants of the church, not to the empire. If the emperor would not admit that, he was cut off from the body of the church. Such was the contention of Gregory.

The contest between Henry IV and Gregory VII is the central chapter of the Middle Ages. Bulls and letters followed one another and the antagonists lost dignity and self-control as the controversy proceeded, and veiled at one another with extreme violence. Pope Gregory VII gave him a lot of troubles from various quarters.

The Penitence of Canossa

The greatest incident of the struggle came in 1077, the year of the famous penitence of Canossa. Henry's power was threatened by various persons. His subjects, bishops, dukes, and counts were failing away from him and siding with the pope; the Saxons were in successful rebellion. Henry found that a reconciliation with the papacy was the only means by which he could preserve his imperial crown. He crossed the Alphs, and humbly approached the papal court which was at the moment is the castle of Canossa. On three occasions he was refused admission. Henry stood as penitent outside the castle for three days, and it was atleast only upon the intercession of the Countess Matilda that he received forgiveness at the hands of the pope. Then he accepted to obey papal orders and then granted him absolution. Thus, 'the spiritual power had triumphed over the temporal'. Canossa had humiliated Henry and compelled him to accept the supremacy of the Pope. But by his act of submission Henry gained a political victory.

Death of Greogry VII

Henry was not sincere in his confession and penitence of Canossa and resumed his support of lay investiture. In 1080 Gregory excommunicated and deposed Henry for the second time. In Germany he won the civil war. A council of German Clergy at Mainz deposed Gregory again. In 1081 Henry led an army into Italy and in 1084 he seized a large part of Rome. He installed an anti-pope Guibert who crowned Henry Emperor.

Immediately Gregory summoned his vassal and ally, the Norman Robert Guiscard to rescue him from his situation. The Normans frightened Henry away in 1085. But they revolted in the Roman towns. Gregory fled to Salermo when he died in 1085, "I have loved the law of God, and hated in equity : therefore I die in exile", are said to have been among his last words. Gregory, therefore, failed to accomplish his aims.

The Concordat of Worms

Henry V succeeded to the empire in 1106 and the struggle between the empire and the papacy continued. During this time thoughts of compromise and conciliation came to the front, and in 1111 it seemed as though a final arrangement might be reached. Henry V had invaded Italy and had negotiated with Pope Parchal. The compromise between the emperor and the pope proved to be a fruitful one. But the terms seemed to the Romans an abject surrender. The coronation was interrupted by a riot in which many Germans were killed. Another war came, and the decision was postponed for eleven more years.

There was an anti-pope set up. The Papal ex-communication was renewed. A Saxon rebellion broke out afresh, and the victory seemed to lie rather with the Pope than the emperor. Pope Parchal died, and his successor also died, Pope Calixtas II came forward to bring the truce. The Concordat of Worms (1122) brought to a close the first phase of this great controversy.

By the concordat it was agreed that the election of bishops should be left in the hands of the church, and that they should receive the ring and the crozier, the insignia of their spiritual office, at the hands of the Pope. The King resigned the long established right of lay investiture.

The long struggle of Henry IV and Henry V with the Papacy was profitable for the Papacy in prestige and power. The papacy succeeded in abolishing the lay investiture. No final settlement of the relations between church and state had been reached. They were still rivals for power.

Second Stage

Frederick Barbanrossa: When the struggle reached its next crisis, political and constitutional questions played a greater part than in the days of Gregory VI and Henry IV. The Emperor Lothair succeeded Henry V and reigned from 1125 to 1137. His successor was Conrad III of Hohenstaufen family. After a reign of 15 years Conrad III was succeeded by Frederick Barbarossa, the greatest of the Hohenstaufen, and perhaps the greatest of all the medieval emperors since Charlemagne (1152).

Frederick reasserted the imperial authority over the wealthy Lombard cities. His Lombard policy paved the way for the hostility of the papacy. As a result Pope Hadrian IV became one of Frederick Barbarossa's most ardent foes. The Lombard struggle reached its height in the Pontificate of Alexander III, Hadrian's successor. To save the Lombard cities the Pope rallied the Lombard cities and formed an association called Lormbard League. A powerful army was raised by him. The emperor had meanwhile thrown his support behind the rival claimant to the Papal throne and Alexander responded by excommunicating and deposing him.

The struggle between Pope Alexander and the Emperor Barbarossa thus started in a fierce manner. In 1176 there took place a terrible battle between them at Legnano (Seventeen miles from Milan). Frederick lost the battle, submitted to the pope and provided to be a dutiful son of the Roman. See, it is described thus, 'He was touched by the spirit of God and abandoning his imperial dignity, threw himself humbly at the feet of the pope'.

After Alexander's death in 1181, the Papcy ceased for a time to be a serious threat and the far — sighted emperor (Frederick) was at the height of his power in 1190. When he died while leading his army toward the Holy land on the Third Crusade.

Third Stage

Henry VI: Henry VI the son of Frederick Barbarossa, married Constance, the heiress of the Kingdom of the Two Sicilies. He was ambitious to make the 'Holy Roman Empire' into a reality, to make the connection between Italy and Germany a real and a close one, and to rule all Europe from Italy. During his rule the struggle existed and the Pope even raised by a rival claimant to his Sicilian dominons. But Henry VI was victorious over all his enemies. He wished to make the empire hereditary like most of the monarchies of Europe, instead of elective with the support of the leaders of Germany. But in the end he failed.

Innocent III: In 1198 A.D. Innocent III became Pope. He is regarded as the greatest of Medieval Popes. He was the greatest maker of Papacy. He was history's most powerful Pope. He claimed for church supremacy over all crowned heads.

It is said in the following manners; 'He stands in the midst between God and man; below God, above man; less than God more than man'. He judged all and is judged by none, for it is written, 'I will judge' and again 'The Lord let to Peter not only the government of the Universal church, but of the whole world'.

Pope Innocent III freed the German church from the State. He vindicated the Pope's right to investigate all candidates for the German throne. In central Italy he made a league with the cities, drove out the emperor's officials and set his own in their place. In 1199, he succeeded in imposing a truce upon Philip Augustus of France and Richard I of England. He also forced King John of England to accept his candidate as archbishop of Canterbury.

Innocent III favoured Otto of Brunswick in the problem of German imperial succession. But after becoming emperor, Otto repudiated his promise to Innocent, asserted his mastery over the German church and even launched an invasion of southern Italy. So he favoured the candidacy of Frederick II. Innocent III died in 1216. Immediately he ignored his promise. The Papacy began to quarrel with him. Popes like Gregory IX and Innocent VI devoted all their diplomatic talents and spiritual sanctions in blocking Frederick's enterprises.

Innocent IV: Innocent IV convened a council at Lyons in 1245 A.D. There the emperor was condemned and ex-communicated. Frederick was deposed. A rival emperor was elected in his place, and a crusade was called to rid the empire of its un-Godly Tyrant. Revolts broke out against him throughout his empire. The royal estates in Germany slipped more and more from his grip and his Italian holdings were ridden with rebellion. Against this unhappy background Frederick II died in 1250 A.D. With the approval of the papacy Conrad the last of the Hohenstaufen was beheaded in Naples and with his death the Hohenstaufen house was extinguished. With this piteous tragedy, the victory of the Papacy ended its conflict with the empire. The empire was overthrown and never revived except in name. At the same time it cannot be denied that the Papacy had been terribly weakened during the contest.

Contributions

Papacy spread very quickly and during the Middle Ages it became a power to be reckoned with. But after some time it also had its fall. We have already discussed the causes responsible for the spread and decline of Papacy. Papacy at the height of its glory made certain very valuable contributions which may briefly be discussed as under.

(1) The Papacy began to help the poor, the needy and the deserving in the social field. The monks began to act as teachers and also began to serve the patients. The result was that among the people survival for morality and character as well as dignity developed.

(2) Then another contribution was that under Papacy, Christians all over the world, believed that they belonged to one fraternity. The result was that among the people, a sense of brother-hood and oneness developed.

(3) Another significant contribution was that under papacy beautiful churches were built. In these churches there were beautiful paintings. As a result of these activities fine arts, paintings, sculpture and architecture developed, which is still appreciated all over the world.

(4) The monks in the monasteries devoted their time and energy in writing religious dogmas, hymns etc. in those days when it was difficult to write and when there were no printing presses. The result was that very precious knowledge which otherwise would have been lost to us could be presented for the posterity and still available to us.

(5) Papacy was highly responsible for the introduction of the idea of universal state, which is even to-day appreciated in the world. Really, it is a wonderful contribution to us.

(6) Papacy was also in a position to inculcate among the people a sense of piety and love for all. The results was that cruelty of the feudal lords could be checked to a great extent. Many feudal lords now stopped unnecessarily testing their peoples.

(7) In the eyes of the Papacy all the high and the low were equal with the result that the Papacy created a sense of equality among all the barries of the high and low or those of superiority or inferiority complexes were narrowed down.

(8) No doubt the most powerful monarchs realised that the Papacy was a force to be reckoned with. The result was that they could not afford to be absolute despots or cruel. They always feared that their high handedness could swing the balance in favour of Papacy, and thus the monarchs thought it worthwhile to sense the people rather than to exploit them.

(9) It was due to Papacy that a sense of charity and giving alms to the needy and the poor developed.

No wonder that Papacy made very significant contributions to world civilisation. Without Papacy much would have been lost, which could otherwise be preserved and is available to us even today. It was due to Papacy that knowledge developed and also could be passed on to the present generation.

20

The Services of Monastic Orders

The rise and growth of Monasticism contributed greatly to the strength of the Papacy. The monastic life in some form was as old as Christianity, and older. But in its early forms it was spasmodic, without discipline and liable to grave excess. The organiser and law giver of monasticism was St. Benedict (480-543 A.D.).

Meaning

Monasticism means the system of living as practised by monks in monasteries. A monastery is a building in which monks live as a secluded community.

Origin and Development

In the 4th century A.D. the popes led a lonely life. Many pious men gave up their properties and families and took an ascetic life in Europe. So these people came to be called as monks. Many pious Christians thus turned to the life of monks in those days. There were some causes for the same.

(i) There arose danger to life and property to the Christians from the barbanans. They destroyed many cities and villages and killed many people.

(ii) The worldliness of the church made the clergymen to lead a saintly life. They felt a sort of disgust in their official work. So many people began to move from their cities to forests and led a saintly life.

(iii) The belief of the Christians about God and Heaven was very firm and they decided to reach heaven through the good deeds and pure life.

(iv) The pious people were very eager to lead the other people in the path of truth and simple life. Hence, the above factors were responsible for the origin of Monasteries.

In the forest each monk had his own hut. But there was considerable distance from one hut to the other. In other words there was no connection between the huts. Even in this life the monks met danger from the wild animals. So they began to live very near to each other. Now the distance between the huts disappeared. The huts were lonelised. Later on they began to live in same hut. Now they came under one common roof. Then they lived together and ate together. The big house where the people lived came to be called as monastery. The life in monastery led by monks is called monasticism.

Many monasteries came into existence during this period. Among them the following monasteries played a significant role.

(1) Benedictine Monastery
(2) The Monastery of Cluny
(3) The Carthusian Order
(4) The Dominican Monastery
(5) The Franciscan Monastery

(1) Benedictine Monastery: St. Benedict of Nursia (480-544 A.D.) was the greatest organiser of monasticism. He was a Roman aristocrat by birth. Inspite of that he did not like the corruptive Roman life in his early days. He attacked the evils of Roman life. Then he took up a hermit life in a cave. Gradually other monks came to him for advice and help and he eventually became the head of a community of monks. He founded a number of monasteries. The most important one was the monastery of Monte Casino in southern Italy.

Monte Casino became a model monastery and for centuries it was one of chief centres of religious life in western Europe.

Features

(i) St. Benedict established certain rules and regulations for the monastery. They were strictly observed by the Abbots.

(ii) Three vows were insisted upon them.

(a) The monks should lead unmarried life.

(b) The monks should not possess personal property.

(c) They should obey the orders of the head of the monastery.

(iii) The monks should lead the life of chastity, poverty and obedience.

(iv) Each monk should work atleast 7 hours a day.

(v) They should study the Holy Bible atleast 2 hours a day.

(vi) The monks should not depend upon the outside world for any requirements. They were not allowed to purchase any goods from outside of their cities. By their own efforts they should prepare their requirements. As a result of this, they produced everything in their monastery.

Contributions

Benedictine Monastery did a lot of service to the humanity.

St. Benedict died in 544 A.D. But his rule survived to inspire and transform Western Europe. Within two centuries of his death, his rule had spread throughout western Christendom hence it is said that 'Benedictine monasticism succeeded in diverting religious enthusiasm from 'record breading' fears of asceticism into the life of an ordered community'.

(i) The Benedictine monastery built many schools. Their schools produced the vast majority of literate Europeans during the Early Middle Ages. One of the greatest of the early Benedictine scholars was an Englishman named Bede who wrote an admirable history of the English Church.

(ii) The Benedictines preserved the writings of Latin antiquity.

(iii) The missionary work of the Benedictines was of utmost value to the Roman Catholic Church. They spearheaded the penetration of Christianity into the forests of Germany and later into Scandinavia, Poland and Hungary. Many Popes, bishops and archbishops were chosen from the Benedictine order.

(iv) They did a wonderful service for the development of Papacy. It was due to their connection with Papacy in religious matters.

(v) The Benedictines received gifts of land from pious donors and they held and managed large estates which became models of intelligent agricultural organisation and technological innovation.

(vi) The Benedictine monasteries highly served as islands of security and learning in an ocean of barbarism.

(vii) The monks in the Benedictine monasteries gave spiritual guidance to its people.

(viii) They developed classical Christian Germanic synthesis that under lay European civilisation.

To put it in a nutshell, 'Benedictine monasticism become the supreme influence in the barbarian west'.

(2) The Monastery of Cluny: The monastery of Cluny was founded in 910 A.D. in Burgandy in France. The Duke of Aquitaine William was the founder of the monastery.

This system of monastery was a highly centralised one.

It was a model for the institutions of Popes and Kings.

Many charitable endowments were created. It was a holy institution; it was free from all sorts of corruption. Hence, it became famous and widely admired. The Cluniac advocated a return to Benedictine rule.

During this period the Cluniac reformers demanded that bishops and archibishops should be invested with the spiritual symbols of their office, the ring and the staff by the proper ecclesiastical authority and not by the King. Pope Gregory VII was the leader of the movement at this stage.

(3) The Carthusian Order: In 1084 St. Buano of Cologne founded the Carthusian order in the Alps.

Under this system each monk worked, ate and slept in his own separated cell, and practised almost perpetual silence.

They strictly observed prayers and mass. They indulged themselves in conversation and common meal. From Alps it spread to other parts of the Christendom.

The Cistercian Order

In 1098 St. Robert of France founded the Cistercian order at Citeaux in Burgandy in France. It was one of the very strict monastic groups founded towards the end of the 11th century A.D.

The monks of this order observed the Benedictine rules and regulations. They restored the manual labour. They took keen interest in large scale sheep breading. They led a vigorous pious life. This attracted many able and zealous men.

The first outstanding leader of this order was St. Bernard. He was the founder and abbot of Clairvaux, one of the daughter houses of Cistercian order.

St. Bernard exercised a tremendous influence during his period. So he became Europe's leading arbiter of political and ecclesiastical disputes.

St. Bernard was responsible for the organisation of second crusade. It was for him that the king of France and the Holy Roman Emperor participated in the crusade. But the crusade ended in miserable failure.

(4) The Dominican Monastery: The Dominican Monastic order was founded by St. Dominic (1170-1221). He was a Spanish priest. He started his career as a pious Christian. He tried to convert the heretics of southern France.

The congregation founded by St. Dominic was called the Order of Friars (Preachers).

St. Dominic emphasised absolute poverty. There should be no fixed incomes; there should be charitable gifts. It was in short a 'mendicant order'.

St. Dominic established many schools. The graduates of these schools dominated the faculties of theology of European universities.

The Dominican Friars carried their evangelical activities across Europe, into the Holy Land, Central Asia, Tibet and China.

(5) The Franciscan Monastery: Francis of Assisi founded the order of Franciscans. His period was from 1182 to 1226 A.D. He was the most revolutionary monk known to Christianity. He was an ideal saint.

Francis was born in the year 1182 A.D. to a wealthy cloth merchant of Assisi in northern Italy. But he lived the life of a beggar. He devoted his life to the service of lepers and orphans. He did a wonderful hospital service.

Francis founded one 'order of friars' with the help of Pope innocent III. The Franciscan ideal was the notion of poverty and humility. They wandered about preaching to the poor, earning for the sick and doing good. He urged his followers that manual labour should be done with faith and devotion.

At the time of his death in 1226 A.D. his order remained the most powerful and attractive religious movement of his age. After his death some modifications took place in his order. By the end of the 13th century the Franciscans had ceased to inspire the society.

Services Rendered by Monasteries

(i) The monasteries played a prominent part in protecting the life and property of the people throughout western Europe when there was unrest and insecurity to the people. In an ocean of barbarism the monasteries served as island of safety and security.

(ii) The monks were employed by the Popes of the Middle Ages to preach Christianity among the Pagans. Many parts of Europe remained under occupation of the Pagans till the 13th century. The people of these parts were converted to Christianity by the monks who carried on missionary work among the Pagans. It goes without saying that the monks were very good preachers.

(iii) The monks were not only good preachers but also good teachers. They conducted schools in their monasteries and gave instructions in subjects like history, arithmatic and philosophy to the children of the locality freely. Further, the monasteries were centers of learning. There were many learned men like Martin Luther, Roger Bacon and Erasmus.

(iv) The monasteries took keen interest in promoting agriculture. Many lands were given by pious men. The monks cultivated these lands and raised all kinds of crops, vegetables, fruits and flowers. Further, they cleared the forests that were near the monasteries and made arable lands. Moreover, they drained the marshy lands and made them fit for cultivation. In these ways the monks contributed to the development of agriculture.

(v) The monks engaged themselves in the work of copying old manuscripts which were about to perish. Many valuable works in Greek and Latin were saved from destruction. In addition to these works, the monks wrote down chronicles in which they recorded the incidents and the happenings of their times. St. Augustine wrote 'the City of God' in defence of Christianity. The most famous chronicle of the monks was the 'Anglo-Saxon Chronicle' which records the great events in the history of England in the Middle Ages. It is from these chronicles that we get much of our knowledge of Middle Ages.

(vi) The monasteries became the centre where alms were distributed to the poor. Pious Christians gave money and other things to the monks for distribution to the poor and the needy. In short, they were in charge of the charitable endowments. Apart from this, the travellers and the pilgrims were given shelter and food in the monasteries. In this respect the monasteries were something like inns or rest houses.

(vii) The monasteries maintained the only hospitals of the time. The monks treated the sick and the wounded in the hospitals and in the monasteries. So the monasteries were converted to hospitals during this period.

(viii) The monks were great builders. They possessed much wealth and this wealth was utilised for the construction of many churches and new monasteries. Many marvellous and beautiful churches of the Middle Ages were built during this time. Manual labour was performed only by slaves. The monks who were slaves of God, showed to the world the value of hardwork.

(ix) The monks improved farming by their careful study of plant growth and animal life.

Decline

The monks gradually lost their respect and regard. The monasteries began to have enormous property from which came a huge income. The wealth of the monasteries made the monks lazy and idle. They forgot their duties and responsibilities and began to lead a comfortable life. They disregarded the three vows. So the people began to hate the worldliness of the monks. This proved to be one of the causes for the Reformation Movement in Europe. As a result of the reformation in many countries the monasteries were destroyed and their property was confiscated by the State.

21

The Crusades

For nearly two centuries (*i.e.* from 1095 to 1270) from the Christian states of Western Europe there went out a series of expeditions against the Mohammedan states of the East, which are known as the Crusades. They wore cross as a symbol of their task. In other words the crusades refer to the military expeditions made by the Christian rulers and people of Europe during the Middle Ages to recover the Holy Land from the Muslims. The most heroic and adventurous chapter in the life of the Middle Ages are derived from these Cursades, and they had a considerable effect upon the life of Western Europe.

Causes

(i) The causes of the Crusades are to be found partly in the condition of the West and partly in that of the East. The crusading movement was started as an offensive against Islam. An active crusade was in progress against the Moors in Spain.

(ii) After the battle of Manzikert (1071) the advance of Seljuk Turks continued into Western Asia Minor, Syria and Palestine. By 1085 A.D. not only most of Asia Minor but also Antioch and all Syria were lost to the Byzantine empire. The Turks had taken Jerusalem from the Fatimite Caliphs of Egypt. By 1092 the Seljuk empire fell apart. Jerusalem was recovered by the Egyptian Caliph in 1098. 'The Holy Land' was a region of pilgrimage of the Christians and people in Western Europe wanted to rescue the holy places and the holy relics of the birth and infancy of their faith from the pollution of infidel fact. Thus, under the leadership of the Pope a mass movement of warriors and non combatants started to recover the Holy Land from the infidels.

(iii) The then ruler of Byzantine was Alexius Comnenus (1089-1118). As the successful attacks of the Turks on the Byzantine empire threatened the destruction of eastern Christendom, the Emperor had appealed to the west for help. The crusaders began to help the emperor.

(iv) Pope Urban II convened a Council at Clevmont in 1095 A.D. It was attended by many nobles and clergy. At this council the Pope Urban II aroused the eagerness for the recovery of Syria and Palestine. He delivered a subtle speech to the large audience. He gave a moving portrayal of the sufferings of the eastern Christians. As a result of this the crusading movement was started against the Muslims.

(v) It was a tug of war between the cross and the crescent. It was due to their great faith in their respective religions. The Christians thought that "it is the will of god". Hence, they shouted this and kept this as their battle cry.

(vi) The immediate cause of the crusade was the attractive speech made by Pope Urabn II. He declared that a Christian army was set out to east in the following year in 1096 A.D. All gentlemen were trained in the practice of war, and most of them loved it.

The First Crusade

The First Crusade was in every way, the greatest and most successful. No king took part in it, but provencals and Italians — French, Germans and Normans went out in a vast undisciplined army, and their great nobles led them. But there was no commander-in-chief. Then groups of crusaders got through to Constantinople arriving in 1096. The last group arrived in 1097. Altogether the warriors of the first crusade numbered around twenty five or thirty thousand.

In the meantime they got the support of the Byzantine emperor.

In April 1097, the crusaders began to enter into Asia Minor. They captured Nical the Turkish capital. After the battle of Doryleanus, they marched towards Syria. Finally, they arrived in Antioch. On the way Baldwin, one of their leaders took possession of the city Edessa. Then the Latin country of Edessa was formed.

In 1097 they attacked Antioch in northern Syria. After the siege of seven months the city was captured. The crusaders won a significant victory against the Turks in 1098. Bohemund, their leader took possession of the city and the second state of the crusaders was founded.

Then the crusaders marched towards Jerusalem under the leadership of Raymond of Toulouse in June 1099. There was no serious opposition. So they easily took the Holy City on 15th July 1099. Thus, the crusaders accomplished their primary aim. The city remained in the hands of crusaders form 1099 to 1187.

Godfrey of Bouillon was elected king of Jerusalem. After his death, Baldwin became the king. Raymond became the count of Tripoli in 1109. In the words of Swain, "The first crusade was the only one to fulfil its major objective."

Results

(1) The first crusade brought great prestige to the Papacy.
(2) Many cities were conquered by the crusaders.
(3) The primary aim of capturing the city of Jerusalem was fulfilled.
(4) A number of individual crusaders decided to settle in the conquered countries.
(5) The conquered countries were properly organised.
(6) Military orders like the Knights of St. John and the Knights of Templars were created to defend their territories.
(7) Romanesque churches and federal castles appeared because of crusades.
(8) European feudalism was established in Palestine and Syria.

The Second Crusade

In 1144 A.D. the condition of the Christian lands was unhappy, because the above mentioned leaders began to quarrel with each other. They had no unity among them; so the lack of unity gave a chance to Turks to attack the city under their energetic leader Zanghi. He captured and destroyed the Latin country of Edessa. Europe was at once aroused by the new Turkish threat to the Latin kingdom Jerusalem. The second crusade was preached by St. Bernard in 1146 and conducted by Louis VII, king of France and Conrad III of Germany.

Conrad III of Germany with his men reached the East. They selected the land route of the first crusaders and suffered a series of defeats. Then Louis came and joined with him. The crusaders laid siege to Damascus; but they failed to take the city. With great disappointment the discouraged kings returned home, with the remnants of their armies. Thus, the Second Crusade ended in utter failure.

The Third Crusade

In 1187 King Saladin, the great Mohammedan leader captured the holy place of Jerusalem. The fall of Jerusalem called forth the Third Crusade.

The Pope appealed to the rulers and the people to take up arms to recapture the city. Accordingly Frederick Barbarossa of Germany, Philip Augustus of France, and Richard I of England took part in the crusade.

The German army advanced towards Asia Minor. Before reaching Antioch, Frederick was drowned while bathing in a stream. So the Germans turned back and abandoned the Crusade.

The French and the English kings arrived by sea and attacked Acre which had been going on for two years. They succeeded in recapturing Acre in 1191. Subsequently they took Joppa. In the meantime Philip returned home. Richard continued the war. But he failed to take Jerusalem. In 1191 a truce was arranged between Richard and Saladin. According to the truce the Christians held a strip of the Levant coast with the right of access to the Holy Land for Pilgrims. Thus, Jerusalem once victoriously regained was lost.

The Fourth Crusade

The fourth crusade (1200-1204) produced great, and in a sense permanent results, through they tended rather to the weakening than the strengthening of the Christian power in the East. Pope Innocent III called for the fourth crusade. His call was responded to by the great nobles of France.

The crusaders made their way to Venice, and there sought ships to sail to the Holy Land. But their funds were exhausted, and without funds they could go no further. They were in consequence bound to bargain with the commercial rèpublic of Venice. Since it was turned aside, they directed their attention first against the Christian town of Zara, a city on the opposite shores of the Adriatic, and later against Constantinople.

Constantinople fell first in 1203 and then again in 1204. In 1204 the Venetians occupied the city of Constantinopie. These followed the barbaric massacre which remains one of the blackest chapters in European History.

Results

(1) The Latin Empire of Constantinpole was established.

(2) The reigning dynasty was deposed.

(3) The Greek form of Christianity was abolished.

(4) Catholicism and Latin empire was instituted.

(5) A great blow was given to Christianity in the East.

Children's Crusade: In 1212 A.D. bands of children from France and Germany started to reconquer the Holy Land. This crusade was preached by a French shepherd boy, Stephen. Under Nicholas they advanced towards Alps. Most of the children died due to exhaustion and hunger. Many were sold as slaves by Venetians. The survivors were asked by the Pope to return to their homes.

The Lost Crusades

The fifth crusade captured Damietta (Egypt) in 1219 A.D. At the same time they lost the city very quickly.

Under the leadership of Frederick II the sixth crusade was started on the advice of Pope Gregory IX. Without any fighting he made a treaty with the Sultan of Egypt in 1229. Accordingly he occupied Jerusalem, Bethlehem and Nazareth.

In 1244 A.D. Morgols invaded and took the city of Jeruslem at the request of the Sultan of Egypt. This necessitated Louis IX of France (St. Louis) to take up the cross. This was called as the seventh comrade. He captured Damiatta in Egypt. But he was defected by the Turks and his campaign ended in disaster.

The Eight crusade was also led dy Louis IX. He achieved meagre things during this crusade. He died of fever on the site of an ancient Carthage (in Africa) and his army returned home demoralised.

There are several other movements after this, which are called crusades, but none that deserved the name. With the death of St. Louis (Louis IX) the crusading movement was at an end.

Causes for its Failure

Many causes were attributed for the failure of the crusading movements which were started by Christians of Europe in 1097 and continued until 1291 A.D.

(1) The crusaders had no training in warfare. They did not have proper weapons. They lacked discipline. So they failed in their attempt of capturing the Holy City.

(2) The Christian army consisted of many feudal nobles and it was impossible to gather a really united force on the Christian side. There was no unity among them. During the third crusade the relations of Philip Augustus of France and Richard of England were unfriendly. Hence, Philip Augustus returned home leaving his troops behind him. So Richard failed in his primary aim.

(3) The crusaders lacked capable generals who were interested in capturing Jerusalem for the sake of Christians so as to enable them to go on a pilgrimage.

(4) The Christian army from Europe had to cross a long land route and as well as sea to reach the Holy land in Asia. But the Turks fought from their land. Difficulties in getting food and war supplies put the Christian army in a disadvantageous position.

(5) The crusaders did not maintain strong and sufficient military force to protect the conquered lands in the East. This facilitated the Muslims for an easy recapture of the Christian lands.

(6) The Eastern Roman Empire did not give any help to crusaders, though the first crusade was undertaken only in response to the appeal of Urban II then Pope of Rome.

(7) The crusaders had no knowledge about the conditions of the East. They had never visited Asia Minor, Syria and Palestine. They had no knowledge about the difficulties they had to face in the east. Hence, they failed in their aim.

(8) The Venetians were selfish and so they diverted the attention of the crusaders from Egypt to Constantinople. The Venetians used the crusaders to destroy their rivals in trade and commerce in the east.

(9) Only the first three crusades are considered as important ones. The later crusades were not so serious as the first three. In the later crusades there was no religious zeal. The crusades ceased because of the dying religious zeal. "The failure of the crusaders was due chiefly to their own short comings. The failure of the Christians to retain their hold upon Jerusalem is therefore, not to be wondered at".

The Results of the Crusades

(1) Political:

(i) The Mohammedan wave had receded for a moment, but soon it advanced again. Nevertheless, the whole movement probably had acted as a useful check to Mohammednanism when it was particularly dangerous and aggressive.

(ii) The nobles sold and mortgaged their lands to get money to go on a crusade.

(iii) The nobles lost heavily in terms of men and money.

(iv) The crusades gave Philip Augustus of France and Henry II of England a pretext for imposing the first direct tax in Medieval Europe, the saladin tithe of 1188.

(v) Feudalism was gradually disappearing and in its place nationalism began to develop rapidly. People began to feel that they belonged to a country.

(2) Social:

(i) The crusading movement hastened the evasion of the common people of towns and country.

(ii) Serfs were freed from their bondage.

(iii) Women had longer responsibilities while their husbands were away. There was a notable change in the status of women.

(iv) The West came to know the demand of Eastern products.

(v) Long flowing robes and full beards seem to have been fashions adopted from the east.

(vi) Social contact was brought by crusades between the west and the east.

(3) Commerce: The crusades reopened the trade between East and West which the Turks had stopped. Particularly cities like Genoa, Pisa and Venice were among the first to benefit from the crusades. They transported supplies, reinforcements and pilgrims from Europe to the east. Their returning ships brought back spices, cotton, sugar, silks and much of the plunder which had been captured from the captured towns of Syria and Palestine, Eastern products like rice, garlic, cotton, silk, maize, muslin, glass, mirrors, spices and perfumes found a ready market in Europe. Europe in turn found profitable eastern markets for commodities like furs, hides, wool cloth and metals. Banking service was also promoted by crusades during this period.

(4) Naval Influence: The Fourth crusade was highly responsible for the naval influence of the Mediteranean. Bigger ships were built for trade and commerce. Mariner's Compass was introduced due to the crusading movements.

(5) The Rise of Towns: Many nobles along with their peasants took part in the crusades. Large numbers never returned home but settled in the growing towns. The crusades thus hastened the urbanisation of western Europe.

(6) Religion: The crusades raised the power and prestige of the Papacy. It was Urban II who preached the first crusade. The first crusade proved to be a brilliant success for the Christians. This resulted the increase of regard and respect for the Pope.

(7) Military Orders: The crusades paved the way for the rise of military monkish orders like the Knight of St. John and the Knight Templars. The members of the two orders were trained in warfare. They were engaged in giving protection to the pilgrims. Besides, they had to take care of the sick and the wounded soldiers.

(8) Introduction of New Things: New articles were introduced into Europe by the crusades. They were wind mill, alcohol, new plants and animals like horse, mule and donkey, Botanical gardens were established in Europe.

(9) Geographical Knowledge: The crusading movement increased the interest in the study of geography. It was intensified more and more. By this the people came to know about the Eastern countries. It induced many adventurous mariners to explore new countries. In other words the crusades were highly responsible for the geographical discoveries of the 15th century.

(10) Arts And Science: The crusades made the Europeans to realise the existence of many Greek-Roman works in literature. Many Greek and Roman literatures were brought to the forefront by this movement. It created an enormous interest in the classics of Greece and Rome. The crusaders brought a collection of oriental tales which influenced Western poets to use the same romantic atmosphere. Architecture was enriched by the round churches built in imitation of the church of the Holy Sepulchre at Jerusalem. Western military science was developed by the crusading movement. In short the crusading activity dominated Europe for nearly two centuries *i.e.*, form 1095 to 1291 A.D.

J.E. Swain says, "The scientific works of Aristotle, Arabic numerals, Algabra, Mariner's compass, and the paper were introduced in the West as a result of discoveries made by the crusades."

22

Rise of National States

The rise of national states is considered as an important event in the history of modern Europe. At the beginning of the modern period, Europe comprised of England, France, Spain and Italy. Among those England, Spain and France became very prominent under monarchies. The monarchs had unlimited powers. Besides, Germany also rose to prominence during this period.

Germany

In Germany there were many principalities. It is said that there were more than one principalities, ruled by the nobles, the Dukes and others. It, therefore, could not be called as single Nation. The German Emperor was their head. In theory they were subject to the higher authorities. He ruled the empire with the help of the Diet.

The Diet consisted of three estates. They were (1) the first estate consisted of electors, the second and third estates represented the towns and cities. The emperor had to consult this diet for each and every thing. If the emperor was weak, the diet would become a very powerful body. This was the condition of Germany during this period.

England

During this period the Hundred Years War (1337-1453) that took place between England and France was an important event in the history of Europe. After that the Wars of the Roses came into existence. At Bosworth the Wars of the Roses reached their final milestone. In the next century the subjects of the Tudors liked to consider that the Middle Ages too had come to a close in 1485 and that a new age had dawned with the accession of Henry Tudor *i.e.* Henry VII. He consolidated much of the work of the Yorkist kings. Certainly the prolongation of strife, waste and insecurity in the 15th century had aroused in all classes an overpowering desire for strong and orderly government. The parliamentary conception which had prevailed under the house of Lancaster had gained many frontiers of constitutional rights. The star of the Renaissance, the storm of the Reformation, here led their new problems on the bewildered but also inspired mortals of the new age upon which England entered under the guidance of the wise, and careful monarch who inaugurated the Tudor dictatorship, as King Henry VII.

Henry VII did a wonderful service to England. He laid the foundation of Tudor despotism. He put an end to feudalism and Manorialism. He was responsible for the rise of national states. He wiped out of the country illiteracy and superstition. He paved the way for eradicating corruption from church and the Pope. During this period critical and national approach was adopted by the people. People became brave and laborious. Long voyages were undertaken and new countries were explored during his reign. To destroy the powerful baroas he established the 'star chamber'. It consisted of the members of the Privy Council. Thus, the path for the glory of later Tudors was also paved by Henry VII.

France

France became very powerful during the time of Charles VII. He crushed the powers of the feudal lords completely. He paved the way for unlimited powers. After Charles VII, Louis XI became the ruler of France. He extended the territories of France considerably. In addition to this he added Burgandy and some other provinces to his kingdom.

Charles VIII became the ruler of France after Louis XI. He had a great ambition to conquer Italy. For that purpose he invited the ruler of Milan. When the Wars of the Roses broke out, his successor tried to gain a big victory over England. At this juncture Henry VII became the ruler of England. He decided to put an end to the war and to maintain peace and order in the country. This was the condition of France during the beginning of the modern age.

Spain

In Spain there were two states *viz.*, Castile and Aragon during this period. These two states were Christian states. In the 7th century the Muslims of North Africa re-entered into Spain. They were called Moors. Naturally there was continuous war between Muslims and Christians. The Christians gradually gained momentum. The Moors at the same time had won the city of Granada. Fortunately, for the Christians the two kingdoms were united together by a matrimonial alliance. Isabella the ruler of Castile married Ferdinand the ruler of Aragon in 1462. This unity gave sufficient strength to the Christians. As a result of this unity Granada was captured from Moors and they were expelled from Spain completely. So Spain became completely a Christian Nation.

Ferdinand was a powerful ruler. He fought against the French king and brought Naples under his control. Mexico, Peru, Philippines etc., were added to his kingdom. America was discovered; alike on land and sea Spain made good her claim to be one of the first powers in Europe. Unfortunately, her greatness was tarnished by the atmosphere of religious bigotry which pervaded the land and in the end did much to ruin it.

Italy

Italy in the 15th century presents us with an extraordinary spectacle. Intellectually it was far in advance of the rest of Europe. The Renaissance had fully begun.

There was no political unity at this juncture. From the Papacy, which was essentially cosmopolitan, no unity could come. There was no state in Italy powerful enough to force its will on the others. Thus, Italy was a "geographical expression", and contained a large number of quite independent states. The chief were :

(i) Genoa
(ii) Milan
(iii) Venice
(iv) Florence
(v) Rome
(vi) Naples

Now we shall shortly examine some of these more closely. Besides these, there was a large number of others, either possessing or claiming complete independence.

Amongst these many states no principle of order was to be found. All alliances were as transitory as they had been among the city-states of ancient Greece. The only constant principle seemed to be that all should join against any state which was for the moment stronger than the others. The factions and frictions took place between them purely on the basis of selfish aims.

Another feature of Italian life, which completes the analogy with decadent Greece, is that the states had for the most part abandoned the employment of citizen troops, and were using mercenaries in their quarrels. The captains of these bonds, the 'Condottieri' and the troops they commanded were drawn from almost every country in Europe. They usually served faithfully the states which paid them.

Of all the cities of Italy, Venice was the most prosperous and the best governed. The inhabitants loved to recall a legend that their city had been founded by Romans who fled from the eternal city, when it was threatened by the barbarians. The whole strength of Venice lay in her commerce. She was at the point of connection between the East and the West. Until the cape route was discovered, all the merchandise of the East was brought to Venice, and from there transported by caravan into Germany, France, and all parts of Europe. The state made vast profits on all goods that passed through her harbour. There was a close oligarchy or aristocracy in Venice. The "Council of Trent" looked after the administration.

Florence presented a great contrast to Venice in every way. There was instability instead of order, fierce factions instead of unity; and democracy gave way not to oligarchy but to the kind of despotism, which the Greeks called tyranny. The popular leader of Florence was Medici. The history of Florence is the history of the Medicean family. In 1469 Lorenzo de Medici became the ruler of France after Cosimo. It was under him that Florence reached the zenith of her fame in art and letters.

MODERN PERIOD

23

Renaissance, Reformation and The Counter Reformation Movement

RENAISSANCE

What is meant by Renaissance? A great change was passing over the thoughts, convictions and feelings of men in the fifteenth century Europe, particularly in Italy. This movement is usually known as the Renaissance, "Renaissance" means "rebirth", and the word is usually used with reference to the revived knowledge of Latin and Greek and of classical literature and ideas which is one of the great features of the time. A spirit of enquiry and freedom of thought developed a new outlook upon all branches of knowledge. The other worldliness of religious dogma ceased to exist. Humanism became the heartbeat of all arts and literatures. This kind of new learning was called Renaissance. It began in the 15th century in Italy and spread all over Europe.

Causes

(1) The barbarian invasions destroyed much of the ancient culture and civilisation of Europe. The Middle Age is characterised as the dark age in the history of Europe. By the close of the 14th century a new age was drawing. It was the age of enquiry which paved the way for Renaissance.

(2) The invention of printing press by John Guttenberg was the most important cause for the spread of new learning far and wide cheaply, quickly and plentifully. The first Latin Bible was printed in 1455 and the first printing press was set up in Italy in 1465.

(3) The city of Constantinople treasured the ancient Greek arts and literature. When the city fell into the hands of the Turks in 1453 the Greek artists sought shelter in Italian cities. The wealthy cities welcomed and gave them encouragement.

(4) In the Italian cities there were enough opportunities and facilities for the study of Greek and Roman classics. In the cities of Italy encouragement was given to education and fine arts. The Italian cities resembled the old Greek cities in every way. Florence in particular resembled Athens. Such conditions were conducive for the study of the old classics.

(5) The crusades opened the eyes of the Europeans to the Eastern and Arab civilisations. The Arab numerical system, gunpowder and other features of a higher civilisation increased their curiosity and enriched their knowledge.

(6) The Italian cities were free from outside control. They were freed from the control of the emperor as well as the people. So it was possible for the Italian cities to break the control imposed by the church on the freedom of thought and expression.

(7) The geographical discoveries were indirectly helpful for the spread of Renaissance. Eastern arts and literatures were brought into Europe through the new routes thus discovered.

(8) Italy was the homeland of Renaissance. The commercial prosperity of Italian cities like Venice, Rome and Florence attracted Greek refugees from Constantinople. Moreover, the merchants, princes and the popes were generous enough to patronise them.

(9) The Humanists were mainly responsible for the movement of Renaissance.

Literature

(1) Dante was the fore-runner in this field. He was an Italian poet. His famous book was 'Divine Comedy'. His period was from 1265 to 1321 A.D.

(2) Boccacio was the author of 'Decameron'. It was a criticism of two short stories of sensual pleasures. His period was from 1313 to 1375.

(3) Petrarch (1304-1374) was another Italian poet. He translated the Roman classics into Italian language. He was called 'the father of humanism'.

(4) Chrysoloras set up a school in Florence and gave instruction in the epics of Homer. It greatly paved the way for the development of literature and philosophy.

(5) Pope Nicholas V (1447-1455) maintained a library of ancient Greek and Roman classics and thus helped the cause of Renaisance.

(6) Machiavelli was a native of Florence. In his book 'Prince' he boldly put forth his political ideas.

(7) Lorenzo de Medici, the ruler of Florence kept the treasures of classical writings and sculptures. He patronised the artists and intellectuals. He spent huge sums of money for this purpose.

(8) Erasmus a Dutch was an outstanding European scholar of the 16th century. His famous book was 'Praise of Folly'. It is a satire upon the evils of the church and the nobility of his time.

(9) Cervantes was a Spanish writer. His masterpiece was 'Don Quixote'. In this book he rediculed the feudal society.

(10) Sir Thomas Moore was an English statesman. His 'Utopia' portrayed an ideal society free from war, injustice, poverty and ignorance.

Arts

In the field of art and architecture many far reaching developments took place. Leonardo da vinci, a painter, sculptor, scientist, engineer and mathematician lived during this period. His paintings of a smiling beauty 'Mona Lisa' and 'Last Supper' were some of his masterpieces.

Michelangelo was an architect and painter of Renaissance period. He designed the dome of St. Peter's church. His creation of 'Last Judgement' on a wall of Sistine chapel is one of his magnificent paintings. His statues of 'Moses and David' reveal the feelings of the spirit of that period.

Another important Renaissance personality was Raphael. He was a great poet and an architect. He helped to design St. Peter's Church. His paintings of 'Madonna and Child' was excellent.

Another famous painter who lived during the time of Renaissance period was Titian. In oil painting no one could excel him.

Giotto, the contemporary of St. Francis, brought a tender naturalism in his religious painting.

Renaissance architecture took its inspiration from the classical architecture. The Vatican palace and St. Peter's Church in Rome were the best examples of the new type.

Science

In the middle of the 16th century Copernicus discovered that the earth was not the centre of the universe and Kepler and Galio, following in his steps revealed the solar system in its main features as we know it today. This discovery implied a great shock to the theory of the universe which men had held all through the Middle Ages, and prepared the way for the adoption of new views on life and religion. "The floor of heaven inlaid with stars, sank bank into an infinite abyss of immeasurable space". William Harvey an English Physician lived during this period. He discovered the circulation of blood in the human body. Sir Isaac Newton was a British Natural Philosopher. He expanded the theory of 'Law of Gravitation'.

Results

(1) The Renaissance spread from Italy to the other parts of Europe. Francis I of France very often interfered in the affairs of Italy. From Italy he took with him scholars, sculptors, architects and Greek works that were unknown to the French.

(2) It was during the time of Henry VII and Henry VIII that the Renaissance spread to England.

(3) Many Germans studied in the Italian universities and when they returned from there to Germany they spread the Renaissance.

(4) It proclaimed the dawn of a new age *i.e.* Modern Age.

(5) The Renaissance created a spirit of critical outlook. An inquisitive questioning mind was fostered. It shook the very foundation of medieval institutions and beliefs. It had done many wonders in the field of science, religion, art and architecture.

(6) Due to the invention of printing press, learning was freed from the control of the religious people. Even poor people could have an access to education.

(7) The Renaissance thanked the conception of nature.

(8) The development of vernacular languages like English, French, Spanish, and German were the direct results of the Renaissance. The Renaissance scholars wrote classical languages but in their own national languages.

(9) As the people began to take special interest in the ancient ruins of Greece and Rome, the study of archaeology also began to develop.

(10) Renaissance movement stirred the spirit of adventure and stimulated the creative power that resulted in geographical discoveries and development of science.

(11) The Renaissance affected the religious ideas also. The people applied the questioning spirit to the religious matters. It paved the way for challenging the authority of church and finally for the Reformation movement.

REFORMATION

During the latter half of the 15th century the Reformation Movement occupied a significant place in the history of Europe. "Reformation" was a religious movement started by Martin Luther in Germany to remove some abuses within the church. This movement was a result against the authority of the Pope. Hence, it was called 'Protestant Revolution' in the history of Europe.

Causes

The causes can be divided into secular and religious causes.

1. Secular Causes:

(i) There was no cordial relationship between the empire and the papacy. There was a long drawn struggle between the emperors and the Popes during the Middle Ages. The Popes had humiliated the emperors. So the emperors hated the authority of the Pope.

(ii) The Pope had the right of making church appointments in all the Christian countries in the west. They usually appointed their own relatives and friends as Bishops and archbishops. These church officials were very influential. Therefore, the Popes used them to create troubles against the rulers. Hence, the rulers of Europe hated the Pope and his officials.

(iii) The clergymen enjoyed immunity from severe punishments. If a clergymen committed a crime, he could be tried only by Church courts and not by the royal courts. In these courts the clergymen were given light punishments. This practice was known as "the benefit of the clergy". Many European rulers did not like the privilege enjoyed by the clergymen. So, the rulers hated the church organisation.

(iv) The nationalists looked at the church and papacy as a foreign institution interfering unnecessarily into the affairs of state. So, they waited for an opportunity to overthrow the power of the church.

2. Religious Causes:

(i) The character of the clergymen was the most important causes among the religious causes. They were leading a worldly life. They maintained their families through the church revenues. Moreover, they were ignorant and lacked proper education. The Bishops and Pope were living in luxury and ease. They abused their power and position to achieve their selfishness. They enjoyed "the Benefit of Clergy". The monasteries also fell into decay.

(ii) The clergymen were not discharging their duties properly. Naturally the people thought that these clergymen had no interest in religion and, therefore, should be dismissed.

(iii) The people did not like the tithe collected by the church. It was a tax which formed 1/10th part of the income of every individual.

(iv) The people did not like the way in which the church funds were utilised by the Popes. The Popes were spending the money in beautifying the city of Rome.

(v) The church was wealthy. It possessed vast lands. The wealth of the church attracted unsuitable men to priesthood. The Kings and Princes were jealous of the wealth of the church and wanted to take over church properties.

(vi) The Popes claimed superiority over the kings and emperors. They could depose kings, excommunicate the high and low. As the power and wealth increased, the corruption and immorality also increased.

(vii) The doctrine of the church needed reforms. There was no authoritative statement of a whole body of Christian doctrine.

(viii) The Germans were very pious and religious by nature. They, therefore, did not like multiplication of the ceremonies and rituals. In short, the Germans felt that the church was dominated by ceremonialism.

3. Other Causes:

(i) The spirit of enquiry which was released by Renaissance movement condemned blind faith and questioned the authority of the church.

(ii) The early reformers like John Wycliffe and John Hus paved the way for the Reformation Movement.

4. The Immediate Cause: The sale of indulgences was the immediate cause for the Reformation Movement. John Tetzel, a Dominican Friar was sent to Germany by the Pope Leo in 1517. He collected funds for rebuilding of St. Peter's church in Rome by sale of indulgences. According to him by paying money to the church anybody could wash off his sins and obtain God's pardon. There was no need for him to repent or confess his sins. His soul would escape divine punishments in Purgatory.

The Course of the Reformation: Martin Luther was the greatest leader of the Reformation Movement. He was born at Eisleban in Germany in 1483 in a peasant family. His parents gave him sound education. They wanted their son to become a lawyer. Luther decided to become a Clergyman. In 1505 he became a priest after studying theology in the University of Erfurt. He had visited Rome in 1510. There he came across the worldliness of the Pope. He hated this life of the Pope and on his return from Rome, he became the Professor of Theology in the Wittenburg University. It was then that Tetzel came to sell the indulgences. Luther could not tolerate the selling of indulgences and so he wrote down "95 Thesis" condemning the practices of the Roman catholic Church and nailed them on the door of the church in Wittenburg. He also began to question the authority of the Pope. This was too much to the Pope and to any one supporting him. Hence, the Pope excommunicated him (rebel). The rebel replied by publicly burning the bull of excommunication.

Charles V was then the Holy Roman Emperor. He was anxious to settle the religious dispute. So he summoned Martin Luther to appear before the "Diet of Worms" in 1521. He was asked to withdraw his statements. But Luther refused to do so. Charles grew angry and by an Edict of Worms he exiled Martin Luther. He was soon the most famous man in Germany. As Luther had the strong support of north German princes, the Emperor could not take effective action against Luther. Then he translated the Bible into German language.

In 1530 Charles V once again turned his attention towards religious dispute to settle the same. In 1530 the Diet of Augsburg was convened. Charles summoned the followers of Luther. In this Diet Charles declared his determination to execute the "edict of worms". The followers of Luther protested against this decision. So they came to be called as Protestants and the religion as Protestantism.

Peasants' Revolt: For at least a century several causes had contributed to worsen the lot of the peasants, While their taxes and other burdens were increasing, the ability of the emperor to protect them was decreasing. They were exploited by every other class including the higher clergy. Their condition was very pathetic and pitiable. Moreover, the preaching of Luther greatly stirred them. In 1524 they broke out into fierce revolt, demanding absolute freedom and anticipating a speedy millennium. Their leaders had hoped for the sympathy of Luther. But the peasants' rising was crushed with great cruelty and serfdom was re-established in Germany.

The Schmalkaldic Wars: The Protestant princes joined together and formed a league called the league of Schmalkaldic for mutual support against imperial coercion. Having realised that a peaceful settlement was not possible Charles decided to take up arms against the Protestants in 1546, the year of Luther's death. He entered Germany in 1547 with a large army and at Muhlberg defeated the army of the Schmalkaldic League, under Prince John Frederick of Saxony. This single victory made the Protestants to submit before Charles.

Charles then decided to introduce a religious settlement of his own. This settlement, called the "Interium" affirmed the unity of the church under the headship of the Pope, and the guardianship of the Holy spirit, but admitted certain doctrines, such as "Justification by Faith", and other rituals and ceremonies. "The Interium" did not fully satisfy the Protestants. Maurice of Saxony, the most important person in Germany too rose against Charles in 1552 and seized Augsburg, and very nearly captured the emperor himself at Innsbruck. With great difficulty the emperor managed to escape into Italy. But he died in 1553.

The Peace of Augsburg: In the meantime Henry II of France helped the Protestants. Charles V lost Metz, Toul and Verdun in the battle that took place between them. So he abdicated his throne in favour of his brother Ferdinand and fled to Italy. Ferdinand agreed to settle the religious affair. In 1555, the 'Peace of Augsburg' closed the war of German Reformation. Thus, a decade of religious war came to an end.

The Peace of Augsburg allowed the rulers of German states to decide the religion of their state.

It realised the necessity of permitting the people to migrate from one state to another where they had their own religion.

It recognised only two divisions of the church *viz.* Protestant church and Roman Catholic church or faith.

Thus, the Peace of Augsburg put an end to the long drawn struggle.

Results

(i) Many Protestant churches sprang up by this movement.

(ii) Western Christendom was vertically divided into two different religious groups. While the North European countries like England, Denmark, Sweden and Northern Germany accepted Protestantism, the South European countries like Portugal, Spain, Italy persisted in the Catholic Church.

(iii) Church became purified and much of its evils were removed.

(iv) The Bible was considered as the supreme authority.

(v) The powers of the Pope were considerably reduced.

(vi) It paved the way for religious wars.

(vii) Religious tolerance was practised due to this movement.

Zwinglianism

Ulrich (Huldrich) Zwingli was born in the year 1484. After finishing his education he showed his interest in religious matters. Zwingli like Luther preached against the sale of indulgences in 1519. Very soon he had large followers from the progressive cantons. The people of those cantons adopted his faith. He effectively organised his movement from the Swiss city of Zurich. He liked simple services of just prayers and sermon held not in Latin but in the everyday language of the people. He abolished the confession of sins to the Priests. Thus, the ideas and reforms of Zwingli brought in the Churches of Switzerland were called Zwinglianism. In this way Zwinglianism became a new sect of Christianity by the year 1531.

During his time the cantons of Switzerland were formed into two groups. They were Roman catholic cantons and the cantons of Zwinglianism. Thus, due to the rise of Zwinglianism the cantons of Switzerland began to split into two divisions.

In 1531 a war broke out in Germany between the protestant cantons and the Roman catholic cantons. In the battle that took place at Cappel the Protestants were completely defeated. Zwingli himself was killed in the battle. However, the Catholics concluded peace with protestants. Even now Switzerland remains partly protestants and partly Roman Catholic in religion. Zwinglianism was for the most part a frank, more independent, more democratic from of Lutheranism.

Calvinism

John Calvin was a French man, born in 1509 in Picardy in the north of France, and destined at first by his parents for a lucrative post in the service of the Catholic Church. But he turned from a clerical to a legal career, and while he was pursuing his legal studies at Orleans he embraced protestant opinions. Then as the government of France was pressing heavily on Protestants, he left the country, and after sometime spent among the protestant communities on the banks of the Rhine, he settled at Geneva; and not without a struggle, became the religious dictator of that city.

The system that he founded became for a century the strongest influence on the Protestantism of Europe. As the energy of Lutheranism declined Calvinism took its place as the representative of Protestant belief in its strongest and most definite form.

Calvin himself is a great contrast to Luther. Luther was passionate, emotional and deficient in logical power. With Calvin all was will and logic; human feelings counted for little in his life and in his religious system. In 1534 before he went to Geneva he had written the 'Institutes of the Christian Religion" and the work afterwards much expanded, became the foundation of Calvinist doctrine and discipline. The work was readily accepted as the best work on protestantism. The people of Geneva gave their whole hearted co-operation and co-ordination to Calvin for the spread of Protestantism.

His Doctrines

From that time onwards Calvin began to preach his faith which came to be called after his name as Calvinism. Calvin declared that the Holy Bible should be highest and the final authority in the matter of religion. Further, it was he who introduced the doctrine of prelestination. According to this salvation depended on the grace of God or the will of God. So it was not necessary to perform any rituals or ceremonies. God decided even at the time of birth whether the man or woman should be saved or should be left unsaved. In other words salvation depended solely on God's grace. Apart from this Calvin insisted the separation of the Church from the state. Further, the administration of the Church should be shared by the priests with his chosen elders of the locality. In other words the affairs of each church were to be ruled, not by bishops, but by a body consisting of pastors and laymen elected by the congregation itself. Moreover, Calvin insisted on a strictly moral and simple life

Opposition

The rigid control exercised by Calvin over the people of Geneva made them hate his leadership. So they brought about his exile in 1538.

However, he was recalled in 1541 and remained in Geneva till his death in 1564.

Martin Luther and Calvin:

(i) Martin Luther strengthened the hands of the Princes; whereas Calvin invested powers in the hands of the people.

(ii) Martin Luther prohibited violence in spreading his faiths but Calvin permitted violence in spreading his faith.

(iii) Luther preached consubstantiation; Calvin stood for Predestnation. It was the very basis of Calvin's whole system.

(iv) It was due to Calvinism that protestantism found a place in France.

(v) It was due to Calvinism that Dutch Netherlands became independent.

THE COUNTER REFORMATION MOVEMENT

Protestantism spread into Italy from Germany. The spread of protestantism alarmed the Pope and the Roman Catholics of Italy. They decided to arrest the spread of protestantism into Italy and thereby save the Roman Catholic faith. At the same time many ardent catholics desired to reform the Roman Catholic church. So it was decided to remove the abuses in the Roman church as a preliminary step in fighting against Protestantism. So a movement was set in motion by the Roman Catholics for the purpose of countering the spread of Protestantism and for purifying the Roman Church. Hence, this movement came to be called as the Counter Reformation Movement.

The following four factors were responsible for the Counter Reformation Movement :

(1) The Jesuits (The Society of Jesus),

(2) The Church Reforms,

(3) The Council of Trent and

(4) The Inquisition.

(1) The Jesuits: The first great instrument of this new movement was the Jesuit order or the company (now Society) of Jesus, as it was officially styled. Ignatius Loyola, the founder of the Jesuits, was a Spanish noble man who had been incapacitated by a wound from further military service (1521). As a result he was confined to bed. While in bed Ignatius spent his time in reading the works relating to the life of Jesus and other Christian saints. This study filled him with desire to become a missionary. After his recovery he visited Jerusalem. Then he realised his lack of knowledge in Christianity. He meditated long; he studied at the university of Paris and elsewhere; he turned over various plans to his mind. While at Paris Loyola organised a new religious order. It came to be known as "Company of Jesus" or "the Society of Jesus". In 1540 Pope Paul III recognised this order.

The society was organisad on the lines of the army. Like the army it had a leader whose orders had to be obeyed by all. Further the members had to take the vows of obedience, chastity and poverty. Moreover, they had to recognise the final authority of the Pope in religious matters and promised to work under the Pope. The Jesuits as the members of the society came be called were not expected to put on any special dress Likewise they were not also expected to do the manual works of the monks.

The Jesuits did a wonderful service in the field of education and learning. As Missionaries they went to far off countries to spread Christianity. Further they established schools in which they taught about Christianity. The Jesuits did a great service for the cause of the Roman Catholic faith. Much of Germany was recovered to the Roman Catholic Church by Jesuits. Thus, the Society of Jesus proved to be the most important factor in the counter reformation movement.

(2) The Church Reforms: The Popes of the later half of the 16th century were different from the popes of the first half in their character. The popes of the first half were renaissance popes. They were interested in everything but religion. They maintained a splendid courts and were leading a worldly life. But the popes of the later half beginning from Paul IV were full of interest in religious duties. They began to lead a very simple and pious life. Paul IV dismissed his relatives from the Church offices and insisted on a strictly monkish life for the clergymen. As a result the morality of the clergy improved. There was then nothing to complaint about the clergymen. The people once again began to respect the clergymen. Thus, the changed character of the popes brought about a thorough change in the life of the clergy.

(3) The Council of Trent: Another factor in the counter reformation movement was the Council of Trent. Charles V, the Holy Roman Emperor wanted to bring about a compromise between the Catholics and the Protestants of Germany. For this purpose he compelled the then Pope Paul III to summon a Council. Paul III summoned a Council in 1545 at Trent in Italy. It was a Council of Catholics. Charles desired certain changes in the Roman Catholic church so that the Protestants could be satisfied. But the Pope was totally against any change and so he transferred the Council from Trent to Bologna the next year. However, nothing came out of the Council, Julius III summoned a Council at Trent in 1551. In this Council the wide difference that existed between the Protestants and the Catholics became clear. But it failed to bring about a settlement. This council was dissolved in 1552. For the third time another Council was summoned at the same place in 1562 by Pious IV then Pope of Rome. The Protestants did not take part in this Council. The Jesuits opposed all changes in doctrine and practices. However, the Council of Trent also did a valuable service to the Roman Catholic faith. The doctrines of the Roman Catholic Church were clearly defined. This removed all possibilities of conflict over the doctrine. Added to this the Council of Trent affirmed the authority of the Pope. Moreover, it reformed the secular and regular clergy. Here-afterwards the services were to be conducted only in Latin and not in the vernaculars. The clergymen were not allowed to lead a married life. Thus, the Council of Trent gave unity to the doctrines of the Roman Catholic Church and reformed the life of the clergy.

(4) The Inquisition: Inquisition was another important factor in the movement. Paul III established the supreme tribunal of the inquisition in 1542 in Italy for dealing with the Protestant heresy but it could only be introduced into any State by permission of the rulers of that State, and it was never admitted into some Catholic States, as for instance, France. The Protestants who opposed the doctrines of the church were brought before the court and tried. It arrested on suspicion; it used torture to force confession; it did not confront the accused with his accusers; it allowed no appeal except to the pope. When the accused was found guilty, he was handed over to the state for punishment. Usually death punishments and confiscation of properties were given for the purpose of uprooting Protestantism. The inquisition worked with terrible severity wherever it was permitted to assume authority.

Paul IV adopted an indirect method to arrest the spread of Protestantism. He published a list of protestant books called the 'Index'. The Catholics were forbidden to read any of the books included in the index. This practice of publishing index was continued by others also. So the protestant literature was suppressed. These factors thus saved the Roman Catholic Faith from total destruction.

24

Geographical Discoveries

At the close of the 15th century many geographical discoveries were made. Before the end of the Middle Ages, the only parts of the world known to Europeans were Europe and the parts of Asia and Africa. They thought that the world was flat. They were afraid of sailing, too far into the sea. But during the 15th century many factors contributed for the geographical explorations.

(1) In 1453 Constantinople, the capital of the Byzantine Empire was captured by the Turks. It closed the usual trade route between east and west. Hence, a necessity to find out a new sea route to east, arose.

(2) The monopoly of eastern trade was enjoyed by the Mediterranean sea ports like Venice, Genoa and Florence. They demanded high prices for the eastern products such as pepper and other spices, silk and cotton goods and precious stones. Countries like Portugal and Spain did not like this attitude. They wanted to break this monopoly by discovering an alternative sea route to the eastern countries.

(3) The invention, of 'Mariners' Compass' increased the knowledge of geography. Moreover, the science of navigation stimulated the spirit of exploration. These things led to geographical discoveries.

(4) Renaissance was highly responsible for the geographical discoveries. By this the Europeans acquired more knowledge about the world and took bold voyages.

(5) People began to realise that the world is round and not flat. This geographical truth gave the confidence of reaching the east by sailing westward.

(6) Another factor which paved the way for geographical discoveries was the interest shown by Prince Henry of Portugal. He had deep interest in shipping and navigation. So he had earned the title "Henry the Navigator". He gave best training to the sailors in his school of navigation.

(7) The crusades also was partly responsible for the geographical discoveries. During the crusading movement the Christians began to know that there was a vast world behind them.

(8) In the 15th century Marco Polo, a Venetian traveller visited China. He stayed in the court of the Chinese Emperor Kublai Khan for some time. Then he reached Venice. He wrote a book called "Book of Marco Polo". In this book he gave a first hand information about the wealth of the eastern world. So the Europeans had a great desire to trade with the east.

(9) The desire to spread Christianity in the east was also another cause. This religious motive urged the Europeans to find out new routes in the east.

The Geographical Discoveries

(1) The Portuguese were the pioneers in this field. Bartholomeo Diaz started his voyage. He sailed to the southernmost point of the African continent. He called the tip "Cape of Storms" as he was caught in a storm. But his king John renamed it the "Cape of Good Hope", as he had a definite hope of discovering a sea route to the east.

(2) Another Portguese sailor by name Vascoda Gama rounded the Cape of Good Hope, sailed along the east coast of Africa, crossed the Arabian Sea and reached Calicut in India in 1498. He was received by King Zamorin of Calicut. Vascoda Gama got commercial privileges for his country. Thus, a new sea route to India had been discovered.

(3) Following the previous sailors, Pedrocabral started his voyage to reach India, But his ships were driven away by storms to South America, the region, he discovered was later called Brazil.

(4) Christopher Columbus started his sea voyage with the kind help of Queen Isabella and King Ferdinand of Spain. After a long and dangerous voyage, he landed in a small island of Bahama in 1492. Subsequently he made three other voyages. He believed that he had reached the south-eastern coast of Asia.

(5) The Italian sailor by name Amerigo Vespucci explored the continental part of America. He found that it is a 'New world' completely separated from Asia. Therefore, the new continent was named as America in his honour.

In the meantime there was rivalry between the Portuguese and the Spanish over the explorations. To settle this issue Pope interfered in the matter. He issued a Bull in 1493 drawing a "Demarcation Line" across the Atlantic. All the lands West to the line would belong to Spain and those east of it to Portugal.

(6) During the time of Charles V in Spain, Ferdinand Megallan, a Portuguese sailor sailed south wards in the Atlantic through a strait which today bears his name 'Straits of Megallan'. Then he sailed across the South sea to which he gave the name "Pacific" because the sea seemed to be very calm. He landed in a group of islands known as "Philippines" named in honour of Prince Philip, son and successor of Charles V. But there he was killed in a battle with the natives.

After this incident, one of his ships continued the voyage and returned to Spain after three months. This voyage was the first circumnavigation of the world.

(7) The English people also took interest in discovering new lands. John Cabbot, a Venetian Navigator in the service of Henry VII of England, was instructed to explore a north western passage to the east. He discovered the northern part of North America (Canada).

(8) The next man who started his voyage was Sebastian Cabbot. He was the son of John Cabbot. He discovered Labrador in the northern part of North America.

(9) Francis Drake was the famous English sailor of Elizabethan Age. He was one of the sea dogs, who plundered the Spanish ships. The Spanish Armada was destroyed by him. He was the first English man to circumnavigate the world.

(10) In the field of explorations French people also took keen interest. Jacques Cartier, a French sailor crossed the Atlantic and entered the St. Lawrence River. He established a trading port, namely Montreal.

Results

(1) The geographical discoveries greatly widened the geographical knowledge of the Europeans. The Europeans were brought closer to the people of the other parts of the world. As a result of

this, the Europeans began to have a better knowledge and better understanding of the people of the East.

(2) Europe was relieved of is problem of over population. Naturally Europe benefitted by these discoveries in very many ways. Among them better and brighter chance of living was the foremost one. Similarly, who went out of Europe also had bright prospects.

(3) European culture and civilisation spread to other parts of the world. The European nations established colonies in different parts of the world and those colonies became centres of European civilisation.

(4) European civilisation itself was affected by the close contact with the other civilisations of the world. The Europeans learnt the use of tea, coffee, tobacco and potato. Thus, new articles came to be used by the Europeans.

(5) A commercial revolution took place. Trade between Europe and the different parts of the world increased enormously. The European countries received raw materials which were abundant in the newly discovered regions. These raw materials were transformed into finished goods. The colonies of the European nations required such finished goods. They exchanged their raw materials for the finished goods. So European become the manufacturing centre for these colonies.

(6) The immense trade and the long and distant voyages necesitated bigger and better ships. Therefore, the construction of ships was developed. Countries like Holland took this task of ship building.

(7) A new powerful middle class came into existence. They challenged the privileges of the feudal lords. This new set up brought vast social changes.

(8) The jealousy and rivalry in establishing colonies and trading centres in the newly discovered lands led to the costly wars of the modern times. The eastern countries felt the bad effects of western colonialism, imperialism and exploitation.

(9) The discoveries and the establishment of colonies by the European nations brought about rivalry among the European countries. They began to compete with each other in commerce, conquest and colonisation. This competition resulted in colonial wars among the countries of Europe. However, by the voyages and discoveries Europe became richer than before. Finally, Europe began to exploit the rich resources of the Eastern countries.

25

Age of Enlightenment — Enlightened Despotism

(I) THE AGE OF LOUIS XIV

Richelieu and Mazarin had done their work effectively. The French monarchy held an ascendancy in Europe greater than had been held by any monarchy since the days of the Carolingian empire. Louis XIV became the King of France in 1643 at the age of five and ruled for 72 years. He was one of the enlightened despots of Europe. He was also known as the 'Grand Monarch". He dominated over Europe during his period of personal rule, and so that the period has been characterised as the age of Louis XIV.

(1) His Character: Louis was very well accomplished bodily as well as mentally. He had a superb constitution and was endowed with abundance of common sense. He was always very cautious in taking decisions. Louis impressed the people of France by the way in which he appeared and acted. He was gracious in behaviour, dignified in appearance, polite in manners and polished in speech. He was not a man of genius, or a really great statesman; but he was capable, energetic and dignified. It was no wonder that Louis was accepted and appreciated by his contemporaries as a "Grand Monarch".

(2) Internal Policy:

(a) Versailles: Louis was fond of pomp and splendour. He caused the construction of a new palace at Versailles. It consisted of stately buildings, broad parks, great grass, beautiful statues and splendid fountains. The palace was well furnished and was filled with beautiful paintings. Added to these it had in its a hall of mirrors. It was in this magnificent hall that Louis held his court.

(b) His Court: The beautiful setting at Versailles was made splendid by the presence of many eminent men in various walks of life. There were poets and priests; there were architects, painters, sculptors and musicians. Among the men of letters Moliere was important. The French drama reached its highest development in the hands of Corneille, Racine and Moliere. Mansart was the great architect who lived in the court of Louis XIV. Besides, Girardon the great sculptor, Le Burn the prominent painter and Lully the famous musician lived in the ourt. In addition to these men there were great nobles with their attendants. The higher clergy also adorned the court. It was no wonder the court of Louis became the wonder of Europe. French literature, arts speech, manners and dress became the model for the Europeans.

(c) His Administration: Louis became great by his personal accomplishments. He also proved to be an industrious monarch. He centralised the administration of France. The provincial differences of France were also to a great extent, destroyed, a uniform system of administration and type of civilisation spread all over France. The officials were brought under the direct control and contact of the King through the ministers. This arrangement enabled Louis to effectively control even the remote districts.

Louis had certain advantages when he assumed the charge of the Government. There was peace in the country. The treasury was full. The nobles, the Huguenots and the representative institutions were no longer rivals to the royal authority. The people were patriotic in spirit. The district officials and the intendants maintained the authority of the King in the respective areas. These conditions enabled Louis to take up a career of conquests.

Louis had strong belief in the "Divine Right Theory of Kingship" advocated by Bossuet. He thought that he had ascended the throne "by the grace of God". He did not allow the States General to meet during his reign. He suppressed the Parliament of Paris. Nobles were expected to live at the court, "The State? I am the State!" Thus, he proclaimed the policy of despotism.

(d) Jean Colbert-Reforms: The early years of Louis XIV's reign were much influenced by his great minister, Colbert, and under his reforming guidance the economic conditions of France wonderfully improved.

Colbert belonged to the middle class family. He had entered the service of the King under Cardinal Mazarin. Since Colbert had talent, he began to hold the high offices one after another. He held the post of the Superintendent of Public Works. He served as Controller-General of Finance for some time. He was the Minster of Agriculture for some years.

He was also Minster of Marine and Commerce. Further he also acted as the Minster of Colonies. Colbert had the confidence of the King and so the King had showed some amount of initiative and independence. Colbert, therefore, took various steps to enrich France.

(1) Finance: Colbert made great changes in the administration of the finances. When he was Controller-General of Finance the direct taxes were rather heavy and they were paid mostly by the merchants and the peasants. The higher clergy and the nobility were free from the direct taxes. Colbert desired to impose the direct taxes on the nobility and the clergy. But thinking that it might lead to some trouble, he increased the number of indirect taxes. He knew that the whole burden of the indirect taxes would mostly fall on the shoulders of the nobility and the clergy.

The increase in the number of the indirect taxes brought about an increase in the revenue to the State. Colbert not only took steps to increase the revenue by increasing the number of taxes and also took steps to avoid the wastage in the system of tax collection. In France, the right of collecting the taxes was usually auctioned and the highest bidder usually obtained the right to collect taxes. They were called middlemen or partisans. He paid down a sum of money to the Government and then made what profit they could get by extracting the taxes from the people. Colbert desired the total abolition of this system. But realising the difficulty in the total abolition of this system he tried to restrict as much as possible. He dismissed the dishonest officials in collecting the taxes. He awarded severe punishments to those dishonest officials. These measures of Colbert strengthened the financial position of the French state.

(2) Agriculture: Colbert wanted to give encouragement to the peasant class. For that purpose he took series of successful steps. He ordered that the tools and implements of the peasants should not be ceased for non-payment of the debt. This relief from the clutches of the creditors enabled the peasants to cultivate the land regularly. Colbert undertook the construction of a number of canals for the purpose of facilitating irrigation of the lands. Likewise he also laid down new roads for the purpose of providing the peasants with easy means of transports.

(3) Middle Class: Colbert was very much interested in the welfare of the middle class to which he belonged. When Colbert came to office, France was importing number of articles from other countries. In consequence much wealth of France was going out of the country. Colbert realised the need for arresting the flow of the wealth to the other countries. For this purpose Colbert wanted to increase the number of industrial products. Subsidies were given to start new industries.

(4) Industries: He further introduced industries into France, and endeavoured to promote and maintain them by means of great protective duties. Subsidies were given to start new industries. Craftsmen were invited from foreign countries. But active craftsmen were prohibited from leaving the country. The newly started infant industries required protection from the competition of foreign merchants. So Colbert began to levy high tariff duties on all foreign imports. Further all foreign ship were compelled to pay very high harbour dues. Having provided protection to the infant industries Colbert expected the French to export their goods to foreign countries. There was great demand for French goods since they were good and durable. For this purpose Colbert began to regulate the production methods and insisted on the use of good stuff in production.

The exports of the French goods necessited foreign markets to satisfy the need for markets. For this Colbert encouraged colonisation in various parts of the world.

(5) Commerce: Colbert did his utmost service to stimulate French commerce. He found that the world's trade was for the most part in the hands of England and Holland, and was carried out by them chiefly through the agency of trading companies. Colbert founded several companies (the most important were the West Indian Company and the East Indian Company) to compete with the English and the Dutch.

Colbert realised the importance of navy at this juncture. He, therefore, brought into existence a navy equal in size and efficiency to that of England, Holland and Spain. He also desired to have Merchant Marine for the improvement of foreign trade. Accordingly he brought the same into existence. These activities necessitated greater facilities for the ship in the harbours. Therefore, the harbours were enlarged and were made more suitable for receiving large ships. Dock-yards and store houses were constructed and greatly improved. All these measures improved to a great extent the economy of the country and reflourished to treasury.

(6) Arts: Colbert was not only an economist and financier but was also a patron of arts and sciences. He developed the Arts Academy and started Cardinal Richelieu. In 1661 Colbert instituted the Academy of the Sciences which still exits as the 'Institute of France'. Colbert established a big astronomical observatory at Paris. The Royal Library which comprised of only 16,000 volumes was made to contain 2-1/2 million volumes by the addition ordered by Colbert. Thus, he proved to be a benefactor of France.

(II) FREDERICK THE GREAT

The 18th Century is sometimes known as the era of benevolent despots, and several countries show us reforms undertaken and carried out by absolute rulers. We have seen how Russia owed her early greatness to Peter the Great; in Austria, a little later, great changes were introduced by the Emperor Joseph; but Frederick the Great is the chief instance of this feature of the age.

Frederick, the Great (Frederick II) ascended the throne in 1740 at the age of 28. He inherited from his father Frederick William I a huge well disciplined army, consisting of about 80,000 soldiers. Further he had inherited a compact kingdom administered by an efficient civil service. In addition to this he had himself being trained in civil and military administration by his father. Therefore he was free to direct his energies to the conquest of new territories. He possessed a good knowledge about warfare and so he decided to launch upon a policy of conquests. Frederick the Great fought two wars, the Austrian war of succession and the Seven years' War.

(1) The Austrian War of Succession (1740-1748): Charles VI the Emperor of Germany had no male heir to succeed him to the throne of the Empire. But he had a daughter named Maria Theresa. Charles wanted to bequeath his territories to his daughter Maria Theresa. So he issued what was called the pragmatic sanction. He declared that in case there was no male heir to the throne of the empire it should pass on to a female heir. Charles secured the acceptance of the Pragmatic sanction by all the rulers of Germany and by the other rulers of Europe. Having secured the acceptance of all those rulers Charles died in 1740.

In 1740 Maria Theresa claimed the possessions of her father and made herself the ruler of Austria. Frederick II of Prussia, Louis XV of France and Charles the Elector of Bavaria refused to recognise Maria Theresa as the ruler of Austria. At this juncture Frederick was the first to attack. The province of Silesia, lying on the both sides of the river Oder, adjoined the territories of Prussia, without any excuse he at once invaded and occupied it. A great European War (the war of the Austrian Succession) at once broke out.

Frederick was engaged in hostilities actual or expected, from 1740 to 1763, European history had known no wars which concerned so wide an area and touched the destinies of so many races and nations; Austria, Russia, France, England and Prussia were all concerned as leading combatants; the whole population of the Indian peninsula and the whole of the continent of North America, were influenced in all their future history by the results of these wars.

There were two main issues in the long struggle:

(i) The future of Prussia to be settled.

(ii) There was the colonial, commercial and naval rivalry between England and France. To which of them was the Empire of the Sea to be settled.

Frederick II had arranged with France that Charles of Bavaria should be made the Emperor with the little Charles VII. He had also accepted the claim of France to the Austrian Netherlands. Further he had made France to agree to his occupation of Silesia. Having made such an agreement with Bavaria and France, Frederick invaded Silesia and occupied it. At the same time the French and the Bavarians entered into Bohemia and occupied It. Maria Theresa had to flee from Austria due to the invasion of France, Bavaria and Prussia. She fled to Hungary and appealed to the Hungarians for help. The people of Hungary flocked under her banner and prepared for the war against her enemies.

Frederick had to fight against the Austrians at first at Mallwitz. In this battle which was fought in 1741, the Austrians were completely defeated. The Prussian victory at Mallwitz made Europe realised the rise of Prussia to a prominent position. The Prussian forces in 1742 gained another brilliant victory at Caslau. Maria Theresa there upon concluded a peace treaty with Prussia in 1742. It was called the Treaty of Berlin. It recognised the Prussian occupation of Silesia.

But Austria continued the war against France and Bavaria. She was now joined by England, Holland and Sardinia. Austria recovered Bohemia with their help and conquered Bavaria also. The French and the Spanish forces were driven out of southern Germany. It appeared as though Maria Theresa would conquer even Silesia. Frederick II got alarmed by the success of Maria Theresa and so declared war on Austria again in 1744.

Frederick invaded Bohemia, but he was not only driven back but was also made to lose Silesia. The Austrian forces occupied Silesia and it seemed as though Frederick would lose Silesia. Fortunately Frederick once again gained number of victories over the Austrians. Maria Theresa, therefore, concluded the Peace of Dresden in 1745. Once again Austria recognised the annexation of Silesia by Prussia. However, Austria continued the war with other enemies. Meanwhile, there was fighting at sea and in India and America, but the contest there was quite indecisive.

Exhaustion and disagreement among the allies brought the war to an end by the Peace of Aix-la-Chapelle in 1748. Accordingly (i) Francis, the husband of Maria Theresa was recognised as the Emperor of Germany, (ii) Frederick was recognised as the possessor of Silesia, (iii) Maria Theresa was accepted as the rightful ruler of Austria.

From the above war it is very clear that France gained nothing though she had taken an active part in the war.

(2) The Diplomatic Revolutions: Before the fighting was renewed eight years later, there had been a great change in the diplomatic relations of Europe. Since the days of Charles V, France had almost invariably been opposed to Austria in any European quarrel; but now France was induced to desert Frederick and enter into alliance with Austria. It was a change more important than the winning and losing of many battles. The French Government was weak and bad at this time: her statesmen and diplomatists lacked entirely the skill and insight which had distinguished them in the days of Louis XIV. Their wisest course would have been to keep out of the European war, and concentrate the efforts of France upon the maritime and colonial struggle. The new alliance exposed France to the blows of Prussia under Frederick and England under Pitt. She lost control of the seas and all chances of domination in Canada and India, in Europe she suffered some of the most ruinous defeats that are to be found in all her history.

(3) The Seven Years' War (1756-1763): Thus, in 1756, the Seven Years' War broke out. England Joined Prussia while the other side were ranged by Austria,.France, Russia and Saxony. Maria Theresa decided to recover her lost territory and her prestige by humbling Frederick. Alliance with France was arranged through the efforts of Kaunitz, the Prime Minister of Maria Theresa. Thus, she turned to Austria's old enemy France for help. It is already mentioned that alliance was termed as the 'Diplomatic Revolution' of Austria. The Battle grounds were in America, India and Europe.

Frederick after occupying Saxony invaded Bohemia and was about to capture the capital of Bohemia. But at this juncture the Prussians were severely defeated at Kolin and driven back into Saxony. Now this defeat was followed by the invasions of the enemies. On the possessions of Prussia the Swedish entered into Pomarenia, the Russians into East Prussia, the Austrians into Silesia and the French and other Germans into Brandenburg. It appeared as though Prussia would be completely destroyed.

It was then that Frederick exhibited his genius in warfare. The tactics he used for the purpose of saving his country had made him rank with the ablest generals of the world. Again it was his success against the enemies that entitled him to be called the great. Fredrick conceived the idea of meeting his enemies separately one after another and inflicting on them crushing defeat. First of all Frederick had to drive the French and the Germans who were advancing towards his capital Berlin. Frederick met the French at Rossbach and inflicted a severe defeat on them. The French retreated back. After this defeat Frederick then turned towards the Austrians and met them at Leuthen. Again he had a brilliant victory over the enemy. After defeating the Austrians, Frederick turned against the Russians and gave battle to them at Zorndorf. Once again it was a victory for Prussia. Thus, Frederick cleared that country by driving out all his enemies by three great battles.

But there was a turn in the time of war. In 1759 the Russians defeated the Prussian forces at Kunersderf. Further England which had been a long supporter of Frederick with men and money withdrew from the war.

The British General James Wolfe defeated the French army at Quebec in 1760. Spain entered the war late and gained some areas.

Robert Clive led British forces against the French and won a decisive victory in the Battle of Plassey in 1757. In the Battle of Wandiwash, Captain Sir Eyre Coote defeated the French army.

At this juncture Czarina Elizabeth II of Russia died in 1762. The new Czar Peter III became the ruler of Russia. France concluded the Treaty of Paris with England in 1763. Thereby it withdrew from the war. So the two major powers, Austria and Prussia were left to face each other. Hence, Austria and Prussia also concluded a peace by the Treaty of Hubertsburg in the same year.

According to the Treaties of Paris and Hubertsburg

(i) Austria gave up her claim to Silesia; Prussia's claim over Silesia was recognised.

(ii) French possessions in India except Pondicherry, Karaikal and Mahe were taken by Great Britain.

(iii) Great Britain received Canada and some parts of French lands.

Results

(i) Prussia's reputation was immensely enhanced.

(ii) Austria was humiliated.

(iii) Prussia's position, power and prestige increased in the political scene of Europe.

(iv) The power of the French Empire was broken.

(v) British empire emerged as the most powerful in the world.

(vi) Prussia had given to Europe an example of efficient and economical Government which made men think that a new type of state had arisen.

(4) Partition of Poland: Frederick joined with Catherine, the Czarina of Russia to check the ambitions of Austria in Poland. Frederick took West Prussia in the partition of Poland in 1772 and with the help of it he was able to link up East Prussia with the rest of his territories.

Reforms

Frederick II spent his 23 years of reign after the Seven years' War in making Prussia a powerful nation. Frederick has been assigned the first place among the enlightened despots of the 18th century. Like all enlightened despots Frederick thought that the power of the rulers should be absolute in character. But the absolutism should be utilised for promoting the prosperity of the people and for raising the power and Prestige of the state. Frederick devoted himself completely to the cause of the nation. Frederick seems to have exclaimed that he was the first son of the state. It is no wonder that he has been given the highest place among the enlightened despots.

(1) Agriculture: Frederick had realised that agriculture formed the backbone of the country's economy. So he promoted the interest of the tillers of the soil and agriculture. He tried to abolish serfdom. He knew well that freemen worked better than the serfs. But he could not abolish serfdom due to the opposition of the nobility. However, Frederick encouraged, like Peter and Catherine, scientific farming. He also took steps to increase the extent of land under cultivation by draining the marshes. Canals were also constructed to facilitate irrigation.

(2) Commerce and Trade: Frederick established a separate department of trade and commerce for the purpose of promoting industry and trade. Frederick like Colbert of France expected his people to import as little as possible and export as much as possible. This was Frederick's conception of political economy. He thought that he must invite foreign craftsmen for the purpose of improving the industries. He constructed numerous houses and Pomarenia offered them free to foreign craftsmen who accepted to settle in Prussia permanently.

(3) Education: Frederick like Peter and Catherine of Russia had realised the importance of education. He ordered the establishment of schools wherever necessary. For those schools he secured the services of efficient teachers. Attendance was made obligatory in those schools. He promoted the cause of learning by himself writing histories, verses and dialogues. He patronised learned men and surrounded himself with eminent men of letters. Voltaire, the French philosopher was a friend of Frederick and he spent a number of years at the court of Frederick.

(4) Justice: Frederick improved the system of judicial administration. Prior to his accession justice was costly. The judges were totally corrupt and sold their decisions in favour of those who gave them much money. Consequently the poor suffered. Frederick awarded severe punishments to those judges who received bribes. Further he collected, consolidated and codified the existing German laws and published them for the information of the public. The publication of the law enabled the people to know whether justice was done to them. Frederick reduced some of the severe punishments awarded to the criminals. He also prohibited the use of torture in criminal investigation. All these measures of Frederick II considerably improved the justice at administration.

(5) Religion: Frederick unlike Louis XIV of France was not a bigot. He realised the need for toleration in the matter of religion. He declared, "let them (the people) think as they pleased, but let them act as I pleased". This statement of Frederick showed that he gave fullest freedom in the matter of faith. But at the same time in political matters he expected the people to follow his direction.

(6) Army: Frederick was responsible for making Prussia one of the greatest military powers of Europe. The standing army of Prussia under him consisted of 200,000 soldiers, having tireless drill, strict discipline, upto date arms, efficient generals and Frederick's own leadership. This made the Prussian army the envy of Europe. Frederick who had at his disposal such an efficient military machine earned a very good name and fame in the military annuls of Europe. Actually it paved the way for the race between Austria and Prussia for leadership in Germany. Frederick has been characterised by Carlyle as the last of the Kings in Prussia and it does not mean that there were no kings in Prussia after Frederick. It only means that there was none after him who could be considered as great as he was. Frederick is, therefore, considered to be the Father of Modern Germany.

(III) PETER THE GREAT

Peter the Great was the most famous among the Romanov Czars. Modern Russia may be regarded as his creation.

(1) His Early Life: Peter was the son of Alexius by his second wife and was born in 1672. Peter had a step-brother and a step-sister Ivan V and Sophia. On the death of Alexius Ivan V became Czar. But he was insane and, therefore, his sister Sophia ruled the country on his behalf. Sophia wanted to get rid of Peter and so conspired against his life. Peter somehow found the plot against his life and seized Sophia and sent her to a convent to lead her life as a nun till her death.

From 1682 when this happened Peter began to rule along with his stepbrother Ivan V. Though he assumed the authority he very rarely sat on the throne along with his brother. He spent most of his time outside the palace. Peter was from his boyhood days very curious to know how things were made. For example, he would try to understand the mechanism of a mechanical toy, Likewise he was interested in learning the principles on which the Government was run. Ivan V died in 1689. He became the sole Czar of Russia in the same year.

(2) His Aims: The aims of Peter were :

(i) To westernise Russia;

(ii) To make his power supreme and

(iii) To secure ports in Black Sea and Baltic Sea.

(3) Internal Reforms: (i) Administration: Peter is acclaimed to be a great ruler not because of his successful military exploits but because of his various internal reforms which completely transformed Russia. Petter was responsible for establishing the system of Government which came to be called in Russia as autocracy. When Peter ascended the throne the nobles, the church and the Streltsi controlled the policies and actions of the Tsar (Czar).

Peter disbanded the Streltsi and in its place created a faithful army.

Peter curtailed the powers of the nobility also. The traditional council of Duma (Council of Boyars) consisting of the nobles was abolished in 1711. In its place instituted the Senate. The Senate came to be consisted of persons elected by Peter himself. So the Senate remained as a subordinate body to the Tsar. The Senate was made the final authority in judicial matters. It controlled all the local courts. Since it was under the control of the Tsar himself, Peter was able to exercise judicial authority throughout his kingdom.

Peter realised that the Church of Russia was something like a state within the state. The Church owned enormous property. The revenues from these properties were also considerable. The Patriarch of the Russian Church was controlling all the Churches in Russia. The monasteries and the convents had taken no vows. They had entered into these institutions only for the purpose of escaping from the temporal burdens. Peter abolished the office of the Patriarch. The Church was to be controlled hence forth by a Church Council, called the "Holy Synod." It came to be consisted of Bishops selected by the Tsar himself. The Holy Synod was to control all appointments to the church. No sermon could be preached and no book could be published without the permission of the Holy Synod.

Peter created a separate department to look after the properties of the Church. This department was to receive the revenues from the properties of the Church and it was to allot the minimum amount of money to the various religious institutions, Thus, Peter brought under the control of the State all the activities of the Church. This prevented the Church from being a check on the authority of the Tsar.

Peter organised the divisions of the empire. He created out of the territories of Russia 43 new provinces. The Governors of these provinces were to be paid a regular salary. Hitherto, the Governors were not given any salary. So they collected money from the people for their own expenses. The introduction of regular salary gave relief to the people of the provinces from the oppression and repression of other Governors.

Peter simplified the system of taxation also. He substituted the poll-tax for the household tax.

(ii) Education: Peter took steps to promote the education of his subjects. He was determined not to allow anybody to hold office if he had no education whatsoever. Hitherto, the nobles by virtue of their superior birth held the posts in the Government. But the nobles were not educated men and, therefore, they were denied posts in the Government. The nobles were sent to foreign countries for the purpose of acquiring scientific knowledge.

Apart from this Peter in 1714 ordered the establishment of elementary and secondary schools in the provinces wherever necessary. Further he was responsible for the translation of number of books in the other languages into Russian. While Peter was at Amsterdam he despatched to Russia a printing machine and a printer. With the help of this printing machine many books were published on different subjects. Peter invited German and English professors and appointed them in the schools. For the first time in Russia a newspaper made its appearance in the reign of Peter.

Peter required skilled men for his army and navy. For this purpose Peter brought into existence a school of Engineering and navigation.

Added to these Peter established a museum of arts and an Arts School. Peter even collected a large number of books and established a big library also.

(iii) Agriculture: Peter promoted agriculture in many ways. He undertook the construction of a net work of canals for the purpose of irrigating the lands and for providing easy means of transport. It was Peter who introduced into Russia the wine, the mulberry and the tobacco. Peter encouraged the farmers to breed horses. The miners were compelled to exploit the natural resources to the maximum extent. Those who did not exploit the natural resources were severely punished. As a result of these measures the national income of Russia rose from 3 million roubles to 10 million roubles within a period of 15 years.

(iv) Commerce: Peter took steps to develop the commerce of Russia. The easy means of communication provided by peter facilitated commerce. Peter introduced gold and copper coins in addition to the silver coins, that were already in circulation. Peter brought into existence a Police force for the purpose of suppressing brigandage on the roads

(v) Industry: Peter took series of successful steps for the development of industries. It was Peter who developed the iron industries of Russia. He required for his navy a good supply of weapons. It was for this reason. Peter gave an impetus to the development of the iron industries. Before the death of Peter there were 200 iron industries in Russia. The indolent nobles were made to work either for seven years in the civil service, ten years in the army or fifteen years in the trade or industry.

(vi) Military Reforms: Peter learnt the technical knowledge of navigation, ship-building and other military science while he was in Europe. He organised the army to the level of western standard. He took special care in recruiting army. Ships were built for the Russian Navy on the River Don. Foreign officers were invited to train the Russian army. Uptodate arms and weapons were supplied to them.

(vii) Westernisation of Russia: Peter desired to transform the life of the Russians so as to make them resemble the West Europeans in every respect. He found Russia barbarous and uncivilised; the power of the monarchy less than that of the boyars or nobles; the country and its resources almost unknown to Western Europe. It was Peter the Great who introduced the rudiments of European civilisation, asserted the power of the monarchy and installed the other elements of Russian Society, founded the new capital of St. Petersburg. The Russians at that time wore long and loose garments. Further they were accustomed to grow beard. Peter ordered the Russians to use short coats and pants as the

French and the Germans. He also ordered the nobles and others to shave off their beards. In addition to these he even compelled them to smoke the pipe. But nobles opposed these reforms.

In social life peter dealt with them severely and made them to obey his orders. Peter expected that the women folk should discord the veil and appear in public. For the purpose of providing opportunities to the women folk to appear in public he arranged for receptions and balls. The marriage laws were also changed. The betrothed couple were expected to meet at least six times before the marriage. This policy of Peter was opposed by his own wife, sister and son. But all the three had to suffer severely for having opposed his policy. Peter was a barbarian in giving severe punishments to those who opposed him. But Peter is considered to be the "Father of Modern Russia", because of his success in transforming Russia into a Western Nation by sheer force of will.

(viii) St. Petersburg: Peter laid foundation of St. Petersburg in the Province of Ingria, when he was engaged in war with Sweden. Then he completed the famous city, his "window to the west", mostly by the labour of Swedish prisoners of war. He made it the capital of Russia and an important commercial port.

4. Foreign Policy: Russia had no coastline when Peter ascended the throne. Therefore, Russia's commercial activities were limited. He wanted to have European trade at the gates of Russia. To fulfil his ambitions he must have sea ports *i.e.* the "Window to the West" on the Baltic Sea and also on the Black Sea. And hence he had to engage in a conflict with both Turkey and Sweden.

At the same time Peter began to feel the need for a fleet for having close contact with the west. This also made him to wage war with both Turkey and Sweden.

Turkey

In 1695 Peter invaded the port of Azov at the mouth of the River Don in Turkey (Black Sea). But this attempt to capture failed. However, he made a second attempt in 1696 and succeeded in capturing the port.

Foreign Visits: After having captured the port of Azov, Peter wanted to construct a fleet; but the Russians did not have a good knowledge of ship building. So on the advice of his friend Peter decided to tour the European countries with the object of learning ship building. Peter thought of visiting Holland and studied at Amsterdam ship building. Then he went over to England and there also he studied ship-building and organisation of Government. From England he went to Prussia and there he studied the organisation of the army. From Prussia he went to Vienna the capital of Austria. Wherever he went he collected sailors, engineers, craftsmen and traders and sent them to Russia While Peter was at Vienna he learnt about the revolt of the royal bodyguard Streltsi. In hot haste he hurried home end ruthlessly suppressed the revolt of the Streltsi.

Sweden

Peter wanted an outlet on the Baltic Sea also. But the Baltic was being controlled by Sweden. Peter had to fight against Sweden for the purpose of getting an outlet on the Baltic Sea. Fortunately for Peter, Charles XII, the then King of Sweden was young in age and Peter wanted to take advantage of this weakness in the King of Sweden. Peter was instrumental in bringing about a coalition against Sweden consisting of Russia, Poland and Denmark. Charles XII came to know about this coalition against him. Charles decided to take up the offensive without waiting for the starting of the war by the enemies. Suddenly he set in motion the Swedish army and fell upon Denmark. The Swedish forces very soon approached the capital of Denmark Copenhagen. The Danish King at once concluded peace with Charles. Charles then turned towards Russia and severely defeated the Russians at Narva. The Russian forces began to retreat into the interior. So Charles turned against Poland and advanced towards the capital, Warsaw. Augustus II was again and again defeated and compelled to conclude peace.

In the meantime Peter took steps to recover what he had lost. He constructed the City of Petersburg and invaded Finland belonging to Sweden. Charles XII was, therefore, compelled again to fight against the Russians. The Swedish forces were utterly defeated by the Russians at Pultava in 1709. Charles fled from the battle field to Turkey. But he again appeared in 1713 and continued the war against Russia. Charles even advanced as far as Moscow but died in 1718. The death of Charles gave an advantage to Peter. Peter conquered a large number of territories along with Baltic. So the Swedish concluded the Peace of Nystadt in 1721. According to it Peter acquired Ingvia, Cornelia, Livonia and Esthonia. Peter also gained a part of Finland. Peter gained for Russia these territories on the Baltic Sea.

(IV) CATHERINE THE GREAT

Catherine the Great, was tire ruler of Russia from 1762 to 1796. She was one of the ablest rulers of the time. She was a very clever and crooked woman and she followed the foot-steps of Peter, the Great. She was an enlightened despot.

Character: Catherine was not a Russian by birth. She was a German by birth. But she was brought up in Russia from the very beginning. Though she was a Protestant, she followed the Russian Orthodox Church. She moved with the Russians freely and frankly and thereby she earned their love and sympathy. She was well versed in Russian language. She was a cautious lady and even a single detail of administration never escaped from her notice. She had a strong will, a power of rapid decision and a spirit of initiative. Her husband Peter III was very inefficient and weak in administration. With the help of some nobles she imprisoned her husband and finally killed him there. Then in 1762 she became the sole Tsarina of Russia.

Internal Policy: Catherine the Great was an intelligent and energetic ruler. She carried out many important reforms like that of Peter the Great in Russia. She wanted to establish absolutism in the administration. She strengtherened it in every way and centralised the authority in the country. She set up a very efficient system of administration but otherwise did not care much for the lot of the people. No freedom was given to the people in any field and her work was low in every sphere. The provincial arid district administration were given new look under the guidance of Catherine. She did a wonderful service for the efficient administration of those divisions. Governors and Vice-Governors were appointed for the provinces and the districts during the time of Catherine. The administration of those divisions was very efficient and excellent in every respect. They were under the direct control of the central government. She summoned legislative Assembly periodically. She was responsible for the establishment of provincial assemblies and municipalities.

In the field of religion also she did a lot like Peter, the Great. She brought drastic changes very daringly in the matter of religion. She scrutinised the Church properties. She made the clergymen to utilise those properties properly for the welfare of the people. No wonder a great transformation took place in the field of religion during the period of Catherine.

Catherine tried to westernise Russia like that of Peter in many respects. She achieved her object in this field. She took pleasure in the company of the learned persons of Europe and patronised literary persons like Diderot. She was the friend of Voltaire. She maintained cordial relations with him. She gave great impetus for the development of French and Russian languages. She made French as the first language and Russian as the second language of the country. She was thus deeply interested in French language, French customs and French manners.

During this period Russian nobles also took great interest in studying French literatures. Like the Academy of France, Catherine too established a similar Academy at St. Petersburg. In addition to this, she established schools wherever necessary for the benefit of the children to improve education in the country.

Agriculture, trade, industry and commerce developed greatly during this period, she took keen interest in the above fields so as to improve the economic condition of Russia. Scientific methods were introduced in agriculture. The agriculturists were given all facilities to improve their conditions. She was responsible for the construction of many canals for irrigation Many roads were constructed for easy means of transport. In short Russia witnessed tremendous development in every walk of life.

Foreign Policy: Catherine's foreign policy was directed against Poland and Turkey.

Poland

The First Partition: Catherine, the Great played the most important part in the three partitions of Poland in 1772, 1793 and 1795. Her main idea was to annex the whole of Poland. Hence, she made an alliance with Frederick the Great of Prussia and Maria Theresa of Austria. Particularly both Catherine the Great, and Frederick the Great, had their eyes on Poland. To begin with, they tried to exclude the House of Saxony from the throne of Poland. They got their opportunity in 1763 when Augustus III, King of Poland died. Both Russia and Prussia put pressure on the Poland nobles and got their nominee elected. The new King of Poland was Stanislaus Poniatowsky who was a great favourite to Catherine. Having put their nominee on the throne of Poland, preparations were made for the partition of the country. The patriots of Poland resented the influence of Russia and formed a league to resist the same. War started between Russia and Poland and Russia was able to break the resistance of the Poles. Frederick proposed the partition of Poland but the proposal was rejected by Catherine who wanted to have the whole of Poland herself. However, the opportunity of Frederick came when war started with Russia and Turkey. When Austria and Prussia joined hands, Russia agreed to the partition of Poland. The first Partition took place in 1772. By this partition, Russia got Livonia and a part of Lithuania and thus advanced upto the Duna and Dnieper, Prussia got West Prussia and Austria got Zips and Red Russia (Galicia). On the attitude of Maria Theresa, the cynical remark of Frederick, the Great was that "she weeps but takes all the same".

The Second Partition: After the first partition of 1772, Poland became dependent on Russia and for some time the patriots of Poland could do nothing on account of an alliance between Russia and Prussia. Things improved after 1791 on account of an alliance between Prussia and Austria which was more friendly to Poland than Prussia. In 1787, there started a war between Russia and Turkey. In 1788 was formed the Triple Alliance which aimed at checking the ambitions of Russia and Austria. The Polish Diet met in 1788 and decided to carry out certain reforms. Unfortunately the work of reforms was delayed because the King of Poland was afraid of Russia and also because the Polish nobles were not in favour of reforms. Opposition came from Prussia also. According to the reforms of 1791 kingship was to be hereditary in the family of the Elector of Saxony. The Polish King was to control the army and executive. The Liberum Veto was to be abolished. Religious toleration was to be given to all. Russia resented these reforms and decided to take action against Poland. She also encouraged Austria and Prussia to take interest in the French Revolution so that she might be able to have her own way in Poland. Prussia also gave up her friendly attitude towards Poland and no wonder the Poles resented this change of attitude. The attitude of Austria was friendly. It was in this atmosphere that Russia attacked Poland and defeated the Poles. The latter was forced to cancel the new reforms. They got no help either from Austria or Prussia and all their resistance collapsed. Poland was partitioned for the second time in 1793. Austria got nothing. Russia got Eastern Poland including Minsk, Padolia, Volhynia and little Russia. Prussia got Danzig, Thorn, Rosen, Genezen and Kalisch. Russia got four times as much territory and twice as many new subjects as Prussia. The partition revealed the shameless selfishness of the powers and their utter distrust of one another. Austria strongly resented the partition which was made without her approach and which brought the Russian territory into touch with Austrian dominions. The relations between Austria and Prussia were strained.

The Third Partition: Russia strengthened her position in Poland and the King of Poland became a mere agent of the Russian Minister at Warsaw. The Poles resented the partition and secret societies were set up to regain their independence and carry out the necessary reforms. In 1794, Russia demanded the disbandment of the Polish troops, but that demand was rejected. There were revolts and the Russians were turned out from many places in Poland. Russia attacked Poland and defeated her. All opposition was crushed. It was then that the third Partition of Poland took place in 1795. According to it, Russia got the land between Galicia and the Lower

Duna covering about 2000 sq. miles of territory. Austria got Cracow and the rest of Galicia and her share included about 1000 sq. miles of territory in all. Prussia received Warsaw and the land between Bug and the Dnieper about 300 sq. miles of territory in all. By a treaty of January 1797, Russia, Prussia and Austria asserted "The necessity of abolishing everything which may recall the memory of the existence of the Kingdom of Poland".

Thus, the rape of Poland by those powers came to an end.

According to Guedalla, the partitioning of Poland was the most shameless and barren act of European diplomacy.

Turkey

After the partition of Poland, Catherine directed her attention towards Turkey. She waged war with Turkey from 1768 to 1774. At this juncture the condition of Turkey was very weak and meak. So the Turks were defeated and forced to evacuate Maldavia and Wallachia. Besides, the Russians captured the Port of Azov and the City, Bucharest subsequently. In the meantime Catherine induced the people of Syria, Egypt, Morea to rebel against the Sultan Mustapha III who was the sole enemy of Russia. The Sultan did not know what to do. He sought the help of France. France also came forward to help Turkey. Russia gained victory after victory over the Turks. Really it posed a danger to the other powers of Europe. In the midst of war negotiations were going on. Finally the war came to an end by the Treaty of Kutchuk-Kainardji in 1774. By the Treaty, Russia got Azov and a number of other places which gave her control over the northern shore of the Black Sea and also over the Sea of Azov. The Black Sea was opened to Russian navigation. The independence of Crimea was recognised. Russia was to have her consuls in Turkey. Russian subjects were to be allowed to visit the holy places in Palestine. Russia was given the right to interfere in the internal affairs of Turkey. Peace between Turkey and Russia did not last long and war was renewed in 1787. At this time, Catherine joined hands with Joseph II of Austria to dismember Turkey. Austria was forced to withdraw from the war in 1791 on account of Triple Alliance between England, Prussia and Holland. However, Russia carried on the war alone which was ended in 1792 by the Treaty of Jassy. By this treaty, Turkey recognised the Russian annexation of Crimea. Thus, she lost her control over the northern coast of the Black Sea upto the river Dniester.

Estimate: Catherine, the Great was an enlightened despot. She further ranked with the enlightened despots of the 18th century because of her varied reforms. She contributed much to the prosperity and prestige of Russia. She humbled Turkey, she was responsible for the partition of

Poland. It cannot he denied that Catherine the Great raised the prestige of Russia in Europe. Her achievements can be summed up in her own words thus: "I came to Russia as a poor girl; Russia has dowered me richly, but I have paid her back with Azov, the Crimea and the Ukraine".

(V) JOSEPH II

Joseph II of Austria has been assigned the first place among the enlightened despots of the 18th century. He was the son and successor of Maria Theresa, the ruler of Austria from 1740 to 1780. Joseph II became the Holy Roman Emperor in 1765 after the death of his father Francis I. He continued in the post of the Emperor till 1790. He inherited the dominions of the House of Austria in 1780 on the death of his mother. He was a typical enlightened despot. Hence, Johnson says that, "Joseph II was a more interesting or more instructive example for the enlightened despots of the 18th century".

His Character

Joseph II was a man of humble character, He was industrious and conscientious. He was deeply interested in the philosophers who lived during this time. He was a liberal minded man. He was sufficiently efficient administrator. He was the hater of old customs and conventions, institutions and legal methods. He was always very cautions and very careful in taking decisions or the important matters of administration. Though he was a hard worker, he failed miserably because he was far in advance of his age in introducing salient reforms to his subjects.

His Aims

(i) His object was to unite all the dominons of the House of Austria by abolishing all differences of race, language and religion.

(ii) His aim was to establish a centralised state *i.e.* one Austrian Nation.

(iii) His another aim was to establish a uniform system of justice.

(iv) His another object was to grant intellectual freedom and religious toleration to the people.

(v) He wanted to give political and social equality to the people.

(vi) He desired to free the church from the Pope.

Reforms

(i) Administration: Joseph II worked day and night for the improvement of his people. He took series of measures to accomplish his aims. He abolished the old territorial and redivided the whole of his empire into 13 provinces. Each province was put under a military commander. Provinces were divided into districts and towns and a uniform system of Government was set up in all of them.

German was declared to be the official language all over the Empire.

Joseph II abolished all privileges of the nobles and the clergymen and everyone was required to pay a tax of 13% on his land. Serfdom was abolished. All peasants were freed from the clutches of the nobles during this time. They were allowed to conduct their marriages without the permission of the nobles. Compulsory military training was given to them. But the people misunderstood those reforms of Joseph II.

The people were guaranteed equality before law, freedom of press and religious toleration.

(ii) Law: Joseph II introduced many changes in the department of law. He made necessary arrangements to collect, consolidate and codify the civil and criminal laws in a proper manner. He simplified the legal procedures. Hence, the poor was also able to know the same easily. He considerably curtailed the expenses of the cases of his land. Torture was abolished. Punishments were given according to the nature of the cases. Judicial department was reorganised, courts were also reorganised. Courts of Appeal were established. A High Court was established. A High Court was established at Vienna. All the lower courts were brought under its control.

(iii) Religion: Joseph II did a lot in the matter of religion also. In 1781 he issued the Edict of Toleration and there by the Catholic religion was recognised as the common religion of the land. But at the same time the other religious toleration was given to the people. Jews were also given religious freedom in the land. He tried to bring the Church under the control of the State and lessen the control of the Pope. The control of the clergymen in educational field was greatly lessened.

(iv) Education: Joseph II took keen interest in the improvement of education. He himself was very interested in learning. He founded a large number of schools. He desired to give free education to the people of his country. The control of the clergymen in educational field was greatly lessend.

(v) Social and Economic Reforms: Joseph realised the importance of the improvement of state economy. At the same time he also realised the importance of social reforms. To improve the state economy, every one was required to pay a tax of 13% on his land. Exemption was not given to the people. Many harbours were constructed. Among them Trieste and Fiume were very important harbours. He tried to improve the commerce, trade and industry of the country. He was highly responsible for the growth of foreign trade. Many commercial treaties were made with neighboring countries.

(vi) Foreign Policy: The main object of his foreign policy was to re-establish the supremacy of the Hapsburgs in Germany and also to readjust the boundaries of his empire. Joseph II co-operated with Prussia in the first partition of Poland to prevent Russia from annexing the whole of Poland. Along with Prussia and Russia, Joseph II got a share of the spoils. He was also able to get Bukovina from the Turks. He forced Holland to give up the frontier fortresses which were allowed to be garrisoned by her by the Treaty of Utrecht of 1713. He unsuccessfully tried to throw open the river Scheldt. He entered into an alliance with Russia to check the growing influence of Prussia. He tried to exchange the Austrian Netherlands with Bavaria but failed to do so on account of the opposition of Prussia. He also declared war against the Turks with a view to dismembering Turks. However, he did not succeed in his mission on account of the hostile attitude of Prussia. Prussia, England and Holland entered in a Triple Alliance to help the Turks and in 1791 Leopold II who came to the throne of Austria retired form the war.

His Failures: However, his reforms were carried out in a hurry, unmindful of the sentiments and traditions of the people. The People were not ready for these reforms. Joseph II boasted that he had made "philosophy the architect of his Empire", but doing so he committed a blunder. He ought to have known that philosophical ideas rarely find a place in the practical life of the people. It was impossible to force the people to rise to the high ideals which were set for them by the genius of Joseph II. The result was that all his reforms failed. His attempt to consolidate his empire almost brought about its dissolution. The Empire of Austria-Hungary was a polyglot Empire and it was impossible to create out of it a homogeneous state. Joseph II was trying to do the impossible and no wonder he failed. However, he had the courage to cancel all his reforms before his death. To quote, "in the most courageous act of the reformer's career, he decreed the revocation of his entire work".

It is said about Joseph II that, "he does not know how to eat or drink or amuse himself or to read anything but official reports". In spite of that he failed because, as Frederick said, "he took the second step before he took the first". Joseph himself suggested the following for his epitaph. "Here lies the man, who with the best intentions, never succeeded in anything".

(VI) TUDORS IN ENGLAND

Henry VII: Enlightened despots came to England with the coming of the Tudors on the throne of England. Before the coming of Henry VII on the throne of England, the country was under feudal system and feudal lords tried to exploit the masses to the best of their capacity. The monarchy was weak. Economic conditions of the people was miserably poor. Law and order situation in the country was at its lowest ebb. In the religious field Roman Pope guided religious affairs of England. When Henry VII defeated the feudal lords at the wars of the Roses and himself came to power, the situation changed. He tried to crush the power of the fuedals and ensured that the people got peace and prosperity. He gave the country a strong and centralised government. Shipbuilding activities were encouraged and industry as well as industrial development was promised. There was of course a Parliament in the country, but he ensured that the king controlled the parliament and not the *vice versa*. In order to improve the conditions of his people, he also maintained better and fitter relations with his neighbouring countries.

Henry VIII: In England enlightened monarchy developed under Henry VIII. He was a very ambitious ruler. He did not allow the interference of Pope in running his national administration. He took care of the welfare of the people. He distributed the lands seized from monasteries, among his people at very low rates. Similarly he used the wealth of these monasteries, both for the welfare of his subjects as well as for strengthening his position. He centralised whole administration and kept the parliament under his control.

In order to check the drainage of wealth from England, he stopped making many payments to Pope. He was responsible for bringing Reformation in England. He gave full patronage to Renaissance scholars in England and in his court many scholars lived and worked. Thus, the work started by Henry VII received considerable encouragement and was considerably strengthened by Henry VIII.

Queen Elizabeth II: Queen Elizabeth followed a wide policy both at home and abroad. She ensured that there was peace and prosperity in the country and also that art, literature and culture developed. She followed a religious policy by which both the Catholics and Protestants came nearer to each other. Thus, religious understanding developed in the country.

Queen Elizabeth gave great impetus to industries and manufacturing concerns. She also took steps to provide employment to every able bodied person. Facilities were provided to the poor, the sick and the needy. Attempts were made to raise the living standard of the people.

It was during her times that Spanish Armeda was defeated and thus England became not only one of the most important and strong naval powers of the world, but at the same time got rid of one of the powerful enemies of England.

In order to provide higher living standard to her people, she encouraged her subjects to establish colonies in far off countries. She also provided facilities to these companies by way of giving financial and legal assistance. It was during her period that East India Company was set up in India.

During this period art and literature was encouraged. William Shakespeare and Francis Bacon were most well known personalities in the field of literature of this period.

In this way Queen Elizabeth took the people of England to the path of progress, peace and prosperity. The people of England gladly tolerated her personal rule. When she died England had become a very powerful and strong nation with pride and self-respect.

Attitude of the People Towards Despotism: Both in England as well as in many parts of the world, the people gladly tolerated enlightened despotism. It was due to very many reasons. The most important of them was the desire of the people to have peace and enjoy a better economic standard. They felt that could be only possible if there were strong monarchs on the throne. They had tasted the feudal authority and their own pitiable conditions, when weak rulers were on the throne. It was this urge for peace and happy life that the people silently tolerated personal rule of these enlightened monarchs.

To put it in a nutshell enlightened monarch for all practical purposes, can be considered as a step forward from absolute despotism to the establishment of democratic systems and institutions. Undoubtedly the system worked well and became a good jumping ground.

26

Era of Revolutions

(i) CAUSES OF REVOLUTIONS IN EUROPE

Europe witnessed many revolutions since 17th century. Each had a far reaching effect on the course of history. As we know, a revolution means a violent change, which could not be brought about by peaceful means. It is desirable to discuss the significant causes for the revolution in Europe in many countries. Though the causes of one revolution differed from the other, yet there were some common causes as well, which might briefly be discussed in the following pages.

1. Indifferent Attitude of the Rulers: The first and foremost cause of the revolutions was the indifferent attitude of the rulers towards their people. They were unkind and unsympathetic towards them. They were not treated well. For example the attitude of the Britishers towards their American colonies was not sympathetic, resulting in American war of Independence. It was this attitude of French and Russian rulers which were responsible for French and Russian Revolutions.

2. Economic Condition of the Masses: Poor economic condition of the masses was another cause for the revolution in many countries. Though the kings and the traders enjoyed a pleasure giving life and were enjoying in their palaces, the economic conditions of the people on the whole were very poor and miserable. They had practically nothing with them though they worked from dawn to dusk. Their pitiable plight on the one hand and comforts and pleasures of the rulers on the other made their rise in revolt against the then established order.

3. Desire for a Change: The people of many European countries had been suffering in their life. They had suffered both from church fathers as well as their rulers. They had also paid heavily and got back nothing as return except rebukes and punishments. As a result they desired a change which could be possible only through revolutions.

4. Divine Right Theory: Another cause of the revolutions was the 'Theory of Divine Right of kings'. Accordingly they believed that the king was the representative of God on Earth. The theory also believed that the subjects had no right whatsoever, to challenge their supremacy and authority. According to them for their every act of omission and commission they were responsible to God and not to the people. Accordingly they developed a very great autocratic attitude, which could be changed only by revolutionary and not peaceful methods.

5. Lack of Contacts: Then another reason was that there was lack of contacts between the king and the people. The kings lived in beautiful palaces with great gay and gaiety. They had no contacts with the people over whom they ruled. They did not know their problems of the day to day life and also about their inconveniences. These problems gradually became deep rooted and since there were no methods of knowing them the result was that these emptied into Revolutions.

6. Nobles' Harsh Attitude: Still another cause was that the attitude of the nobility towards the masses was very harsh as well as unsympathetic. The nobility surrounded the Kings and kept them in dark. They took the laws of land in their hands and ruled as they desired. They completely and conveniently ignored the ignorant masses. Moreover, the masses paid and the nobles enjoyed. This became intolerable in due course and so they rose in rebellion.

7. Wasteful Wars: Another cause of the revolutions was the wasteful wars of the kings. These wars were not fought for the welfare of the people. On the other hand these costly wars were fought either to satisfy the personal ambitions of the kings for their territorial expansions or to settle their dynastic disputes. It greatly affected the economy of the country. The people were required to pay. Hence, they rose in revolt against their kings.

(ii) GLORIOUS REVOLUTION OF 1688

There had been a continuous struggle between the Stuart Kings and their parliaments. This struggle started during the reign of James I (since 1603) and ended with the plight of James II to France in 1688. The Parliament got succeeded in this struggle and the country's sovereignty was transferred from the King to Parliament. This great historical event has been termed as "Glorious Revolution".

Causes for the Revolution:

(1) James II, who ascended the throne of England in 1685, was a Catholic. He openly attended Mass (prayer in Catholic Church)

which shocked the Protestant people. Not being content himself being a Catholic, he wanted to restore Catholic religion in England against the wishes of the people. He tried to repeal the Test Act of 1673, which stated that every holder of military or civil office had to be a member of the church of England (Protestant). James appointed Roman Catholics to his Privy Council, in the army and navy. He also appointed Catholics to the various departments of Oxford University. Therefore, the people were much concerned about the activities of the king.

(2) The Stuart monarchy had been based on the principle of the Divine Right of Kingship. Particularly James II was very much eager to adhere strictly this principle. So, he believed that he need not answer to any representative of the people. He claimed to have for himself the right of dispensing and suspending power and tried to promote the cause of Catholicism.

(3) A rebellion was led against James II by the popular Protestant leader Duke of Monmouth, illegitimate son of King Charles II, brother of James II. After the rebellion was suppressed in a battle, Monmouth was executed. The Lord Chief Justice Jeffreys then held series of court sessions — known as the "bloody assizes" — in which he condemned or banished many of Monmouth's supporters. This step taken by James really shocked the people.

(4) James wanted to have standing army violating the law of the country. Therefore, when James asked for a standing army commanded by Catholic officers, Parliament protested and reduced the king's subsidies. Angered by their criticisms, James dissolved the Parliament.

(5) In 1687 and 1688, James issued two 'Declarations of Indulgence' by which he suspended all the laws passed against both Roman Catholics and Dissenters. The crisis came to head when he gave orders that his second Declaration of Indulgence should be read in all Churches, Seven bishops including Sancroft, the Archbishop of Canterbury refused to read it. James became furious when he came to know this. The seven bishops were arrested and brought to trial. But they were acquitted.

(6) Another shocking news that intensified the fear of the people was the birth of a son to James II. The new prince would, of course, be brought up as a Catholic. Then there was every prospect of long continuance of Catholic rule in England, which the people could not tolerate.

(7) Hence, the prominent leaders of both Whig and Tory parties, extended invitation to William of Orange (the Protestant ruler of Netherlands) and his Queen Mary (daughter of James II) to save Protestant religion and liberties of the English people.

The Revolution of 1688: William and Mary landed in England with a small force. James found that it was useless to resist and so he fled to France. Parliament was summoned. It voted that James II had abdicated the throne by his plight to France and that the throne had thereby become vacant. It drew up a 'Declaration of Rights' where in James' unconstitutional and unlawful acts were denounced as illegal. The Declaration was presented to William and Mary who ratified it. There upon the throne was offered to William and Mary as joint sovereigns. On their acceptance of the throne the Glorious Revolution was completed.

The Nature of the Revolution: According to G.M. Trevelya "The true glory of British Revolution lay in the fact that it was bloodless; that there was no civil war, no massacre, no prescription, and above all that a settlement by consent was reached on religious and political differences that had so long and so fiercely divided men and parties".

It is a resolution to avert a bloody revolution. It was the creation of the moderates who wanted to preserve the ancient traditions and liberties of the people. It was not progressive in nature but conservative in character.

The Revolution Settlements

(1) The Declaration of Rights was changed into a constitutional law called 'Bill of Rights'. It denounced the illegal acts of James II, such as levying tax without the consent of Parliament, dispensing and suspending powers and setting up prerogative courts like the Court of Ecclesiastical Commission etc. As regards Parliament, freedom of election, freedom of speech, frequency of meeting were established. Standing army should not be kept during peace times. Thus, the royal arbitrary powers were stripped off and made it impossible for future kings to rule on despotic line.

(2) For the ordinary expenses of civil government it voted a fixed grant. Annual Parliament summoned every year granted money for maintaining an army.

(3) To ensure summoning of Parliament at least once a year the Mutiny Act was passed one year only.

(4) The Triennial Act limited the duration of Parliament to three years.

(5) The Licensing Act which restricted the freedom of press was allowed to lapse.

(6) By the Toleration Act of 1689 religious toleration though in a limited form was granted to all sects of Puritans except the Unitarians.

(7) The passing of the Act of Settlement of 1701 ensured Protestant succession, and restricted some of the powers to be issued by the king.

By these above measures the executive was made responsible to the Parliament.

Results of the Revolution

(1) The Glorious Revolution marks the transition from despotism to constitutional monarchy; and the triumph of Parliament over the crown. The sovereignty of Parliament was firmly established.

(2) It destroyed the old theory of divine hereditary right, and made the king an official, subject to dismissal if he neglected his duties. It indirectly emphasized a fact that there was a kind of contract between the king and the people were justified in asking him to go.

(3) It ended an era of prerogative and arbitrary actions of the kings and the liberty of the people were put on a sound and secure footing.

(4) The Parliament's authority over succession to throne, justice, army, finance, trade and church was well established.

(5) Although the Revolution settlement helped the whole Parliament to emerge victorious yet it was the House of Commons that was the greatest gainer. It became the dominant body in the matters of revenue and taxation.

(6) The Glorious Revolution resulted in the grand success of Anglican Church.

(7) Finally, the Revolution settlement put forth the theory of limited monarchy and served as the bulwark of English liberty.

(iii) AMERICAN WAR OF INDEPENDENCE

The American War of Independence was an epoch-making factor not only in the annals of America but also in the history of the whole world. The tyrannical practices of colonising and inhabiting many tracts of lands had been in vogue from the times immemorial, but America was the first country to launch a war of independence against oppression, enslavement and exploitation. This movement opened a new era of liberalism, revolution and independence in the dictionary of nationalist movement.

The causes for the American war of Independence were deeply embedded in the life of colonists. The idea of revolt was surging in the minds of the people, for the mother country had become a great hindrance rather than that of help for the development of colonies. The day of American Independence was precipitated by the passage of laws of British Parliament to establish a strong imperial organisation in the colonies.

Causes of the Revolution

1. Spirit of Liberty of Americans: The settlers in America had developed a kind of self-reliant attitude for there was enormous growth of their economy, agriculture and trade. This resulted in the emergence of a spirit of liberty for, most part of the settlers were dissenters and radicals expelled from Britain. The divergence of these people from England had enabled them to develop new ways of life. A sense of national awareness was unfolded by Americans. The self-reliance, self-governed and a fairly religious freedom had developed a spirit of liberty among the Americans which ultimately was accomplished by an unavoidable conflict with Britain. The vigorous southern planters wanted to escape from the burden of debt to British merchants. The energetic northern traders felt that their developing trade was being crushed by the imposition of British trade regulations. Moreover, the urban mechanics and some farmers were clamouring for more political and economic freedom. The whole episode of American Revolution was the work of such minority people who were bestowed with superior ability, courage, liberality and dynamic enthusiasm.

2. Mistress Attitude of the Britishers: Simultaneously Great Britain too had been developing an exactly opposite attitude against Americans. Their conviction was that the colonies existed primarily for the benefit of the Mother Country and must, therefore, be kept in subordination. Hence, many colonies like Virginia, Plymouth, New York etc., were brought under royal control. Governors and military commanders of all these colonies were appointed by the British Government. The imperial control was increased and hence friction between Governors and Assemblies had become frequent. The conflict was between the imperialism of Britain and Colonial autonomy of Americans.

3. Act of Mercantilism and Navigation: The basic philosophy under which the English settlement were ultimately exploited was Mercantilism. This meant roughly that the colonies existed for the benefit of the Mother Country, they should add to its wealth, prosperity and self sufficiency. This policy led to the passage of a number of Navigational Acts.

Navigation Act of 1651 insisted that all goods entering England must be carried in ships owned and manned by British citizens.

In 1660, Enumerated Commodities Act provided a long list of commodities like sugar, tobacco etc. prohibiting their export to other countries. The same list was expanded in the years 1706 and 1722.

Subsequently, the Staple Act of 1663, The Duty Act of 1673, the Enforcement Act of 1696, and the Molasses Act restricted the colonial trade to the benefit of Britain and to the detriment of Americans. So, the American merchants and manufactures were annoyed, irritated, infuriated and denounced these Acts as an infringement of their rights obtained under Royal Charaters.

4. Freedom from the Gallic Peril: The defeat of France in the French and Indian Wars had eliminated its menace in northern and western America. Along with It, the need for the military reliance of Americans over their mother country too had vanished. After the Seven Years' War the relations between England and the Colonies completely changed. The colonies had acquired valuable military training and expanded — their militia during these wars. They had also developed inter-colonial co-operation in facing common problems. Thus, colonies slowly strengthened their positions and gradually tried to sever their connection with the mother country.

5. Proclamation Act of 1763: After the war with France, the natives of Virginia poured across the Appalachian ranges into the Ohio Valley. The native Indian tribals under the leadership of Partiac fought back the whites which caused the enormous loss of men and money. In order to avoid further clashes with tribals and to preserve the already existing trade centres on the coastal region, the British Government issued a proclamation prohibiting any settlement beyond the Appalachian ranges. Besides, the British Government decided to maintain an army of 10,000 troops in North America, in order to guard against possible Indian raids and French attempts at reconquest. Since they had to be posted for the defence of the colonies, they were required to pay part of the cost. George Grenville, a brother-in-law of Pitt, the Elder, became Prime Minister and he set himself in raising fresh resources by strictly enforcing the customs duties and preventing smuggling.

6. The Grenville Measures:

(a) *Sugar Act, 1764:* Smuggling of Molasses from French and West Indies was carried on at a large scale, transgressing the Molasses Act of 1733. Grenville wanted to make this Molasses trade a source of revenue by reducing the duty of six pence per gallon to 3 pence. He passed the Sugar Act in 1764 to this effect and collection of the duty was made strict. Besides, new taxes on wines, silk, indigo and·other luxury items were imposed.

(b) *The Currency Act, 1764:* It prohibited the Colonial Assemblies from the issue of any more paper currency. By this Act the colonial debtors were prevented from settling their debts in depreciated currency.

(c) *The Stamp Act, 1765:* Sugar Act was followed by the Stamp Act in 1765 which declared that Stamp Duties were to be paid on Newspapers and legal and commercial documents. This tax was calculated to yield a revenue of 100,000 pounds for meeting one third of the cost of the army stationed in America. This was considered to be the first direct tax levied by the British Government.

(d) *Storm of Protests of the Colonies:* Lawyers, Ministers, Legislators and Editors expressed their resentment over this Act, considering it as violation of their fundamental and natural rights. Massachusetts led the other colonies in organising their protest against this Act. Virginia exhibited its vigorous opposition through its resolution called "Virginia Resolves". These acts raised, a storm of indignation of the Americans against the British Government. "Sugar Act made the people to think and Stamp Act to talk". They could not tolerate the tyranny of taxation without representation.

(e) *Stamp Act Congress:* In response to the call given by Massachusetts to formulate protest against the Stamp duty, nine states assembled in New York in 1765. The first meeting to take concerted action in the history of U.S.A. published a "Declaration of Rights and Grievances" which challenged the right of British Parliament to tax Americans.

(f) *Stamp Act Agitation:* A revolutionary organisation called "sons of liberty" was founded. Its exponents like Sam Adams of Boston, Charles Thomson of Philadelphia had caused a lot of havoc and made life miserable for the British agents appointed to sell the stamps. Riotous popular demonstrations became rampant. The most effective weapon used against the Stamp Act was a general agreement to stop importing British goods.

(g) *Quartering Act, 1765:* This Act enforced the colonists to provide lodging and supplies for British troops whenever they were stationed for a time in their towns.

(h) *Repeal of Stamp Act:* British merchants suffered heavy losses and urged the Government to give way. Symphathisers like Pitt, Burke and Fox too opposed the right of British Parliament to tax the colonies. Practically the Stamp Act was not implemented and it became defunct, for transactions were carried on without stamps. Hence, Marquis of Rockingham, the successor of Grenville repealed the Stamp Act in March 1766, lowered the molasses duty to one penny and passed a "Declaratory Act" which affirmed the principle of Parliamentary supremacy over the colonies.

Townshend Duties

Rockingham was succeeded by the Earl of Chatham, Charles Townshend was his Chancellor of Exchequer. Since Parliament reduced the taxes in England, Townshend had to turn to colonies in order to make up the deficit and passed the Duty Act in 1767 which imposed import levies on glass, lead, paints, tea and paper. Townshend also suspended the New York Assembly since transgressed the Laws of Quartering Act of 1765 by refusing to provide supplies for the troops stationed in the colony.

Opposition Against Townshend's Policies

(a) *Non-Importation:* John Dickinson, a Pennsylvanian Lawyer wrote a series of "Letters from a farmer" which questioned the right of British Parliament to tax the colonies, condemned the Townshend Acts and suspension of New York Assembly. Agreements were signed to refrain from importing British goods in August 1768 by merchants. Merchants engaged in illegal trade were protected from Cutoms officials by the "Sons of Liberty".

(b) *Boston Massacre:* Two regiments of British troops were stationed in Boston to prevent smuggling. The Sons of Liberty roused popular hostility to the presence of these troops. On March 5, 1770, a ding dong battle was fought in which soldiers opened fire upon the crowd which provoked the altercation by throwing snowballs. This resulted in the so-called Boston Massacre of five Bostanians.

7. Lord North and Conciliation: Lord North, King George's favourite became the Prime Minister in January 1770. He promised to heal the breach that had been developing between the colonies and the mother country. He persuaded the Parliament to repeal all Townshend duties except a small tax on tea in order to assert the principles of parliamentary authority. Peace prevailed in the period between 1770 and 1773 due to the conciliatory policy of Lord North. His conciliatory attitude strengthened the conservatives in the American colonies, who wished to avoid trouble. But the radicals who disputed North prepared to meet any future infringement of their political and economic rights. In 1772 Sam Adams and his associates set up throughout Massachusetts a net work of "Committees of Correspondence" composed of men who would carry on agitation and organise resistance.

8. The Final Crisis:

(a) *The Tea Act of 1773:* None of the frictions excited so much people until the British Government under Lord North committed the most crucial mistake of passing Tea Act of 1773. It was a clever scheme to dispose of the East India Company's surplus tea by means of bypassing the American wholesalers. What made the scheme unacceptable to the Americans was that the East India Company was given a virtual monopoly of the colonial tea market.

(b) *Boston Tea Party:* The result was that many of the merchants again joined forces with the Sons of Liberty. The Tea Act was opposed everywhere. When the first shipments of tea arrived in the autumn, the ships were compelled to sail back. But in Boston, Hutchinson, the Governor of Massachussetts, was determined of unloading the ships, for the consignees were his own sons and a nephew. Hence, a group of "Sons of Liberty" disguised as Indians, boarded the ships and threw the tea worth of 15,000 Pounds in the harbour. This Boston Tea Party precipitated the crisis.

9. The Intolerable Acts: The Bostonians were promptly punished by the passage of the "Intolerable Acts" which closed the Boston Port until compensation should be made, royalised the Government of Massachusetts, re-enacted the Quartering Act and provided for the trial of accused royal officers outside the colony.

Quebec Acts: Parliament also passed the Quebec Act which extended the boundaries of the Quebec to include all the areas West of the Alleghenies and North of the Ohio river. It also permitted collection of tithes by the Roman Catholic clergy. This act was passed in accordance with the wishes of the French-Canadian population. Thus, the Quebec Act seemed to the Americans to be quite as intolerable as the Coercive Acts.

First Continental Congress: These Coercive Acts made it obvious that Americans were not entitled to any legal rights. Nearly all the colonies expressed solidarity with Massachussetts. The Virginia House of Burgesses passed a resolution calling for the First Continental Congress meet in Philadelphia. Fifty six delegates representing all colonies except Georgia assembled on 5th September 1774. Even though there were three factions radicals, moderates and conservatives, they unanimously adopted "The Declaration of Rights and Grievances" and petitioned King George for a redressal of political and economic grievances. They appealed to the French Canadian to join them and once more adopted an economic boycott of Britain.

A "Continental Association" was formed to watch the effective adherence of the boycott. The people of Massachussetts were busy gathering arms and ammunitions and were training themselves as "minutemen" ready to fight at a minute's notice. In the Second Continental Congress at Philadelphia it was resolved to adopt the New England Militia as nucleus of a continental army. One of the most fortunate decisions of the Congress was its choice of George Washington as its Commander-in-Chief of its forces.

Developing Desire for Political Separation: The colonists were licensed by the policy of the British Government in hiring foreign mercenaries to fight Englishmen in America. Before, General Washington took the command of the army the colonials were pushed off Bunker Hill near Boston at a terrible cost to the British, who evacuated Boston nine months later. During the seize of Boston, Americans began to conclude that independence from Britain offered the only safety for their liberty. Press and pulpit along with Thomas Paine's argument in his pamphlet, "common sense" expressed this common sentiment.

THE DECLARATION OF INDEPENDENCE

The Irrevocable Step: During the Spring of 1776, several colonial legislatures instructed their delegates in the continental congress to work and vote for Independence.

Richard Henry Lee of Virginia moved a motion for Declaration of Independence. One of the strongest arguments for such a step was that it would make it easier for the Americans to secure help from France. The Congress responded by naming a committee headed by Thomas Jefferson to draft a Declaration of Independence. The Declaration, largely the work of Jefferson, was accepted by the Congress on July 2nd and was formally signed by most of the delegates on July 4th 1776.

The Declaration was designed to strengthen the radical cause in America and to win foreign support for the American rebellion.

It was also a Revolution: The American War of Independence barely lasted only eight years and in a broad sense the American revolution was not the same thing as the American war of Independence. But the American revolution commenced even when the first Permanent English Settlers set foot on the new continent and the revolution lasted over a century and a half. Insurrection of deeds always followed such revolutionary ideas. The revolutionary ferment was burning in the minds of the people in America even before their bullets began to fly. America was a revolutionary force from the day of its discovery.

This revolutionary spirit was the natural result from the dissenters, radicals and descendants of discontented people who migrated from Britain. They emigrated with a view to enjoy large share in Government, richer portion of properties, and an opportunity to worship God in their own way. American continent gratified all their expectations. After crossing three thousand miles of ocean, the settlers were relatively free and enjoyed independence. The deep and dense fertile forests had changed the patterns of living and consequently habits of thought. When the Americans attained maturity they set up their own parliaments and adopted the parliamentary methods of Britain.

It was not a revolution in the sense of a radical or total change. It was not a sudden and violent overturning of the political and social frame work as occurred in France and Russia later on. Significant changes were ushered in but they were not breath-taking. What happened was accelerated evolution rather than outright revolution.

Results of the War: The American War of Independence had accomplished a number of things which are placed in the first order. It was the war which liberated a colonial country and elevated to the level of a democracy in which emerged a written constitution, with federal features for the first time in the annals of the history of the world. The constitution of U.S.A. came to include the Bill of Rights, seeking to protect the right and liberties of the citizens.

All the thirteen colonies which were functioning as separate entities were now brought under a single National Government. This helped the development of the National Culture of America.

(iv) FRENCH REVOLUTION

The French Revolution was a great event in the history of the world. It gave to humanity three new ideas *viz.*, liberty, equality and fraternity. They have found their way in every nook and corner of the world. The following causes were responsible for the outbreak of the great revolution in 1789.

1. Social Cause — Social Divisions: The first and foremost cause of the French Revolution was the social cause. "The Revolution of 1789 was much less than a rebellion against despotism than a rebellion against inequality". On the eve of the French Revolution there was too much of inequality in French Society. The French Society was divided into two parts. They were :

(i) The privileged class and
(ii) The unprivileged class.

The following were the privileged class people.

(i) The nobility,
(ii) The Clergy and
(iii) The members of the royal family.

The following were the unprivileged class people.

(i) Peasants,
(ii) Professors,
(iii) Lawyers,
(iv) Physicians,
(v) Bankers,
(vi) Merchants and
(vii) Common people.

Nobles: In the total population of 24 million, there were 1,50,000 nobles and 1,30,000 clergymen. Roughly, their combined strength was about one percent of the total population. But they excelled all others in the matter of rank, possessions, positions and privileges. Ordinarily, a noble's coach was decorated with an ancestral coat of arms. The best seats were reserved for him both in the Church and in the theatre. He had a monopoly of practically all the jobs in the army and the Church.

Clergymen: Like the nobles, the clergymen also occupied a privileged position. They led a pompous life. They lived in luxurious palaces. They had castles, cathedrals, palaces invaluable pictures, golden chalices, rich restaurants and rentals from land in the form of tithes.

Particularly, the Cardinal of Rohan had enormous wealth so also the Archbishop of Strasbourg had an income of 300,000 dollars a year, even the sauce pans of his (Archbishop of Strasbourg) kitchen were made of silver. There were 180 horses in his stables for the pleasure of his guests.

The Church: The Church was a state within the state. Favoritism, nepotism, corruption, bribery and extravagance prevailed in the Church administration. So the people felt indignant. Most of the income of the Church went to the Church officers. Thus, they enjoyed pomp and power in France.

In this connection it is stated that one per cent of people owned about 40 per cent of property in the country, while they enjoyed privileges, they were exempted from taxes. There was a French Maxim that, "the nobles fight, the clergy pray, the people pay".

Peasants: The lot of the peasants was unhappy. They did a lot of work to their lords. A peasant had to work on the land of the landlord from sunrise to sunset. During this, time there was no rotation of crops. So the yield was very low. The lord's domestic animals and birds were fed on the crops of the peasant. In addition to this there was no fencing. He was bound to grind his corn at the mill of the landlord and as the mill was situated at a great distance, he was put to a lot of inconveniences. Heavy punishments were given to the peasants by the lords.

Taxes: The peasant had to pay the following taxes to the Lord, the Church and the King.

(i) Double rent was to be paid on the death of the peasant.

(ii) If the farm was sold one fifth of the price went to the landlord.

(iii) Tithe was paid to the Church (1/12 or 1/15 part of the gross produce).

(iv) Taille or land tax paid to the King.

(v) Vingtiome or income tax paid to the King.

(vi) Gabelle or Salt tax paid to the King.

(vii) Corvoe or road tax paid to the King.

It has been estimated that after paying all the taxes the French peasant was left with only about 20 per cent of his total produce. Their condition was pathetic and pitiable. They experienced untold sorrows and sufferings, inspeakable dangers and difficulties and indescribable miseries and misfortunes. A dry summer or a long winter completely finished them. Starving peasants tried to satisfy their hunger with roots and herbs and thousands of them died of starvation. No one seemed to bother about them. It is hence said, "in France, nine-tenths of the population died of hunger, and the tenth of indigestion".

1. The Middle Class: The bourgeoisie or the middle class also belonged to the unprivileged part of the French Society. To this class belonged the professors, lawyers, physicians, bankers and merchants. This class was all powerful in the field of finance, trade and industry. But they suffered a lot during this time. So they became the leaders of the people of France in their revolt against the "Ancient Regime".

According to Prof. Salvemini, "the privileged classes plundered the Exchequer, disrupted the administration and paralysed the country's economic life".

2. Lack of Good Administration: Another cause of the French Revolution was the rottenness of the French administrative system. The king was the head of the state. He had all powers in his hands. So he acted in an arbitrary manner. In short, the French Monarchs were virtuality dictators. The people suffered seriously in their hands.

The King did not go on tours to visit the various parts of the country and consequently lost his personal touch with the people. Moreover, he had no knowledge of the sufferings and aspirations of the people. The King centred all his attention at the capital when the nobles assembled from all over the country to participate in the frivolities of the royal court. In the time of Louis XV his mistress influenced the politics of the country. So also in the time of Louis XVI his Queen Maria Antoniette interfered in state affairs. It was pointed out that "the court is the tomb of the nation".

The members of the royal family led a luxurious life. The court of Versailles was composed of 18000 persons out of which 16,000 were attached to the personal services of the King and his family. The rest were courtiers. Everyone in the family had separate establishment. It is stated that queen alone had more than 500 servants.

The administrative system of the country was highly rotten. Under this system various units possessed ill-defined and overlapping jurisdictions.

There were many types of administrative divisions. For example, there were judicial districts, educational districts and ecclesiastical districts. Naturally, there was conflict of jurisdiction among them. Those conflicts added to the difficulties and troubles of the people.

There was full of confusion in the legal system also. There was no uniform law for the whole of the country. Different laws were in the force in different parts of the country. While at one place German law prevailed, at another place the Roman law was in force. In short, there were 400 different systems of law in the country. The laws were written in Latin. The people were not able to understand the same. Added to this the laws were cruel and unjust. Severe punishments were given even for ordinary offences. Torture was a common feature. There was no regular criminal procedure. Any body could be imprisoned on the whim of influential person. Men like Voltaire and Mirabeau were imprisoned like many others.

There was also confusion in the field of law courts. There were royal courts, military courts, church courts and courts of finance. Their overlapping jurisdictions added confusion and injustice.

There was no uniform weights and measures. It created confusion in the country.

Parliament claimed and exercised certain political powers. Those powers actually crippled and crushed the common people.

Above all, the method of collection of taxes was hopelessly faulty. The worst type of method made the people to rise in rebellion against the Ancient Regime. The right of collecting taxes was given to highest bidder. The result was that while the contractors paid a specific amount of money to the state, they tried to get as much as they could from the people. It resulted in a lot of oppression and tyranny. It goes without saying that the whole of the administrative system of France required a through overhauling.

3. Weak Successors of Louis XIV: Another cause of the revolution was the incapacity and inefficiency of the meak and weak successors of Louis XIV.

Louis XIV: Louis XIV was a grand monarch. He left a legacy of financial bankruptcy for his successors. While on death bed he advised his great grandson Louis XV not to indulge in wars and tried to relieve the people from great difficulty as early as possible. But it fell on deaf ears and he initiated his (Louis XIV) fondness for war.

Louis XV: The advice given by Louis XIV did not have any effect on Louis XV. Instead of giving any relief to the people he added to their miseries by his wars and frivolities. He used to say, "After me, the deluge" (destruction).

At the Court of Louis XV there was nothing but confusion, scandals and injustice. He did not take any effort to carry out good principles of Government. He left everything to chance. It, therefore, caused inspeakable disgust and discouragement in the country.

Louis XVI: He became the King of France at the age of 20. He was very ugly. He was very weak in all fields of administration. He was worthless but not a worthy ruler. He was lazy and stupid. He was very inefficient. He was very weak and meak. His helplessness to manage the state of affairs can be noticed by the following statements made by him. "It seems as if the universe is falling on me". Again, "God, what a burden is mine and they have taught me nothing". From this we know his inefficiency.

Louis XVI was awkward and too shy to preside over the meetings of the council. His hobby was lock-making and shooting deer from the palace window. He did not seem to be interested in the art of government and this is clear form his following remarks to Malsherbes on the latter's resignation : "How fortunate you are. I wish I could resign too".

Louis XVI came to the throne in the year 1774 and his reign lasted upto 1793. During this period the administration was actually run by his queen Marie Antoinette.

Marie Antoinette was the daughter of Maria Theresa, Empress of Austria-Hungary. She was the sister of the great benevolent despot Joseph II of Austria. The object of her marriage to Louis XVI was to unite Austria and France into a blood of friendship. She was beautiful, gracious and vivacious. She had a strong will power of rapid decision and spirit of initiative. However, she was lacking in wisdom and breath of judgement. Since she was born in a royal family, she could not understand the problems of the unprivileged. At the same time she was extravagant, proud, willful, impatient of retraint and fond of pleasure.

She committed a large number of mistakes and was hated by the people of France. Particularly, in the Seven Years' War she committed lawful mistakes and thereby paved the way for French humiliation. She was the centre of a group of greedy persons. Who were opposed to all reforms. At this juncture it is stated that she was the virtual ruler of France. Added to this "She tossed the King hither and thither" by various means. All these things irritated the people of France. So they rose in rebellion against the Ancient Regime.

4. Responsibility of the French Philosophers: Another cause of the French Revolution was the effect of the preachings and teachings of the French philosophers. Three great intellectual giants were very prominent and predominant during this revolutionary era. They were Montesquieu, Voltaire and Rousseau.

Montesquieu (1689-1755): Montesquieu played a significant role in paving the way for revolution. He was a polished and efficient lawyer. He was well versed in history. He was a profound student of human institutions. He was a master of a terse and pointed style. His criticism and satire were highly responsible for shaking and shattering the foundations of the Ancient Regime in France.

Montesquieu stood for a constitutional form of Government. He believed in the supremacy of law. He advocated the theory of separation of powers. The three organs of the governments *viz.* the legislature, the executive and the judiciary should be kept in watertight compartments and then alone could there be liberty of the people — according to Montesquieu.

In 1748 he published his famous book "The Spirit of Laws". It wag his great work. It was the product of 20 years of labour. It is stated that 22 editions of this book were published in 18 months. It was a study of political philosophy. Prof. Salvemini says that "The Spirit of Laws", enabled the 18th century revolutionary theories to prosper quickly in the country.

Voltaire (1694-1778): Another great intellectual giant was Voltaire. He attacked traditions, beliefs and abuses through prose, verse, history, drama and romance. He expressed their short comings mercilessly. He attacked the church vehemently and vigorously. He called in the infamous things. He was a deist and he attacked Christian bigotry and fanaticism and stood for religious toleration. Voltaire's writings were widely read and he commanded tremendous influence on his age.

Voltaire was one of the master minds of European history. He was a warrior all his life. He was a pillar of cloud by day and of fire by night. He was never tiresome. He was always interesting and generally instructive. He opposed tyranny tooth and nail in any shape or form. He was always ready to take up the cause of the oppressed and suppressed in nook and corner of the country. He stood for a benevolent despotism and had no love for democracy. He is said to have remarked that he would prefer to be ruled by one lion than by a hundred rats.

Voltaire was the best friend of Frederick the Great of Prussia, the enlightened despot of the 18th century.

Rousseau (1712-1778): The most prominent philosopher of this period was Rousseau. He exercised a tremendous influence during this period.

He did not like the study and analysis of the past. He did not care for the spread of knowledge and art. It appeared to him that study of knowledge and cultivation degraded man. All societies were artificial. All accepted forms of political organisations were tyranny and abuses.

Rousseau published his famous book "The Social Contract" in 1762. It was considered as the Bible of the French Revolution. In this book he says that "man was born free but he was every where in chains". According to Rousseau the surroundings of society destroyed the natural simplicity of man, tainted his virtues and were responsible for his sufferings and sins.

Rousseau gave his own conception of the state of nature in which people were virtuous, equal and free. He also explained how by means of "Social Contract" the state was created and the state of nature was ended. He advocated the idea of the sovereignty of the people. According to him the people had the right to revolt against the government. He condemned all the existing institutions. His writings created a profound impression upon the people. "The Social Contract" supplied the text and lit the fire of revolution.

Other Writers: Besides these three giants, there were writers of small stature, who were highly responsible for the revolutions during this period. They considerably influenced the thoughts of the people. Among them the foremost was Diderot.

Diderot was original, ingenious, reckless in expression and most intense and imaginative in thought. He possessed a magnetic power, and thereby he attracted the people. He had an indomitable perseverance and thereby he improved the conditions of mankind.

Moreover, Diderot was the editor of the Encyclopedia to which many writers made their contributions.

Helvetius, Holbach, Quesntey, D' Alambert and Turgot did a wonderful service to the people. In short, they hated unjust things; they condemned slavery; they criticised the inequality of taxation; they vehemently condemned the corruption of justice and wastefulness of war.

Mallet says that "the seed sown by these remarkable writers fell upon fruitful soil..... Thinkers and talkers alike were full of illusions, full of curiosity, full of unselfishness and full of hope". Prof. Thompson says that "their teachings became more important later" during the revolutionary era.

5. Influence of American War of Independence: The French nobles and military officers took part in the war of American Independence in support of American Colonies. They gained glorious victory for the Americans. After the war was over, they returned to their native country and induced the affected people of France to revolt. Some enlightened nobles like Lafayete spread the idea of a parliamentary form of Government. Thus, the influence of the American war of independence greatly paved the way for French Revolution.

6. Financial Cause: Another cause of the French Revolution was the financial condition of the French Government. It has been said very aptly that "The Revolution was precipitated by the economic factor and the train which had been laid by philosophy was fixed by fiance". "The fiscal causes lay at the root of the Revolution".

The "Grand Monarch" Louis XIV engaged in many wars. As a result of this the treasury became empty. The financial condition of the country was deplorable when the Grand Monarch died. He advised his great grandson Louis XV to desist from wars. But he acted contrarily.

Louis XV not only wasted a lot of money on palaces and mistresses, but also had the audacity to take part in many wars. He took part in the following wars :

(i) The war of Polish Succession.

(ii) The war of Austrian Succession.

(iii) The Seven Years' War.

By these wars the financial condition of France became more deplorable.

France was on the verge of bankruptcy when Louis XVI ascended the throne, but in spite of that France joined the war of American Independence. It cannot be denied that it was the French participation in that war of American Independence which precipitated the financial crisis which led to the French Revolution.

We have seen already in the previous pages that the nobility and the clergymen who owned about 40 per cent of the total wealth of the country did not make any contribution towards the state exchequer. No wonder the burden of taxation fell on the unprivileged classes. It thus paved the way for bitterness and anger against the Ancient Regime.

In the meantime the National debt had increased tremendously and is estimated to have reached the figure of 4,467,478,000 louvers. Interest also had increased regularly. The government had to meet out the various expenses at the same time. Some radical remedy was urgently needed to solve the problem.

In 1774, Louis XVI appointed Turgot as the Controller of Finance. He was an efficient administrator. He outlined his programme in these words: "No bankruptcy, no increase of taxation, and no more borrowing". Turgot succeeded in saving many millions by stopping useless expenditure. There arose more borrowing". Turgot succeeded in saving many millions by stopping useless expenditure. There arose great opposition from the nobles. They all joined hands with Marie Antoinette to put pressure on the King to dismiss Turgot.

In 1776 Necker was appointed in his place. He was a banker of Genoa. He was the first person to publish a financial report which showed the annual income and expenditure of the state. Formerly, the whole thing was kept as a secret. It created indignation in the country. So, he was dismissed.

In 1781 Calonne became the Controller of Finance. He wanted to please all. He followed a wonderful philosophy of borrowing. To quote him "A man who wished to borrow must appear to be rich and to appear rich he must dazzle by spending freely". The result of his philosophy was the money flowed like water. But the acts of omission and commission made the royal treasury empty later on. There was no more fools willing to lend to the State. He came forward to impose tax both on the privileged and unpriviledged. But at this juncture he was removed from office.

In 1787 De Brienne became the Controller of Finance. He tried to improve the condition of the French finance. He too failed miserably in his attempt.

Once again Louis XVI invited Turgot to tackle the financial problem. In 1787 the Assembly of the nobles was summoned. They refused to give their consent to impose tax on the privileged. So the King tried new loans, but the Parliament of Paris refused to register further loans or taxes. There was a lot of hue and cry. The situation was very serious. Crowds demanded the convocation of the Estates General. It was under these circumstances that the King was forced to summon the Estates General after a lapse of 175 years (1614-1789). This led to the French Revolution.

The Course of the French Revolution

The French Revolution is said to last from 1789 to 1799. During that period there was a series of revolutionary governments and a series of leaders. The most extreme revolutionary period was reached in 1794 under Robespierre. The events of the French Revolution are narrated below.

Estates General: Louis XVI called the Estates General to meet and solve the financial problems. The Estates General was made up of the representatives of the clergy, nobles and commoners — the three estates each electing its own representatives by an indirect method. Louis permitted the Third Estate to elect double their representation. As a result there were as many Third Estate representatives as for the first and second Estates combined. The Third Estates consisted of lawyers, judges and scholars. At first the three estates sat separately. But many Third Estate members insisted that they should meet as one body and not as three.

Formation of National Assembly: When the Third Estate's demand was not granted, it proclaimed itself a National Assembly. Then the members went to neighbouring Tennis court and took an oath called "Tennis Court Oath". Under the leadership of Mirabeau they swore that they would not separate until they had drawn up a constitution for France. The lower clergy now joined with the Third Estate.

Attack on the Bastille: The signal for the French Revolution was the fall of the Bastille. The poor workers of Paris and the hungry village people joined together and formed the Paris mob. The mob lost hope with the king and nobles. They attacked and destroyed the Bastille in July 14th, 1789. This was a prison in Paris and a symbol of royal tyranny. Only six of the prisoners were set free.

March of Women to Versailles: Women of Paris marched to Versailles in October 1789, hoping that there was plenty of food there. On their way back they brought the king and his family. "We have brought the baker, the baker's wife and the baker's little boy", they shouted. Violence began to erupt in many villages. The peasants attacked their lord's houses and burned them. Many of the noble and their families fled from France and they were called "Emigres".

Reforms of the National Assembly: By this time the Revolution was well started. The National Assembly started proclaiming reforms and passing new laws. The new laws and reforms are : (1) It abolished the system of feudalism, seridom and class privileges. Louis XVI was officially provlaimed by the National Assembly as "Restorer of the French Liberty". (2) It issued the "Declaration of the Rights of man". The Declaration contained many of the ideas of the French reforms. It was also influenced by the American Declaration of Independence. (3) It set up a uniform system of Administration all over the country. (4) It issued paper currency known as Assignats to tackle the financial problem: (5) It took lot of steps to reform the church. The "Civil Constitution of the Clergy", was enacted. (6) It framed a new constitution for France, in 1791 and hence it was known as the "Constituent Assembly". It was the first written Constitution of France.

Plight of the King (June 1791): After the Constitution was enacted, a government was formed with the king as its head but without powers. Now Louis and his queen tried to get away secretly from France, but were found out and brought back by force.

The Legislative Assembly (1791-92). The new Legislative Assembly, elected under the constitution of 1791, met at Paris on 1st December. None of the National Assembly members was eligible to become member of the new assembly. Hence, there were no talented members in the new Assembly.

There were two groups fin the Assembly, they were the moderates and extremists. The moderates were called the 'Girondists' While the extremists were called the 'Jacobins'. The Girondists demanded that the Republic in France should be set up through non-violent methods, while the Jacobins wanted to set up through violent methods. The Jacobins dominated the Assembly. The chiefs among them were Danton and Robespierre.

Execution of the King (1793): The other European countries feared that the revolutionary movement would spread into their countries. So the new republic was threatened by foreign invasions especially from Prussia. The French armies faced defeats. The people blamed the king and queen for the defeat. They also doubted that the queen was negotiating with the enemy to restore absolute monarchy. Therefore, the Legislative Assembly imprisoned the king. The Assembly then, ordered an election for National Convention to frame a new constitution.

The National convention took over the Government of France. It declared France as a Republic in September 1792. Louis XVI was tried and executed in January 1793, though Girondists opposed. In a wild uprising known as the "September Massacres", thousands of royalists were killed. In the meantime the French army won the battle and drove back the Austrians and Prussians.

Reign of Terror (1793-94): A strong central Government was formed with the "Committee of Public Safety" as the head. Robespierre became the leading figure in the committee. The committee instituted a "reign of terror" in which thousands were guillotined as they were suspected. Among those put to death were Queen Marie Antoinette, Danton and finally Robespierre. With the death of Robespierre ended the reign of terror.

Constitution of 1795 and the Directory: The National Convention drew up a new constitution. It provided for a representative assembly of two bodies and five more executive committees called the 'Directory'. The legislature chose the Directory. The Directory became corrupt and weak. So the people marched towards the Assembly Hall in 1795. A young general Napoleon Bonaparte was called to help. He controlled the mob by using artillery. This is known as 'the whiff of grape-shot'.

Results

(1) The French Revolution gave a death blow to the Bourbon dynasty of France.

(2) It gave a decent burial to the Ancient Regime. The autocratic rule of the Kings came to an end.

(3) It was not a local event. It influenced profoundly not only the people of France but also those of Europe and the world.

(4) The three principles of the Revolution the liberty, equality and fraternity spread nook and corner of the world.

(5) The Declaration of the Rights of Man by the National Assembly emphasised the fact that sovereignty resides in the people and law is the expression of the general will.

(6) The French Revolution asserted that all men were equal before law.

(7) Serfdom was abolished. Freedom was given to all.

(8) Feudalism was abolished. There was no feudal restrictions.

(9) The French Revolution also asserted the principle of nationality.

(10) The principle of nationality spread all over Europe. It created a new star in the minds of the European master minds.

(11) The French Revolution also gave a stimulus to humanitarianism. Slavery was abolished root and branch.

(12) The French Revolution also helped the revival of romanticism. The influence of the French Revolution can be seen in Victor Hugo's 'Les Miserable', Southey's 'Joan of Arc', Wordsworth's 'Prelude', Shelley's 'Mask of Anarchy', Goethe's 'Faust' and in the early works of Coleridge.

(13) The influence of the Roman Catholic Church was strengthened.

(14) The confiscation of property by the Government weakened the idea of the sanctity of property.

(15) According to Kropokin, the French Revolution made France stronger and prosperous. He also points out that it brought

about the abolition of serfdom and absolutism. He pointed out that the French Revolution left a legacy on the principles of communism.

(16) The French Revolution paved the way for the rise of Napoleon and the establishment of an empire.

(17) It created a feeling of patriotism.

Napoleon Bonaparte

Napoleon Bonaparte was born on August 15th, 1769, in Corsica, an island in the Mediterranean. Hence, he was an Italian by birth. Educated in military school at Brienne and Paris, he joined the French army. The French Revolution gave him a splendid opportunity to display his talents and capacity. He was sent to recapture Toulon from the British in the year 1793. He expelled the English from there. In 1795 he dispersed the Parisian mob.

Italian Campaign (1796-97): The Directory sent Napoleon to lead the French army against Austrians in Italy. He won brilliant victories. And, therefore, he became an idol not only among the soldiers but also among the French people. Fearing his popularity, the Directory turned his attention towards the English in Egypt.

Egyptian Campaign (1798-99): In 1798, Napoleon defeated the Sultan of Egypt in the "Battle of Pyramids". But in the 'Battle of Nile' in the same year the French navy was defeated by Nelson, the British general. Napoleon kept this defeat a secret.

Coup D' Etat (1799): In Europe the French Army without Napoleon was repeatedly defeated. So the Directory became unpopular. Napoleon returned to France and overthrew the Directory. He established the Consulate with himself as the First Consul. This is known as the coup d' etat of Brumaire.

Napoleon *Vs.* Second Coalition: Napoleon had to face the new coalition of Russia, Britain and Austria. He defeated again the Austrians at the battle of MARENGO (1800) and Hohenlinden (1801) in Italy. Austria was compelled to make peace with France. Now Britain was left alone. Both France and Britain were tired of war and a treaty was signed in 1802 at Amiens. "It was a treaty about which everyone was glad but no one proud".

Napoleon as an Emperor (1804): Napolean's popularity grew tremendously. In 1804 the people voted him to become Emperor. The right of his descendants to succeed him was also accepted.

Nepoleon *Vs.* Third Coalition (1805): There was an outbreak of war in 1803 between France and Britain. In the Battle of Trafalgar in 1805, Nelson defeated the combined French and Spanish fleets.

A Third Coalition consisting of Britain, Russia, Austria and Sweden against France was formed by William Pitt the Younger, the British Prime Minister. Napoleon defeated the Austrians at Ulm (October 1805) and again the combined armies of Austria and Russia at Austerlitz (December, 1805). The Coalition broke into pieces and Austria accepted the "Peace of Pressburg in 1805. He combined all the independent chieftaincies in Germany (about 350) into a political union of 39 states in 1806. The Union was called the "Confederation of the Rhine" being himself its Protector. Prussia was then defeated by him in the Battle of Jena (1806). Russia was again defeated at Friedland in 1807. Tsar Alexander of Russia concluded the Treaty of Tilsit with Napoleon in 1807.

The Continental System: To overcome the British, Napoleon decided to starve the "nation of shop-keepers", by closing the entire continental trade with Britain. With this aim he issued his "Berlin Decrees" in 1806, by which he asked his allies and members of his Empire to boycott British goods. This boycott of British trade is known as the "Continental System". Many countries defied the Berlin decrees. The Continental System proved very harmful to the people of Europe. Prices of goods shot up. Thus, it failed and led many wars.

The Peninsular War (1808-13): When Portugal defied the Continental System, Napoleon's army invaded Portugal. Napoleon deposed the King of Spain, Charles VI and appointed his own brother, Joseph as King in 1808. Britain sent an army under Sir Arthur Wellesly (afterwards Duke of Wellington) to expel the French from Portugal and Spain. This is known as the Peninsular War. Wellesly obtained the victories of Salamanca and Victoria in 1812 and 1813 respectively and expelled the French from the Peninsula.

The Invasion of Russia (1812): Austria and Russia too defied the Berlin Decrees. Napoleon easily defeated Austria in 1809. Napoleon's Grand Army invaded Russia and defeated the Russians at Borodino. Napoleon advanced towards Moscow. The Russians retreated swiftly destroying everything on their way back. Even the city of Moscow was evacuated. By the time Napoleon decided to turn back to his country, winter had set in. The soldiers died due to cold and starvation. Napoleon lost half a million men and this invasion of Russia proved to be a fatal blunder in his career.

The War of Nations or the War of Liberation (1813): The Fourth Coalition, consisting of Britain, Russia, Prussia, Austria and Sweden was formed. The armies of the Fourth Coalition met Napoleon in the Battle of the Nations at Leipzig in 1813. Napoleon was badly defeated. He fled to Paris. The enemies quickly surrounded the city. Napoleon abdicated in March 1814. He was exiled to the Island of Elba near Italy. Louis XVIII brother of Louis XVI became the king of France.

The Hundred Days (Defeat At Waterloo-1815): A few months later Napoleon escaped from Elba and returned to Paris. He was accepted as the king by the people and army. Louis XVIII fled to Belgium. Napoleon ruled only for a hundred days. The allies met him at Waterloo in June 1815. He was defeated by the Duke of Wellington assisted by the timely arrival of Prussian army under General Bluncher. Louis XVIII was once more restored to the throne of France.

At last Napoleon was taken prisoner and sent to the island, St. Helena in the Atlantic. There he spent the last 5½ years of his life writing his memories and meditating over the past. He died in 1821.

Causes for the Downfall of Napoleon: There were many causes for the downfall of Napoleon. They are as follows : (i) His policy of militarism and despotism earned enemies rather than friends, (ii) His policy of "Continental System" failed and led many wars, (iii) Britain's sea power and economic strength shattered the French domination, (iv) The ill-fated Russian Expedition took away half a million men and destroyed the spirit of his army, (v) Continuous wars exhausted his resources and energy.

Reforms

Napoleon was a rare combination of a conqueror and a statesman in one. His victories did not endure whereas most of his internal reforms proved to be lasting and beneficial. His reforms are explained below.

I. Reforms in Local Government: In 1800 Napoleon made the entire system of local government subordinate to him.

(1) France was divided into Departments, Each Department was controlled by an officer called 'Perfect', appointed by the Central Government.

(2) Each Department was divided into Arrondissements which were controlled by an officer called "Sub-Prefect", appointed by the Central Government.

(3) Each Arrondissement was divided into Communes. The Commune was controlled by an officer called "Mayor". Mayor was advised and assisted by an elected local council.

II. Reforms in Education

(1) Secondary schools were opened. These were managed by the Communes.

(2) Grammar schools in French, Latin were opened for special training.

(3) University of France was founded.

(4) Intellectuals and academicians were encouraged, through the 'Legion of Honour' which was established by Napoleon.

III. Economic Reforms

(1) The Bank of France was established.

(2) He introduced the metric system and a stable currency based on gold.

(3) He established advisory boards to encourage trade and commerce.

(4) He tried to protect the infant industries by imposing high duties on imported goods.

IV. Reforms in Communications

(1) He built new roads, canals and bridges.

(2) Ports were improved.

(3) Highways of France were planned by Napoleon.

V. Reforms in Finance

(1) He developed the Secretariat of State for levying and collection of taxes.

(2) Many indirect taxes were levied and strictly collected.

(3) He received large indeminities from defeated countries.

(4) He introduced severe economy in public expenditure.

VI. The Concordat (1802): The people must have a religion and that must be under the control of the state. This was the religious policy of Napoleon. As the French men were mostly Catholics he entered into an agreement with the Pope, known as the Concordat. According to this, churches were reopened. Napoleon agreed to nominate bishops in consultation with the Pope and to pay their salary regularly

VII. Reforms in Judiciary — The Code of Napoleon

(1) Napoleon constituted a committee to codify laws : (a) Civil Code, (b) Code of Civil Procedure, (c) Code of Criminal Procedure, (d) Penal

Code and (e) Commercial Code. These were called 'Code Napoleon'. It abolished feudal privileges and established civil equality. (2) The rules of the Code were uniformly adopted throughout the country. (3) The Code was a clear and definite book of Laws and Procedure, (4) Three important principles were enumerated in the Codes (a) All classes were equal before the law, (b) toleration for all religions, (c) trials should be conducted in public and under the jury system.

Conclusion: Napoleon's administration is differently estimated by different people. It is argued that his internal reforms were mostly necessitated by his foreign policy. Some say that there was nothing original in his system as the ground has been prepared for the Revolution. Anyhow his administrative reforms were far and wide. Hence, Napoleon can be called "The Founder of Modern France".

(v) INDUSTRIAL REVOLUTION

Introduction: The 18th century saw great changes pass over the life of England. Among the great changes the Industrial Revolution is considered as an important change in the history of England. Industrial revolution is a change in industrial methods and organisation. The great changes that took place in English industries between 1760 and 1830 have been called the "Industrial Revolution".

Favourable Factors

(1) Existence of freedom of thought and expression.
(2) Free scope of experimentation.
(3) Few restrictions on the manufacture of goods.
(4) Nearness of coal and iron mines to the industries.
(5) Supply of large-scale surplus agricultural labourers to the factories.
(6) Availability of more capital.
(7) Political stability.
(8) The naval supremacy and
(9) The supply of raw materials from the colonies.

Causes

(1) Due to an increase of population in the 18th century, the demand for the goods increased. The existing system of manufacturing goods could not meet the increased demand. Necessity became the mother of invention. Hence, new machines were invented to produce goods on a large scale.

(2) England had many colonies in the 18th century. The colonies preferred the English goods. Hence, more goods were to be produced by using new devises to cater to the new markets in the colonies.

The Inventions

I. Textile Industry

(1) John Kay invented the "Flying Shuttle" in 1733. This helped the weavers to increase the speed of weaving.

(2) James Hargreaves invented the Spinning Jenny in 1765. This helped the spinners to spin the spindles at the same time.

(3) Arkwright invented "Water Frame" in 1769. This helped the manufacture of hard and firm yarn suitable for weaving.

(4) Samuel Crompton invented 'Mule' in 1779, by combining the advantages of both the spinning Jenny and Water Frame.

(5) Edmund Cartwright invented "The Power Loom" in 1785. This helped to speed up the weaving.

II. Power

(1) Newcomen was the first to invent the Steam Engine.

(2) James Watt improved the Steam Engine and this replaced the water power.

(3) Abraham Derby discovered that coke could be used instead of charcoal for smelting purposes.

III. Other Improvements

(1) Henry Cort invented new methods of rolling and pudding iron.

(2) Humphrey Davy invented the "Safety Lamp" which enabled the miners to carry out their work safely.

(3) John Macadam, an Engineer of Scotland was responsible for good road construction.

(4) George Stephenson, the father of steam locomotive, succeeded in building locomotive engine in 1830.

(5) Charles Wheatstone contributed a lot in the invention of electric telegraph.

(6) The Duke of Bridge Water popularised the digging of canals which provided a cheap means of transport.

Results

(1) The revolution increased the national wealth of England. England became "the workshop of the world".

(2) The growth of industries and the employment of the large number of people in them necessitated the establishment of factories and towns. Manchester, Lanckashire and Sheffield were some of the factory towns. There were no provisions for drainage and town-planning in the new towns. Hence, in order to tackle the social problems and public health many laws had to be enacted.

(3) The revolution resulted in the creation of a Capitalist society in which the rich grew richer and the poor poorer. There were conflicts between the labourers and the employers. Therefore, trade unions were formed.

(4) The revolution led to the shifting of population from the South and East of England to the North and West of England.

(5) The improved facilities of communication widened the market for manufactured articles.

(6) The growth of large populous towns made parliamentary reform necessary as these towns were not represented in the parliament.

(7) The distress of the workmen under the factory system led to the Chartist Movement and socialistic demands for reforms.

The industrial revolution resulted in vast and far reaching changes in the social, economic and political life of the English people. The changes in industrial system were, from the domestic system to the factory system; from the work done by hands to work done by machines; from human power to steam power, from self-sufficient production to large scale production and from internal market to the international market. Thus, England became the worship of the world and came out a decisive power in the two world wars.

(vi) THE AGRARIAN REVOLUTION

The word "Revolution" denotes a fundamental change. A political revolution is a complete change of Government. An industrial revolution is a change in industrial methods and organisation. Similarly an agrarian revolution is a change in the methods of agriculture. The methods of farming and cattle breeding underwent many changes in the 18th century. This great change was called "Agrarian Revolution".

Early Agricultural Conditions: Until the middle of the 18th century little change had occurred in English agriculture. The primary occupation of the English people was agriculture. The chief features of the English agriculture were : (1) Open-field system was prevalent. Therefore, fencing was absent. The absence of enclosures led to boundary disputes (2) Three field system of cultivation was also common. According to the system, in one field wheat was grown and in another, barley while the third-field was kept fallow. (3) Old methods and traditional ways of cultivation were followed. (4) There were customary rights over common pasture and woodlands to all in the village. (5) Peasants carried on textile work in cottages in their leisure time.

Causes for the Agrarian Revolution

(1) In the 18th century population of England increased. So, there was a great demand for food. It was difficult to produce enough food under the existing system of cultivation. Hence, new methods of cultivation had to be found out. (2) Scarcity of food led to a rise in prices. Due to the outbreak of war with France it was also difficult to import food for Europe. Hence, the farmers had to adopt new methods of cultivation to increase food production. (3) The coming of the factory system separated weaving from agriculture. Hence, the peasants who lost their part-time work had to gain a living solely from agriculture. This led to producing more by following scientific methods of cultivation.

The Improvements made in Agriculture

Sir Robert Westerm: He published a book called "Discourse on Husbandry" in 1645. According to him if rootcrops were introduced, there was no necessity of leaving one-third of land uncultivated every year. This crop also would provide fodder for cattle in winter.

Jethro Tull: He invented a machine called "Drill" in 1701 for sowing seeds. It could sow deep in rows. The Drill method prevented the birds from picking up the seeds.

Lord Townshend: He founded a new system of "Rotation of Crops" called the "Norfolk Course". He advocated a four-field rotation instead of a three-field system. The crops were to be grown in the order of wheat, turnip, barley and clover. He was nicknamed as "Turnip Townshend".

Sir Aurthus Young: He published a book called "Annals of Agriculture" in 1784. He was responsible for setting up of "Board of Agriculture" and became its first secretary.

King George III: He took keen interest in agriculture and hence he was called as "Farmer George". He established a model farm at Windsor.

Robert Bakewell: He introduced a new type of sheep called "New Leicester". This new type of sheep has been known for its weight.

Charles Colling: He specialised in a new breed of cattle called "Durham Shorthorn". These cows have been famous for their milk yield.

The Enclosure Movement: To prevent the destruction of crops by cattle, the Board of Agriculture encouraged enclosing the field. The small peasants could not adopt the improved method of agriculture as they had small strips of land. Hence, consolidation of holding was necessary. The small strips of lands were also brought into big blocks. The enclosure was undertaken by mutual consent in some cases and in other by Acts of Parliament. About 1500 "Enclosure Acts" were passed between 1760 and 1800. And in the same period about 3 million acres were enclosed.

Results of the Agrarian Revolution

(1) By adopting new methods of cultivation the yield of crops increased tremendously. More wool, more milk and meat were available for the demands of the town population.

(2) The Enclosure Movement removed the scattered lands from peasants and made big compact farms. Thus, capitalistic basis of cultivation came into practice.

(3) There was a practical disappearance of the small farmers, many of whom sank to the position of labourers.

Between 1750-1820 the face of England was completely changed. The English farming was the best in Europe and long remained the model which the continent tried to follow.

(vii) RUSSIAN REVOLUTION

Russian Revolution of 1905 was an important event in the history of Russia. It brought about fundamental changes in the social, political and economic life of Russia on the one hand and changed the balance of power in Europe on the other. The following events were very important :

The first and foremost cause of the Russian Revolution of 1905 was the autocracy of Czarism in Russia. In 1905, the condition of Russia was like that of France in 1789. The monarchy was very weak. The condition of Russia was very chaotic. There was growing discontent among people due to the autocracy of the Czars. The rulers of Russia were autocrats and self-willed, and their autocracy had created discontentment all over the country.

Secondly, the social discontent paved the way for the revolution. Like France, where in 1789, the clergy and the feudal lords or the nobles enjoyed special privileges, in Russia also in 1905 the same type of atmosphere had been created. The clergy and the nobles in Russia enjoyed special privileges. It created a high tension and discontent among the Russians.

Thirdly, the population of Russia was illiterate and suffered from blind faith in religion. It gave ample opportunities to the priests to prosper on their credulity. It was in favour of the czars. Moreover, the czars followed the theory of divine right. Accordingly the king was the representative of God on earth and for that reason he could not be made responsible to anyone but God.

Fourthly, nepotism and corruption in Russia was highly responsible for the revolution of 1905. The Russian czars administrated the country with the advice of the fawning and cringing flatterers of the court. These flatterers were the symbols of ugly bureaucracy. This tyrannical behaviour had created discontent among the people of Russia.

Fifthly, the Russian Army was highly responsible for the outbreak of the Russian Revolution in 1905. The Russian Army was rigid in its attitude towards the czar. It remained busy in promoting the autonomy of the czar. It was defeated in the foreign countries. It indulged in many nefarious activities. Those activities created terror among the people. Naturally the people hated this type of army.

Sixthly, the czar was under influence of Czarina and her favourite Rasputin, clever wicked wizard of Russia. He could compel the czar to indulge into act of tyranny. Under the influence of Rasputin he lost the love of his people. Now the people being fed up with his tyrannical acts were looking forward to any opportunity to strike the czar.

Seventhly, the influence of Czar Nicholas II who ruled Russia from 1894 to 1917 was also responsible for the revolution.

Eighthly, political parties like Liberal Party, Socialist Party and Socialist Revolutionary Party played a significant role in bringing the revolution.

Ninthly, the Czar made Russian language compulsory for all the races living in Russia. It was made also compulsory in the university, schools and for the libraries. The people of Russia opposed the policy of Czar vehemently, and they started taking an active part in the activities which might put an end to his regime.

Finally, the rise of nationalism paved the way for the Revolution. Besides, the Russo-Japanese war greatly affected the people of Russia and so they turned towards revolutionary activities. They wanted to put an end to Czarism.

Course: The defeat of Russia in the war encouraged the revolutionaries. Soon they started slaying the government officers. There was virtual terror in the land. The revolutionaries combined the entire country and killed the government officers. They raised slogans against the Czar. "Long Live Revolution" became the common slogan of the people. In this manner, the whole of Russia became a holocaust of revolution, the blazes or conflagration leaping sky very high.

Bloody Sunday: The moderates were placing their demands before the Czar. The revolutionaries were freely indulging in massacre. Peasants also started their agitation. Strikes were staged in the mills and factories, and the workers started parading on the streets. All the races joined together and raised their standard of revolt.

On 22nd January 1905, which is known as the Bloody Sunday in the history of Russia, an incident occurred which ignited the key of the gunpowder. That day a mass of labourers were moving towards the royal palace of St. Petersburg under the leadership of Father Gabon, to place their grievances before the Czar. But the forces of Czar attacked the people treading their way towards the palace. Thousands of people were shot dead. Men were killed in large numbers. Czar was condemned for all. All Europe was electrified by the terrible piece of news.

In spite of all this, the demonstrators could not achieve their aim. Yet it influenced the country. But there was strike everywhere. There was military revolts in the country. The houses of the landlords were set on fire. The uncle of Czar, Grand Duke Sergius was assassinated. The man was a great reactionary. The Poles revolted in Warsaw, Finland, Lithuania etc. and declared themselves to be independent kingdoms.

Declaration of Nicholas II: The following reforms were announced by him :

(1) Religious freedom was given to the people.

(2) The small officers like Treypoff were dismissed from service.

(3) Certain rights were given to the people.

(4) Complete freedom was given to all the races in the country.

(5) It was declared illegal to punich anyone without trial.

(6) The Japanese war was stopped by making a treaty.

(7) The Czar promised to convene the Duma, the Parliament of Russia.

(8) The members of the Duma should be elected by the people.

(9) The sanction of Duma will be essential for framing a law.

(10) The king also promised to took after the welfare of the people by his officers.

(11) The people will be given freedom and right to make platform speeches and writing articles.

The above declaration satisfied the people of Russia. Any how the revolutionaries achieved veiy little success.

Causes for its Failure:

(i) The revolution was localised in certain areas. Since Russia is a vast country it failed to attract the people of other parts of the country. So, it failed miserably.

(ii) Lack of nationalism among the different races paved the way for its failure.

(iii) There was no unity among the people.

(iv) Poor organisation of the demonstrators was highly responsible for its failure.

(v) There was no strong leader to conduct the revolution with great vigour.

Results

(i) A great impediment was brought to the autocracy of the Czar.

(ii) Duma was established in Russia.

(iii) Czar dissolved Duma twice asserting his autocracy, but the concept was buried for ever.

(iv) It gave a green signal to the succeeding revolution in Russia.

Russian Revolution of 1917

The Russian Revolution is considered as the most important event in the history of the world. There were many causes for the Russian Revolution of 1917. Let us discuss the causes in the following pages:

1. Weak Czarist Regime: The defeats Russia had suffered in the Crimean war and at the hands of Japan brought out the weaknesses of the Czarist regime. They also showed that the Russian autocracy only know how to rule cruelly and not how to defend the national interests. The inefficiency of the autocratic government to the foreign attacks during the Great War of 1914 goaded the people into overthrowing the government.

2. Economic Disparity: As in France, in Russia too there was wide disparity between the upper and lower classes. Previously the Russian society was composed of two classes, nobles and serfs. The nobles owned the land and also held the government offices. About the condition of the serfs it was said that they were no better than "hewers of woods and drawers of water". Alexander II had emancipated the serfs from the bondage of the nobles, but even after their freedom from serfdom their living condition did not improve. They led a wretched life. These people living in penury and poverty were the most potential elements for any kind of movement which promised them relief from their misery.

The poverty of the people in general had also increased due to the ills produced by the industrialisation in Russia. The labourers did not get due return for their hard work and toil. They were also ready to take part in a movement which assured a better living to them.

The economic distress compelled the poor people to feel attracted towards the new force of communism which sought to abolish capitalism. This force influenced a large populace of Russia, for it assured that it would end all economic ills by setting up such a regime and would give maximum economic power to the laboures and workers. The proletariat felt very impressive by the communistic ideology and joined the communists in large numbers. Thus, it was economic cause that precipitated the Revolution of 1917.

3. Influence of Western Ideas: The Czarist Regime tried its best to prevent infiltration of the western ideas into Russia. But it was all in vain. The liberal and radical ideas of the Russians produced an explosive situation, threatening the Czarist regime. These ideas got their expression in literature. The novels of Tolstoy, Turgenev and Dostoievsky impressed the youth most under their influence, the intelligentia began clamouring for political reforms on the western lines. The radical section of the people raised their demands for reforms on the Marxist principles. Out of this ferment grew the creed of Nihilism, which sought to destroy everything in the existing order of Russia. It was, however, eliminated by the force of socialism.

4. Russian Hatred of Soldiers: The Russians hated the soldiers who had been given many facilities by the Czar. These soldiers lived comfortably and, therefore, always favoured the government and perpetrated cruelties on the common People.

5. People's Desire for General Welfare: The Allies in the First World War had declared that they were fighting the war for the general welfare of the people. This encouraged the Russian to overthrow the Czarist Regime.

6. People's Deplorable Condition: The condition of general people became very acute and deplorable when Russia began losing in the first

World War. The prices of essential commodities soared very high and on acute shortage of fuel, cereals and cloth gripped the country. Starvation stalked the land.

7. Czar's Apathy Towards People's Appeal: The best attempts to improve the situation was made by a committee of experts. The committee appealed to the Czar to personally look into the affairs of the Government and mend the things. But the Czar turned deaf ear to the appeal and his officials became more and more corrupt. Now there was no other way than a revolution to get rid of the Czarist apathy.

Bolsheviks: By the time the nineteenth century came to a close, Russia witnessed great economic changes. Several new towns sprang up and factories were set up like mushrooms. These changes led to the growth of the capitalist class and the proletariat. With them arose new problems of factory life and the new outlook of the town workers. The exploitation by the capitalists made the life of the workers miserable. It was at this time that the socialism spread in Russia. It was received with great enthusiasm by the workers and labourers. The ideas of Marx were propagated in Russia by radicals like the novelist Maxim Gorky. The intellectuals were also impressed by the socialist ideology.

In 1895, was founded the Workers Social Democratic Party with a socialist programme. It worked unitedly in the cause of the workers and labourers. But in 1903, it was split up into two on the question of party discipline and tactics.

The radical group consisted of the Bolsheviks who believed that only a revolution could end the Czarist Regime and help to set up a communist regime in its place. They were also ready to adopt violent means to achieve their main object. They were led by Vladmir-Ulianov, better known as Lenin.

Mensheviks: The other group consisted of Mensheviks who wanted to set up a communist government gradually and through the dissemination of education. It abhorred violent means to achieve their object.

Lenin: Lenin was a influential leader. Being a disciple of Marx, he had no faith in parliamentary republic of the middle class. He wanted a government which had the representatives of the labourers, soldiers and farmers.

When the war broke out in 1914, he took up the causes of the common people. He charged the Czarist Government with giving war to the people when they wanted bread, land and peace. He inspired the commoners with his speeches. He said to them.

"Comrades, the workers and the labourers, in you resides the greatest power on earth".

He also told them that they would be the custodians of their country's sovereignty and enjoy its benefits.

Lenin's Aim: Lenin wanted :

(a) Confiscation of all big estates,

(b) End of Government control over all kinds of trades,

(c) Declaration of the national debt as illegal,

(e) Abrogation of all treaties made by the Russian emperors,

(f) Right of vote for the commoners,

(g) Boycott of all capitalists and rich from Government offices,

(h) Checking of the foreign interference in Russian affairs and

(i) Economic and social changes according to the policy of the Bolshevik Party.

Course: The weaknesses of the Czarist regime were exposed thoroughly in the course of the First World war 1914. The Russian autocracy failed to meet the situation. A reactionary party advocated immediate end of war by making peace with Germany. The party thereby wanted to halt the breaking out of any revolution in Russia. This party was headed by Czarina whose guru was Rasputin. The public opposed any peace arrangement with Germany. Rasputin was murdered. Riots also broke out in the country side. The workers struck work and there took place large scale desertions in the army. The acute shortage of bread made the matter worse.

Riot in Petrograd: The workers in Petrograd created a serious crisis in 1917. They struck work and rioted for bread. The Czarist soldiers did not do anything. On the contrary, they sympathised with the workers. The workers set up a Soviet, or Council including soldiers to direct the rising and to run the local Government. In the meantime, the Duma (the Russian Parliament which had very limited powers) set up a provisional Government and forced the Czar to abdicate. Now, the Revolution had broken out.

Contrary to the expectation, the Provisional Government came into the hands of middle class people (Bourgeoisie). It was composed of mainly of cadets (Constitutional democrats) led by Milinkov, a liberal Professor-politician. He introduced several liberal reforms on the western lines. He announced that very soon a Constituent Assembly would be elected to form a permanent Government. He also announced the continuance of the war.

But, backward as the Russian people were, the political reforms did not influence them very much. What they wanted were peace, land and bread. They wanted rapid social and economic changes to free them from their distress. They favoured the ideology of socialism. More and more Soviets of working men and soldiers sprang up all over the country and they encouraged agitation and propaganda.

The workers struck work everywhere for higher wages and fewer working hours. The peasants seized the lands of the nobles. The soldiers refused to obey their officers and even murdered some of them. They also began fraternising with the German soldiers. To make the situation worse, the Poles and Fin in the Russian Empire began agitating for their freedom. The war policy of the Cadets became highly unpopular with the people. They were, therefore, turned out and replaced by the Mensheviks under the leadership of Alexander Kerensky, a moderate socialist.

But Kerensky found it very difficult to run the Government smoothly. His constitutional approach towards the economic problems was disliked by the people. The Bolsheviks opposed him strongly and agitated for the establishment of the dictatorship of the proletariat. They also wanted an honourable peace with the Germans. Their leaders were Lenin and Trotsky.

Kerensky's foreign policy made some success and Russia made some victories on the Germans. But all this success proved temporary. Influenced by the pacificist Bolsheviks, the soldiers refused to fight and rose in mutiny against the Government. Taking advantage of this situation, Germany captured Riega and threatened Petrograd itself. In the meantime, the Bolsheviks had improved their strength considerably. They overthrow the Kerensky Government by a Coup d'etat, in November 1917.

Results

The following were the results of the Russian Revolution of 1917 :

(a) The Government took under its control all trades.

(b) Every peasant was given sufficient land to till.

(c) The council of Workers took over the management of the factories.

(d) All national debts were cancelled.

(e) Everyone was called upon to earn his own food by working.

(f) Every capitalist was compelled to do physical work to entitle himself to the right to vote.

(g) Educational facilities were provided to the workers.
(h) All treaties made previously by Czars were abrogated.
(i) Every race in Russia was free to create its own kingdom on the principle of Bolshevism.
(j) Education was nationalised.
(k) Every person was given equal treatment.

27

Romanticism in Art and Literature

During the 18th and 19th centuries a significant development took place in Europe in the field of literature, painting and science. In other words that period gave birth to a new era of greatness, heroism and progress. Further the Revolution had brought new lights on the 19th century philosophy and as well as in the literary field.

Literature: During this period the Enlightenment of rational tradition which was anti-classical existed in France. At this disappearance of this nationalistic approach, a new age called "Romanticism" appeared.

The word "Romantic" merely indicated the historical character of the work or that the subject matter was drawn from the 'Romantic' of a past age. The movement was in full swing both is Germany and Britain. In the same way it spread to France too. The following were the noted German Romantic scholars :

(1) Nowalis,

(2) Morike,

(3) Kleist and

(4) Hoffman.

In the same period the following English Romantic poets contributed very much to English literature :

(1) Wordsworth,

(2) Coleridge,

(3) Byron,

(4) Shelley and

(5) Keats.

Vicomte de chateaubriand and Madame de Stael were the chief exponents of the new literary movements in France. The former is believed to be one of the great masters of French prose of those times. His outstanding works were La Genie du Christiani due and Rene. Madame de Stael, another French scholar travelled widely in Switzerland, England, Germany and Italy.

Goethe was admired and conferred the Legion of Honour by Napoleon.

Stael's most famous book was "De J. Allamagne" (a Romantic portrayal of an ideal Germany). Since it had political implications, it was confiscated in France. Therefore, she went to London and published her book.

Arts: Painting revived great impetus during this period. A French painter by name Louis David was very famous for his canvas painting. His great contribution was "The oath of the Heratti". It was painted and deployed in 1785. In 1804, he was appointed as a court painter by Napoleon and he was also made commander of the Legion of Honour. He also painted powerful realistic portraits for instance, Pious VII and Napoleon. His other paintings were "Correction of Napoleon" and the "Distribution of the Eagles".

Gerard and Gross were the best pupils of David. Gerard's portraits of "Madame Recounier" and the "King of Rome" were very much appreciated. Gross produced many dramatic and picturesque paintings. The important of them were "Bonaparte at the Bridge of Arcola", "Napoleon visiting the plague — stricken at Jaffa and the Battle of Eylau".

Science: Scientific developments were very great during this period.

In Chemistry, the French scientist Lavoisier carried on the investigation of oxygen and hydrogen. He established the fact that matter may alter its "State" but not its quantity; and studied the connection between oxidation and respiration. Thus, he placed nomenclature on a scientific basis. Lavoisier was guillotined in 1794.

Herschal and Laplace were very prominent in astronomy. Their conception of the origin of the planets opened new vistas for the study of the universe.

Laplace made a significant contribution in Mathematics. He was known as the "Newton of France". He was very famous for the development of the calculus.

Lagrange was another leading figure in Mathematics. His special contributions lay in his investigation of geometrical problems.

Medicine and therapeutic studies were greatly advanced during this period.

Tissue philosophy was investigated and vaccination was improved by Edward Jenner.

Galvani discovered electricity and this led Volta to work on electric currents and on the storing of electricity in batteries.

Besides Charles Darwin, Louis Pasteur, Thomas Alva Edison, Madame Curie, Michael Faraday, Margoni, Baird, Wright Brothers Edward, Jenner, Joseph Lister, Roentgen, James Simpson Mendel and Julius Cohen contributed a lot for the promotion of science.

28

Rise of Nationalism

(i) EUROPE

In Europe nationalism played a significant role in bringing drastic changes. Many causes were responsible for such nationalism in Europe. They were :

(1) One of the most important causes for the rise of nationalism in Europe was the decline of papacy. Once the Pope of Rome was the religious head of the state. He was so powerful that he kept all the Christian kings under his power, authority and control. As long as the Pope was strong there was international state and international religions. But when papacy declined, all the states began to exert themselves. In fact rise of nationalism was one of the major causes of the decline of papacy.

(2) Another cause was the decline of feudal system. After the decline, great impetus was given to nationalism. In the words of Swain, "Most of the nation states grew out of the activities of the feudal lords. France was unified by the efforts of the Ile De France; Spain came out of the unity of feudal provinces of Aragon and Castile, and feudal House of Hapsburg ultimately unified Austria".

(3) The war of 18th and 19th centuries Europe (American war of Independence, Seven Years' War, War of Austrian succession and so on) created feeling and love for one's own state and thus nationalism got strength.

(4) Another cause for the rise and spread of nationalism was the struggle for colonial supremacy. Each country looked after its own colonies. It led to clash between one country with another country. Thus, struggle for supremacy in the colonial gave birth to nationalism in Europe.

(5) Still another cause for the rise and spread of nationalism was the change in social structure.

(6) French Revolution was a major cause responsible for bringing nationalism in Europe. The writings of Russian and slogans of liberty, equality and fraternity awakened the people all over the world and aroused among them the feelings of nationalism.

Growth: It was in this background that nationalism developed in Europe. Renaissance played a prominent part in the process. People began to take pride and pleasure in their own culture and civilisation. It resulted in many struggles to achieve nationhood in Europe. Machiavelli's Prince exercised a tremendous influence in this respect. It opened the eyes of Italy and other countries in the succeeding years. Gradually, the spirit of nationalism arose in different countries. It might briefly be discussed as under.

1. England: Under Anglo-Saxons, England was divided into small principalities. It was King Edgar (959-75) who united England.

William established a strong government in the country in 1066.

Spirt of nationalism, however, developed more vigorously under Edward I (1272-1307). He conquered Wales and reduced the powers of barons.

Under Tudors, spirit of nationalism witnessed a considerable growth. Henry VII defeated the feudals at Wars of Roses. Henry VII severed all his connections with Pope to end his supremacy. Queen Elizabeth defeated Spanish Armeda and set up colonies abroad. Under them church was nationalised and national pride went up due to development of fine arts and growth of literature. When England became a colonial power, she had to fight many wars, both in Europe and in the colonies, with many European countries to establish her colonial supremacy. Her victory in these wars gave momentum to the feelings of nationalism in England.

2. France: In the 10th century, France was ruled by Capet dynasty, which ruled over the country till 14th century. It was under this dynasty that feelings of nationalism developed. Philip IV compelled Roman Pope to shift his headquarters from Rome to Avignon and thus raised national prestige of France.

It was during European period that feeling of nationlism in France gained strength. Englishmen were driven out of France. Louis XIV by his ability and wisdom, created feelings of nationalism in the country. In bringing nationalism in the country a major and very important role was played by Napoleon and French Revolution. It was during Napoleonic wars that whole France stood as a strong nation against whole of Europe. It has rightly been said that during the later part of 18th and early part of 19th century, French nationalism dominated whole of Europe.

3. Spain: In the middle ages Spain was divided into five small kingdoms. It was during this period the Spanish Christians tried to drive their Arab rulers out of the country. Spain emerged as a nation by the union of Aragon-castile and Grenada. When Columbus discovered America, Spain emerged as a colonial power and thereafter it began to expand in America. In order to check the interference of other European powers she got a Papal Bull by which all the catholic states were asked not to interfere in America.

Congress of Vienna: Congress of Vienna, which made after the fall of Napoleon, did not care for nationalist feelings in Europe. It gave Belgium to Holland, Norway to Sweden and Poland to Russia. Many states of Italy were given to Austria and thus unification of Italy was not allowed. A confederation of states of Germany was created. Thus, the congress of Vienna did not care for the principle of nationality.

After the Vienna Congress: Particularly after the congress of Vienna many rebellions and wars broke out to have nation states. In 1820 Spain rose in revolt against the misrule of Ferdinand who was forced to surrender. It was crushed by the forces of Austria, Russia and Prussia and thousands were killed. Thus, the cause of nationalism received some setback. In 1821, Greece rose in revolt against their Turkish rulers and it was only with the help of Russia that she could get independence, with the Treaty of Adrianople.

4. Belgium: During the congress of Vienna, Belgium was given to Holland. But the country was not wisely ruled with the result that the people of Belgium were supported in their national struggle by England and France and opposed by Austria and Russia. In 1839 Belgium got her independence and her nationality was guaranteed.

5. Poland: When Belgium got her independence, Poland also got inspiration and revolted against her Russian masters. It was, however, fortunate that Polich nationalism could not stand against the strong and powerful Russian armies, with the result that nationalism in Poland was not much success. It was only after First world war that Poland could win her freedom and independence.

6. Italy: The congress after Vienna stood on the way of unification of Italy. It divided the country into small states. Naples and Sicily were ruled by France, Central states by Pope; Lombardy and Venetia by Austria.

Parma, Modena and Tuscany were ruled by the heirs of Australian Princes. Soon nationalism spread like wild fire in Italy. A slogan "Italy for Italians" became very popular.

At this juncture Italian youth extended their whole hearted cooperation to a nationalist secret society called "Carbonari". Moreover, at that time in Italy there were three political parties. One favoured to have united Republic of Italy; other wanted to have in Italy a parliamentary form of Government under the king of Sardina whereas the third party wanted to have in Italy a confederation of all Italian states under Pope.

There were a number of secret societies which were working for the Independence of Italy at that time. The party which wanted to see Italy a Republic was headed by Joseph Mazzini who was a native of Genea. In 1831 he founded "Young Italy Society". Mazzini was several times arrested and at last forced to leave his country for Paris, where he started his paper "Young Italy". It was now with the help of this paper that he began to guide the movement in Italy. But all the revolutionary movements were crushed with iron hands. Mazzini, who could establish a republic in Rome in 1848, was thrown out by French troops. There was great discontentment against Austria in the states of Modena, Tuscany and Parma. But Austrians were in a position to put down the revolt.

Unification of Italy: Thus, upto 1848 all attempts made by Italian patriots to have their freedom and also a united Italy failed. Another great patriot Joseph Garibaldi rose to prominence took up the task of unification. He was a born revolutionary. He was an ordinary member of Mazzini's 'Young Italy'. He was responsible for inflicting a defeat on Austrians.

In 1848, King Charles Albert of Sardinia declared a war on Austria but was defeated. The king then abdicated in favour of his son Emmanuel II. In 1852, the king appointed Court Cavour as his Prime Minister, who began internal reforms in Sardinia. He gave liberal constitution to the country and also promoted education, agriculture and industry. He also reorgainsed his armies and paid his attention towards the problem of unification of Italy. In the Crimean War he sided with England, France and Turkey against Russia. He could also get the support of France against Austria. Having thus strengthening his position certain border incidents were instigated by which Austria declared war on Sardinia. France joined Sardinia and the combined forces were in a position to occupy Lombardy. It was at this stage that France decided to withdraw her support from Sardinia with the result that she had to conclude a treaty with Austria with which war was brought to a close.

Thus, Lombardy was added to Sardinia.

In 1860 Garibaldi conquered Sicily and Naples and those joined Sardinia.

The states of Parma, Modena, Rosmagna and Tuscany were also added to Sardinia.

As a result of Austrio-Prussian war, Austria was forced to accept ceding Venetia to Italy.

In 1870, as a result of Franco-German war, Italian forces were also in a position to bring Rome under their control and thus the talk of unification of Italy was completed with great difficulty.

7. Germany: The congress of Vienna did not care for the unification of Germany. Instead it created a confederation of 39 states with Austria as one state. This confederation was opposed to the unification. But in 1854, many states joined in a tariff union called Zollverin. Subsequently, the union was joined by all the states except Austria. In 1848, representatives from different states met at Frankfurt Parliament and created a united Germany under a democratic constitution.

In 1862, Prince Bismarck was appointed as the Prime Minister of Prussia who completely reorganised Prussian army. He was clear in his mind that as long as Austria was member of the German confederation, Germany could not be united. By his able policies Bismarck won the co-operation of Italy and neutrality of France. He followed his famous policy of 'Blood and Iron' in achieving his object of German unification.

In 1871 a war broke out between France and North German confederation, in which France was defeated and Bismarck was in a position to bring the remaining states under his control. In this way by 1871, whole process of unification of Germany had been completed.

Thus, a powerful and strong struggle for nationalism came into existence in Europe.

(ii) AFRICA

For quite some time Africa was uncared and unnoticed by the Europeans. The discovery of gold and the slave trade attracted the European powers to expand in Africa.

Gradually, and slowly powerful colonial powers began to occupy more and more territories in Africa by the beginning of 19th century. Consequently almost the whole of the continent had gone under European influence. These powers had divided the continent under their spheres of influence.

Africans realised the exploitation of the Europeans in the land. Being dark complexioned they were ill-treated by the white complexioned people. They were not allowed to mix with them. Moreover, they were mal-treated and humiliated. They were considered uncultured, uncivilised and Europeans considered it below their dignity to mix, dine or to play with them. They were not given any share in the running of administration. Hence, all these exploitation and humiliation paved the way for Nationalism in Africa.

1. Egypt: As regards Egypt it was under the control of England upto 1882. In the construction of Suez canal Britishers spent heavy amounts. But due to policy of economic exploitation and cultural arrogancy Egyptians did not like the Britishers.

During First World War, Egypt was ruthlessly exploited by the Britishers. The incompetent and inefficient officers ruled the state without caring for the sentiments of the masses.

In the circumstances stated above the nationalist forces united under Zaghlol Pasha. A demand was made for complete independence. Their rising was crushed ruthlessly. Thousands of Egyptians were put to sword. Zaghlol Pasha was arrested.

In the meantime Lord Milner was sent to Egypt to study the situation and make an agreement. But the Egyptians boycotted him. After a long pursuation he met Zaghlol and made an agreement. By this Britain agreed to have constitutional monarchy in Egypt. In turn Egypt agreed to protect special British interests in the country and also allow stationing of British forces in the country. In 1922 Egypt was granted independence and in 1924 Zaghlol became Prime Minister of the country. King Faud became monarch of the country. But soon a conflict between the king and the parliament started in which the king dissolved the parliament. Till 1936 he ruled Egypt with the active support of the British. But Britain interfered in the internal affairs of Egypt.

During the Ethiopian invasion of Mussolini in 1935 the Britishers sought the co-operation of Egypt. Accordingly Anglo-Egyptian Treaty was concluded between them. The then ruler of Egypt was Farouk I. He failed to give the country clean administration. In 1948 Egypt was defeated by Israel.

A revolution under Nasser ousted the king in 1952. Egypt was made a Republic. Later on Naguib was removed and General Nasser became President of the United Arab Republic. After the death of Nasser, Anwar Sadat had become the president of Egypt. Israel later on invaded Egypt and captured certain territories. So Egyptian Nationalism is again awakened to get back her lost territories.

2. Ghana: Ghana was previously known as gold coast. It was under British control. The people were uncivilised and illiterate. They were ill-treated by the British. Dr. Nkruma spear headed the revolution in the country. In March 1957 they achieved their aim of getting independence of Ghana.

3. Congo: Independence of Ghana brought awakening in other African territories as well as Congo was one such territory. It was known as Congo Free state in 1908 under Belgian Government. The people were ruthlessly exploited. So in 1950 a nationalists movement started in Congo. There was bloody riots in the territory. The Belgian Government followed the policy of Divide and Rule and tried to create split in the ranks of the nationalists. In 1957 there was a great economic depression in the territory. So the movement gained momentum. It was in June 1960 that Belgian Government decided to grant independence to the territory and a Congolese Republic was established.

4. Nigeria: Nigeria was under British control till 1960. As against the Britishers they started their nationalist movement. In 1960 Nigeria got her independence and in 1963 it became a Republic. It decided to stay as a member of the Commonwealth.

5. African French Colonies: France had many colonies in Africa. The people of these colonies started their nationalist struggle against the French domination. So Guinea was set free. In 1960 Cameroon Republic was born. The Federation of Mali, Malagasy, Senegal and Sudan all got their independence.

6. Algeria: Algeria was brought under French control. As against the French the Algerians raised their standard of revolt. It was virulent and violent. In 1962, Algeria was granted independence and France withdrew from the country.

7. Tanzania: It was in 1884 that Tanzania went under foreign domination. But soon after that nationalist movement started in the country. League of Nations recognised the same. So it kept Tanzania as mandate territory under England. After the Second World War U.N.O. also recognised the force of nationalist movement in the colony. In December 1961 the colony was declared independent. Later on both Tanganika and Zanzibar combined together and a state of Tanzania came into existence.

Thus, African nationalism, though of comparatively recent origin, soon got much strength and achieved great success.

(iii) ASIA

Like Africa, Asia also remained under colonical rale for centuries. Many countries of the Asian continent remained under British control and sphere of influence. Actually many European countries exploited Asian countries to their full. So nationalism gradually came in Asian continent. It was the awakening in Asia which made European powers to leave the colonies and thus empire began to crack down.

The following were main reasons for awakening in Asia :

(1) The foremost reason for the rise of nationalism in Asia was the rise of U.S.A. and U.S.S.R. They posed a great danger and a challenge to those powers in Asia.

(2) Another reason for awakening in Asia was emergence of Japan.

(3) Still another reason for such nationalism was the war of freedom waged by many countries after the Second World war.

(4) Sense of unity was another cause for the awakening of Asian nationalism.

(5) By supporting England in the Second World War, the Africans and Asians thought of winning their own independence with their united strength.

(6) After the war was over, the Asian countries were awakened with the support of European countries.

(7) Spread of education particularly the western system of education was highly responsible for the rise of nationalism in Asia.

(8) The Europeans had created a myth that they were a superior people as compared with Asians. But during the war this myth was exploded. It gavd a great vigour for their nationalism.

(9) Finally, one also finds that nationalism is a natural phenomenon in all the colonies.

1. Japan: Japan led a solitary life till the middle of 19th century. She followed a closed door policy. She kept aloof from other countries. It was in 1854 that Commodore Perry an American opened the door of Japan for trade and commerce. Thereafter, trade facilities were granted to England, Russia and Holland. At this time Japan was a backward country with feudal economy. Later on it began to grow strength to strength. She penetrated into China and got Korea from her. She was also in a position to defeat Russia in 1904-05. After the First World War, Japan emerged as a powerful nation. Thereafter, she followed a vigorous aggressive policy. But it was defeated by U.S.A. in the Second World war. But due to her nationalism U.S.A. could not maintain her hold over Japan, for long and had to vacate the country.

2. China: China too followed policy of isolation during the 19th century. She believed that her culture, her institutions and systems have no parallel in the world. She also thought it below her dignity to mix with European country. But the European countries wanted to have trade relations with China. England was the first country to have such relations. She defeated her in opium wars and China was forced to throw some parts open for trade to Britain. U.S.A. did not tolerate the influence of England in China. Gradually, other European countries also got trade and other facilities from China. China was nakedly exploited and her economy completely went out of gear.

At this juncture Dr. Sun-Yat-Sen created national awakening and nationalist Government in the country. In addition to Dr. Sen, Chiang-Kai-Shek involved in the national struggle. He fought with the communists later on. Ultimately the communists under Mao-Tse-Tung and Chou-En-Lai emerged victorious in the civil war. Chiang had to take shelter in Formosa. Today Communist China is a member of U.N.O. and one of the powerful countries of the world.

3. Malaysia: Malaysia was a part of British Empire for long. It was rich in rubber and mineral resources. The population of Malaysia consists of Malaysians, Indians and Chinese. There was a national movement in the country. In 1957, the country won its freedom.

4. Burma: Burma was part of India till 1935 and it was under British control. In that year Burma was separated from India. But it continued to remain under British domination. There was nationalist movement in the country and during Second World War Japanese were in a position to have their hold over Burma. In 1943 Japan declared Burma as an independent state. After the defeat of Japan in the War, Burma again went under British domination. Nationalist Movement cropped in Burma severely in 1948 and it had to be granted her independence. Burma then became a republic and continues to be so.

5. Ceylon: Originally Ceylon was a Dutch colony. During Napoleonic Wars, the colony was passed to Britain. It is a tea exporting country. Hence, Britain showed great interest. Ceylon National Congress started the nationalist movement. After First World War it was very severe. In 1929 British agreed to give Ceylon very liberal constitution. The people did not satisfy with that constitution. So they continued their struggle. It was in 1948 that Ceylon could win her freedom. It has decided to stay as a member of the commonwealth.

6. Indonesia: It has rich mineral resources. It is dominated by Muslim population. It was ruled by Dutch people. To drive out the Dutch the nationalist movement was started by the Muslims. In 1918 a Parliament with limited powers was set up to satisfy the people. Even then they continued their agitation under an able leader Soekarno. He formed a Party called Indo-Asian Nationalist Party. During the Second World War they raised the slogans 'Asia for Asians'. After the defeat of Japan in the war, Dutch again got back their colony of Indonesia. But the nationalist struggle continued. U.N.O. interfered and forced the Dutch to withdraw form the country. In 1949 Indonesia got her independence.

7. Indo-China: Indo-China consists of Annam, Tongking, Laos, Cambodia and Cochin-China. It went under French control in 1886. They showed great interest in exploiting the country. This gave birth to the rise of nationalist movement under Ho-Chi-Minh. He formed his communist party on scientific lines. His great movement was ruthlessly suppressed in 1930 by the French government. During Second World War Japan conquered Indo-China. With the help of China Dr. Minh continued his activities. As the war was over, France again got back the country. But Annam was brought under Dr. Minh's control. There he established a republic. He himself became its president. On the basis of Geneva convention France withdrew its force in 1954. North Vietnam is under communist domination whereas the capitalists control South Vietnam. The struggle for supremacy and efforts for supremacy and efforts for unification are still continuing.

Thus, Asian Nationalism was so vigorous in many countries during the 19th century.

(iv) INDIAN NATIONALISM

The East India Company was established in India in 1600 A.D. The British people came to India as traders and they turned as rulers due to our disunity. As against the British exploitation, the people of India rose against the company. It was oppressed and suppressed by the British. As a result, the administration of the country passed on to the British country. Queen Victoria also promised to give fair and honourable treatment to the Indians. Nothing was done to this effect. So national awakening came in the country. As a result of this Indian National Congress was established in 1885. Under this banner our national movement was started rigorously and vigorously. Many causes were responsible for this awakening. They were :

(1) Both the East India Company as well as the British Parliament formulated policies which resulted in the exploitation of the people. It was not tolerated for long.

(2) Spread of western education was another cause for the rise of nationalism in India.

(3) Another cause for the nationalism in India was the contact of the Indians with Europeans. They were inspired by the ideas and institutions of the Europeans.

(4) Improvement in the field of transport and communication paved the way for out nationalism.

(5) In 1904-05 Japan, an Asian country, defeated mighty Russia. This inspired confidence among Indians as well. If Russia could be defeated why could not India throw Britishers out of the country.

(7) The two world wars were highly responsible for the rise and spread of nationalism in India.

(8) Another cause of the nationalism in India was the revival of Indian culture.

(9) Indians press also awakened the people by bringing to the notice of the acts of omission and commission of the government.

(10) The attitude of the rulers created a sense of hatred in the minds of the Indian masses. Hence, they began to defy them by agitations and demonstrations.

Nationalist Movement: Out Nationalist Movement started in 1885 when a British officer A.O. Hume founded Indian National Congress. Educated Indians like Raja Ram Mohan Rai, Dada Bhai Nowroji, M.G. Ranade, Pherozshah Mehta, Surendra Nath Banerjee and Gopala Krishna Gokhale added flesh to the Congress. These people were called liberals. They did not believe in violence. Under their influence the Government of India Act of 1909 was passed. But Indians were not given adequate representation in running their own administration.

So the Congress went under the influence of the extremists like Lokmanya Tilak, Lala Lajpat Rai, Bipin Chandra Pal and Subhash Chandra Bose. They believed in violence.

When Gandhiji appeared in the scene and took the leadership of the movement in his own hands, the whole situation changed. He believed in non-violence or Ahimsa. So he introduced nonviolent methods like civil disobedience and non-cooperation to oust the British from power. The Government of India Act of 1919 was introduced to satisfy the

Indians. Instead it created discontent and dissatisfaction. The struggle continued. The government sent Simon Commission. The commission suggested grant of more rights to the people. Round Table conferences were organised by the British Government to find out a solution to the Indian problems but without any success.

In the meanwhile under Gandhiji's leadership thousands and thousands of people courted arrest. British courts and educational institutions and clothes were boycotted.

At this juncture violence took place in India sporadically. Sardar Bhagat Sigh, Chandra Shekar Azad, Aurobindo Ghosh and Netaji advocated violent methods. During the Second World War in Japan Netaji organised Indian National Army.

When war broke out, India decided not to cooperate with the British government, unless she agreed to grant independence to us after the war was over. To find out a peaceful solution the government sent Cripps Mission. The Mission failed. So in 1942 India launched Quite India Movement under Gandhiji. Simaltaneously the Muslims also joined the movement with different slogan i.e. "Divide India and quit". The movement was a wonderful success. Baffled by this, British Government sent to India a Cabinet Mission and Wavel Mission to find a way out. The Indian people continued their agitation till full freedom was granted to them. It was on 15th August 1947 that India got her freedom.

Pakistan: The Muslims in India, under the leadership of Mr. M.A. Jinnah had been agitating since 1930 for separate country of Pakistan. So in June 1947 the British Government decided to partition India and a separate state of Pakistan was created in August with two wings namely West Pakistan and East Pakistan.

Bangla Desh: The people of East Pakistan suffered seriously at the hands of West Pakistan. So nationalism erupted in the country. Indian army gave its whole hearted support for their nationalism. East Bengal won freedom and a new state of Bangla Desh was born in 1971.

29

World Peace Movement

(i) THE LEAGUE OF NATIONS

During the First World war the people experienced untold sorrows and sufferings. All thinking men decided to put an end to the war and maintain peace and order in the world. The First World War thus gave birth to a child called the League of Nations in 1920.

The original membership of the League consisted of the Allies, the new states that emerged after the war and a number of neutral states. The covenant recognised the national sovereignty of each member, but no member could withdraw from membership without fulfilling its international obligations under the covenant.

Organs: The organs of the League were : (1) The Assembly; (2) The Council; (3) The Secretariat and (4) Permanent Court of Justice.

1. The Assembly: It was the supreme body of the League. All the member states represented in the supreme body. Each member state had only one vote. New members were admitted by a two thirds majority vote. Decisions were taken unanimously.

2. The Council: It was the executive body in the League of Nations. At the inception of the League there were four members. They were permanent. In addition to this there were four non-permanent members. In 1926 Germany became a permanent member. Each member had only one vote. Each state was represented by one delegate. Decisions had to be unanimous.

3. The Secretariat: Its Headquarters was fixed at Geneva. Secretary General was the leading personality in the Secretariat. He was appointed by the Council with the approval of the majority of the Assembly. He was assisted by a large number of staff. The expenses were borne by the member states. They engaged in official business.

4. The Permanent Court of International Justice: It was created to settle international disputes; it had its Headquarters at the Hague. It consisted of 15 judges elected jointly by the Council and the Assembly. Their term of office was 9 years. It settled many disputes.

The mandatory system was adopted in the league. The inherent principles of this system were that there should be no annexation by anyone power, mandated territories should be exclusively given to the League and the League could delegate its authority to one state.

The Covenant of the League of Nations out and out dealt with the measures for the prevention of war. Limitation of armaments, maintenance of territorial integrity and maintenance of international peace were the main principles of the League.

International Labour Organisation was established by the League to improve the labour conditions in various parts of the world.

Estimate: The League had three primary functions. They were (1) The settlement of international disputes, (2) Wipe out the germs of war and (3) The organisation of international cooperation. The League met a miserable failure in its first object. However, it settled more than 40 disputes. But it was unable to prevent the Sino-Japanese and Italio-Abyssinian Wars. Finally, the rise of Hitler and Mussolini gave a great shock to the League. But it had tremendous success in respect of international cooperation and social and moral betterment.

It performed a lot of useful work in organising action against malaria, small-pox, leprosy, rabies, cancer, tuberculosis, syphilis, heart diseases etc. Added to this it controlled opium trade and did a lot of intellectual, social and humanitarian work.

The League failed in its marvellous mission of preserving peace in the world. It was due to the lack of forces, rise of nationalism in Germany, Italy and Japan, economic nationalism and the attitude of America which was not a member in the League. It would have been successful had the U.S.A. been a member of the body. But it cannot be denied that the League had maintained international cooperation for nearly 20 years.

(ii) THE UNITED NATIONS ORGANISATION

Origin: When the Second World War was going on intensively Roosevelt, the American President and Winston Churchill, the British Prime Minister met in a ship in the Atlantic Ocean on August 1941 and decided to put an end to the war. There the seeds were sown by them for another world body to maintain peace. As a result of this the Atlantic Charter was issued. It was succeeded by the Tehran Conference in October 1943 by U.K., U.S.A., U.S.S.R. This was followed by a conference at Dumbarton Oaks in the U.S.A. held in 1944. There an agreement was reached on the general principles and purposes of such an organisation. Then another Conference was held at Yalta in Crimea, in February 1945. U.K., U.S.A. and U.S.S.R. participated in the deliberations of Yalta Conference. As a result of this the Charter of the United Nations was signed at San Francisco on June 26, 1945 at a meeting of the representatives of 50 states. They represented two-thirds of world's population. The United Nations Organisation actually came into existence on the 24th October, 1945.

U.N. Charter: The preamble to the Charter contains III 'articles'. It sets out the aims of the United Nations as :

(1) To save the succeeding generations from the scourge of war;
(2) To reaffirm faith in fundamental human rights;
(3) To establish justice and respect for international obligations;
(4) To promote social progress and better standards of life.

Aims and Objects: The first and foremost aim of the United Nations is to maintain international peace and security. Secondly, its object is to develop a spirit of co-operation, and friendly relations among the nations of the world. Thirdly, it is to promote and encourage respect for human rights and for fundamental freedom. Fourthly, its aim is to solve international problems of economic, social, cultural and humanitarian character. Finally, its object is to employ international machinery for the promotion of economic and social advancement of all people.

The Headquarters of the U.N.O. is at New York. The Secretariat building is situated on a 17 acre tract of land donated by John. D. Rockefeller on the Manhattan Island, a suburb of New York. It has 39 storeys. More than 8000 office workers are functioning in the building. The official language of the U.N.O. are English, French, Chinese, Russian, Arabic and Spanish. The flag of U.N. is white in colour with U.N. emblem (two bent olive branches open at the top, and in between them is the world map) on a light blue back ground.

Organs: The Organs of the U.N.O are :

(1) General Assembly;
(2) Security Council;
(3) Economic and Social Council;
(4) Trusteeship Council;
(5) International Court of justice and
(6) The secretariat.

1. General Assembly: Every member state of the United Nations is a member of this body. Each state had one vote though it may send upto 5 members. Two-thirds majority of members are required to decide important questions. It meets regularly once a year, Special and emergency sessions can be convened under certain circumstances. It elects ten non-permanent members of the Security Council, all the 27 members of the ECOSOC and certain members of the Trusteeship Council and also Judges of the International Court of Justice. The President of the General Assembly is elected for a year. It can discuss and recommend for the maintenance of international peace and security. It directs and supervises international economics and social co-operation. The budget of the U.N.O. is prepared by this body. It admits, suspends and expels members. Now there are 149 member states in the U.N. General Assembly.

2. The Security Council: It is mainly responsible for maintaining international peace. It is composed of eleven members-five permanent members and six non-permanent members. The "Big Five" the U.K., U.S.A., U.S.S.R., France and Communist China are permanent members. The non-permanent members are elected by the General Assembly for 2 years from among the member States. Each member in the Council has one vote. But the unanimous opinion of the Big Five is essential in every case. The Big Five has the power of veto. Among the five if anyone says "no" to a proposal by a veto the resolution is negatived.

3. The Economic and Social Council (ECOSOC): It consists of 27 members elected by the General Assembly. Their term of office is for 3 years. It meets thrice in a year. Its primary function is to make studies and reports with respect to international economic, social, cultural, educational, health and other related matters. It co-ordinates the activities of the specialised agencies.

4. The Trusteeship Council: The mandatory system of the League has been improved as the Trusteeship system. It has to consider reports submitted to it by the administering authority. The Trusteeship Council seeks to ensure the political, economic, social, and educational advancement of the people living in 'Trust Territories'.

5. The International Court of Justice: It consist of 15 Judges elected for a 9 year term by the Security Council and General Assembly. Five judges retire every three years. The seat of the Court is at the Hague. It decides those cases which are the subject of dispute between two or more states. It gives advisory opinion on legal matters to the various organs and specialised agencies of the U.N.

6. The Secretariat: It is headed by the Secretary General. He is appointed by the General Assembly in consultation with the Security council. He is the Chief Executive Officer. He is assisted by a large number of officers.

Special Agencies: Apart from these organs there are many specialised agencies like I.L.O., F.A.O., UNESCO, UNICEF, W.H.O., I.C.A.O., I.B.R.D., I.M.F., I.F.C., I.D.A., and I.A.E.A. (International Atomic Energy Agency), in the UNO.

Estimate: The U.N.O. has rendered remarkable services to the world. It has played the part of international policeman, economist, scientist, Jurist, doctor, social worker and banker. Many burning problems such as mediation in Indonesia, and Palestine, cease fire between India and Pakistan, stopping of aggression in Korea and liquidation of colonialism in Asia and Africa have been solved by the U.N. It was responsible for the passing of historic document "The Universal Declaration of Human Rights" on 10th December 1948. It gives personal, civil, political, economic social and cultural rights. It played a vital role in Congo. Moreover, it helps to solve the economic problems of the world. In the social field too it gives a lot of useful advice.

The U.N.O. has been criticised from various quarters. It is called the disunited Nations. It is said that in the U.N. there is neither unity nor nations. It is not able to function effectively due to the veto power of the Big Five. The small states are ignored by the great powers is another reason for its ineffectiveness. There is no sovereignty and separate force for U.N.O. There is no universality of the membership of the U.N. Proper representation is not given to the various regions of the world. All these things are to be rectified for its successful functioning and for bright future.

30

Contemporary Civilisation and its Features

1. Political Trends: After the First World War monarchism was given a decent burial in many countries. In Europe, at least a dozen republics were established, including Poland, Czechoslovakia, Lithuania, Latvia, Estonia, Finland, Austria, the Ukraine, Turkey, Spam, Germany and Russia. In other countries, there was a general liberalisation of political procedure. Progress of democracy was a significant event during this period. Wilson pleaded for the recognition and the right of self-determination of all nations, large and small.

Signs of an economic collapse were evident in world economy as early as 1926. Unemployment was widespread in many European countries, and throughout the world production was in excess of demand.

At this juncture dictatorship became the order of the day, superseding the absolute monarchies and popularised constitutional republics whose doom was written by World War I. The government provided for in the Union of Soviet Socialist Republics (U.S.S.R.) was very different from other forms of government. Economic development has been considered by the Soviets to be their most important activity.

After the Second World War dictatorship in Germany and Italy disappeared without any indication. Japan was brought under the control of the U.S.A. The United States emerged from World War I with considerable gain in experience and with some fundamental changes in her historic step. Industrially the United States had climbed to the top, and at the same time, had become the world's greatest creditor nation. Lloyd George was at the helm of the English ship of state when the nation emerged from World War I. Political turmoil gripped France after World War I. After the failure of the League of Nations, another World peace organisation i.e. U.N.O. came into existence in the world in 1945.

2. Economic Trends: Recent economic theorists have turned against the *laissez faire* idea of economic control, largely because of the world depression and the general collapse of economic enterprises.

Adam Smith and the physiocrats introduced the classical school of economics, which included Bentham, Malthus, Ricardo and John Stuart Mill. They defended the new capitalism on the basis of natural law and natural liberty. Alfred Marshall revived the classical economy.

Marshall, Clark, Tausing, Carver, Classel, Fisher, Devenport, Hobson, Fetter, Pigou, Veblen, Mitchell and Tagwell have been considered as important members of present-day school of Economic Thought. Among them Veblen occupies an important place in the development of modern economic thought. He attempted to distinguish between "business" and "industry". The changes brought about by the depression in the United States were revolutionary. A leading American economist, W.C. Mitchell wrote, "a crisis is expected to be followed by a depression, the depression by a revival, the revival by prosperity, and prosperity by a new crisis".

In 1850 many experiments were made in the field of co-operatives in Great Britain. Since then the movement got great impetus. Membership in English cooperatives represents almost one-half of the entire population.

Sweden has made greatest progress in the establishment and the successful operation of cooperatives than has any other country.

During this period co-operatives are just beginning to make headway in the United States.

International co-operatives are beginning to attract considerable attention. The first effort along this line was the establishment of the Scandinavian Cooperative wholesale during World War I. Another important one was the International Co-operative Alliance in Paris. Due to these co-operatives retail prices were considerably reduced; promotion of thrift was improved; control of monopoly and improvement in labour standard were achieved.

One of the greatest threats to be met in a war economy is that of inflation. The inflation was controlled more effectively by increasing the taxes and by controlling the prices. Similarly the post-war economic problems were also solved carefully.

3. Social Trends: In modern society, the social position of the individual is determined by his economic status. Poverty is considered as a chronic and at the same time an acute problem of economic society. A great amount of time and money is being spent on the scientific study of poverty, in the hope that some solution other than alms giving may be found.

Crime is just as persistent and, seemingly, just as uncontrollable as poverty. In fact, some contend that this evil is growing worse. Many steps are being taken to wipe out the nefarious practices of criminals. The ancient theory of "an eye for an eye and a tooth for tooth" was superseded by imprisonment and isolation of criminals in more recent times. Prison conditions have been improved considerably.

The battle to combat diseases in still raging, with the scientists gradually gaining ground. In general infant mortality has decreased, but the death-rate among the adults of middle and old age has not been materially reduced in the last half of the century. The American people spend 400 corers of Dollars annually for medical service.

The social outlook has been changed considerably. Many changes took place in the society from the beginning of the First World War. The relationship between the employer and the employee has been improved tremendously. The Beveridge Plan (1942) in England has attracted considerable attention regarding labour problems.

4. Cultural Trends

Education: Education continues to be principal hope to promoting progress. Mr. Foster emphasised the importance of Mathematics, Natural Sciences, History, Literature, Philosophy and Religion in the curriculum. Adult education has taken on an increased significance. In the United States it has been given more importance. "Brain Trust" established by President Roosevelt was a step in the right direction. Geopolitics was introduced in Germany. Finally, UNESCO has been considered a remarkable institution in this field.

Religion: Religion always has played an important part in the development of civilisation. Church influence lost its control over schools. They need cooperation to solve their problems. Union of Protestant denominations has been accomplished in Canada and Rhodesia. Roman Catholics are following religious toleration towards other faiths. In Russia the great religious bodies were deprived of legal recognition and their wealth was confiscated.

Literature: Truly, this is an age of mass production in literature, as well as merchandise. George Bernard Shah, H.G. Wells and John Galsworthy helped to introduce the new age in literature. Besides Jayce, D.H. Lawrence, O' Neill, Conrad, Mansfield, T.S. Eliot and Davis have made a significant contribution in the field of literature.

Painting and Sculpture: Post impressionism, or expressionism in painting has been expanded in many directions. Matisse and Picasso, two outstanding contemporary painters, are most prominent for their achievements. Picasso is a prominent figure in modern art development. The French painters Seurat and Derain and the Italian painters Chirico and Modigliani are very famous in this line. Moreover, the English painters Orpen and John are prominent in this line of painting. Salvador Dali, a Spaniard, is one of the best known exponents of surrealism (portray the reactions of the mind of man rather than to present the world of nature). Later on the art of common man has appeared. Two Mexican artists, Diego Rivera and Jose Orozco are the chief representatives of the "social art" in the Western Hemisphere. Bellows has been acclaimed as a distinctly American painter of American life. Grant Wood found inspiration for his painting in his own section of the country and its people. "American Gothic" is one of his most widely known paintings.

In the field of sculpture Germany stands in the fore front. Lehmbruck, the master sculptor is a great significant figure. In France Maillos Bourdelle and Brancusi are leading modernists. Mestrocic, a Yugoslav, attained great favour for his decorative sculptures. In England Gill became known for his extraordinary work. Epstelim and Lachaise are very prominent figures in this field.

Architecture: During this period architecture advanced conspicuously, Classic models, Romantic, Gothic and Byzantine forms have been employed, particularly for churches and war memorials. Even the skyscraper, with all its modernism, is often decorated with Gothic ornamentation. Another best example is the Imperial Hotel in Tokyo. Moreover, the Wordsworth Building in New York is famous for its ornamental structure.

Music: Modern music has followed the same tendency like that of painting and sculpture. The Russian Scriadin produced a mystical system of harmony in his "Poem of Five". The Austrian Schonberg and Igor Stavinsky are best known musicians. Perhaps the most sensational ultra modern contribution to music has come from Russia.

Popular Music and Jazz are famous during this period. Victor Herbert produced breezy and melodious operettas, but he followed the conventional style. Jazz was more revolutionary. Its main characterists are exaggerated rhythm, melody and emotional appeal.

Science: More has been accomplished in the field of science in the 20th century. The quantum theory, the principle of relativity, the atomic structure and activity have revolutionsed the study of Physics in the 20th century. Plank, Einsterin and Rutherford have done a lot in this field. Bohr combined the quantum and atomic theories that led to the conception of

"Cosmic rays". The creation of the atomic bomb has opened an entirely new aspect of science.

Studies in astronomy, physics, chemistry and geology have been contributed a vast store of new information. The value of preventive medicine has been emphasised, with encouraging success in the results. Tetanus and Diabetes have been checked considerably. Many endowments like the Rockfeller Foundation and the Carnegie Institution are doing yeoman service in this field. There is every reason to be hopeful for still further progress in peace time.

Index

A

Aachen, 143
Abbasids, 124
Aeschylus, 62
Akkad, 21
Alexandria, 19
Alyattas, 50
Amenhotsp III, 14
American War of Independence, 211, 215
Aragon, 168
Archilochus, 62
Archimedes, 63
Aristophanes, 62
Aristotle, 61
Aryan Civilisation, 75
Asoka, 87
Assyria, 27-31, Decline, 28
Athens, 56
Augustus, 71
Aztec, 105

B

Babylonia, 23, Civilisation, 23-25
Bartholomeo, Diaz, 184
Bastille, 232
Battle of Leuctra, 57
Battle of Marathon, 56
Battle of Salamis, 56
Benedict, St., 152
Bloody Sunday, 245
Boccacio, 171
Boston Massacre, 219
Boston Tea Party, 220
Bridge Water, 240
Buddha, 84-88
Buddhist Literature, 86
Buddhism, 84-88
Byzantine Civilisation, 117

C

Caliphs, 123
Calvin, 149-150, Calvinism, 178-180
Cambyses, 34-35
Canossa, 146
Capitularies, 142
Carthusian Order, 154
Castile, 167
Catherine the Great, 201-203
Cato the Elder, 71
Cavour, 258
Cervantes, 172
Chaldea, 31-33
Charlemagne, 136, 139-143

Charles Darwin, 2-4
Charles V, 176-177, 181
Charles VII, 167
Charles VIII, 167
Chinese Civilisation, 92, 98
Christopher Columbus, 184
Chrysoloras, 172
Cistercian order, 154
Cleisthenes, 57
Cleopatra, 19
Cluny, 154
Code of Napeoleon, 238
Confucius, 93
Conrad III, 160
Continental System, 236-237
Copernicus, 2
Cro-Magnan Man, 7
Crusades, 158, 160-165
Cyrus, 34-36

D

Dante, 171, Divine Comedy, 171
Darius, 34, 37
Dasyu, 78
Davis, 274
De Brienne, 231
Decameron, 171
Delphic oracle, 59
Demarcation Line, 185
Demosthenes, 63
Diet of Worms, 176
Digambara's, 91
Diogenes, 62-63
Divine Right Theory, 212
Dominican Monastery, 152, 155
Dryden, 71

E

Edward I, 256
Egyptian Civilisation, 13, 18
Eightfold Path, 85
Enlightenment, 84
Epicurus, 62, 66
Erasmus, 172
Euclid, 63
Euphrates, 9, 15, 20, 31

F

Ferdinand, 168
Fertile Crescent, 20, 28, 31
Feudalism, 128-132
Flying Shuttle, 240
Four Great Truths, 85
Francis Drake, 185
Frederick Barbanrossa, 147-148
Frederick, the Great, 191
Fujiwara, 99

G

Galen, 73
Galileo, 2
Gallic Peril, 217
Galsworthy, John, 274
Garibaldi, 258-259
George Stephenson, 240
Gift of Nile, 13
Gilgamesh, 26
Glorious Revolution, 212-215
Gokhale, 265
Greek Civilisation, 55, 64, 66
Gregory VII, 146-147
Grenville Measures, 218

H

Hammurabi, 24-25, 28, Code, 24
Hannibal, 68
Harsha, 87
Hebrew Civilisation, 39
Hejira (Hegira), 123
Helen of Troy, 55
Henodotus, 62
Henry Cort, 240
Henry IV, 146-148

Henry V, 147
Henry the Navigator, 184
Henry VI, 148
Hesiod, 61-62, 65
Hippocrates, 64
Hittite Civilisation, 43
Hojos, 99
Holy Roman Empire, 136-139, 141
Holy Synod, 198
Homer, 58, 61-62, 65
Horace, 62
Hume, A.O., 265
Humphrey Davy, 240
Hundred Years War, 166

I

Iliad, 62
Incas, 104, 108-112
Index, 182
Industrial Revolution, 239, 241
Innocent III, 148-149
Innocent IV, 149
Inquisition, 180, 182
Isaiah, 42

J

Jainism, 88-91
James Hargreaves, 240
James I, 212
James II, 212-214
James Watt, 240
Japanese Civilisation, 98
Jassy Treaty, 205
Jataka, 86
Jazz, 275
Jean Colbert, 188
Jehovah, 41
Jeremiah, 40, 42
Jesus Christ, 113-114
John Cabbot, 185
John Kay, 240
Joseph II, 206-208
Julius Caesar, 19, 69, 71
Justinian, 117-120

K

Kanishka, 87
Kapilavastu, 84
Kutchuk-Kainardji Treaty, 205

L

Land of Pyramids, 13
Land of the Pharaohs, 13
Lao Tze, 94, 97
Last Judgement, 172
Last Supper, 172
Lawrence, St. River, 185
League of Nations, 267-268
Lenin, 248, 250
Leo, Pope, 175
Livy, 72
Lorenzo de Medici, 169
Louis XI, 167
Louis XIV, 187-188, 193, 226
Louis XV, 226, 230
Louis XVI, 231-233, 237
Lydians, 49-51

M

Machiavelli, 172
Madonna and Child, 172
Mahavira, 88-90
Manorialism, 133
Manzikert, 158
Marco Polo, 184
Mariners' Compass, 127
Martin Luther, 174-177
Mathew Arnold, 1
Maya, 103
Mayadevi, 84
Mazzini, 258
Megallan, 185
Memphis, 15
Mencius, 94

Menes, 13
Mesopotamia, 9
Michelangelo, 172
Middle Kingdom, 13, 17
Milton, 26
Mohammed Prophet, 122-123
Mona Lisa, 172
Mongol Rule, 94
Montesquieu, 228
Moses and David, 172

N

Napoleon Bonaparte, 234
Nasser, 260
Neanderthal Man, 6
Nebuchadnezzar, 25, 40
Nebular Theory, 2
Necker, 231
Neolithic Age 9-12
New Kingdom, 14
New Testament, 40
Nicholas II, 244-245
Nicholas V, Pope, 172
Noah's Arc, 22

O

O'Neill, 274
Odyssey, 55, 62
Old Testament, 40, 42
Origin of Life, 3
Origin of Species, 4

P

Paradise Lost, 26
Partition of Poland, 195, 204
Paul IV, 181-182
Peace of Augsburg, 177
Peasants' Revolt, 176
Peking Man, 6
Peleolithic Age, 5
Peloponnesian War, 57, 63
Peninsular War, 236
Pericles, 56, 63
Persian Civilisation, 34
Petarch, 171
Peter the Great, 191, 196, 199, 201
Phoenicia, 52, Civilisation, 52
Phrygians, 46-48
Plato, 61
Pliny, 72
Primordial, 3
Prince, The, 172
Ptolemy, 72
Punic Wars, 68
Pythagoras, 58, 61

Q

Quartering Act, 219, 220
Quebec Act, 221

R

Rahula, 84
Raphael, 172
Reformation, 174, 177
Reign of Terror, 233
Rig Veda, 75, 79
Robert Western, 242
Roman Civilisation, 67
Rousseau, 228

S

Schmalkaldic Wars, 177
Sennacherib, 28
Seven Year War, 191, 193-194
Shoguns, 99-100
Social Contract, 229
Socrates, 58, 61
Solon, 57
Sophocles, 62
Sparta, 55-57
Stamp Act, 218
Streltsi, 197
Stuart Monarchy, 213
Sugar Act, 218

Sumerian Civilisation, 20
Svetambaras, 90
Swain, J.E., 165

T

Taoism, 94, 97
Ten Commandments, 85
Tennis Court Oath, 232
Thebes, 57
Theodosius I, 74
Thomas Moore, Sir, 172
Thucydides, 63
Thutmosis III, 14, 18
Tigris, 9, 20
Tirthankaras, 88-90
Titian, 172
Toju, 100
Tokugawas, 99
Townshend Duties, 219
Trent, Council, 180-182
Tri Ratna, 90
Tudors, 209
Turgot, 229-231

U

Ulrich Zwingli, 178
Ummayyad, 125
United Nations Organisation, 268
Urban II, 159
Utopia, 172

V

Vaisali, 88
Vascoda Gama, 184
Versailles, 187
Virgil, 71
Voltaire, 226, 228

W

Wars of the Roses, 166
Wells, H.G., 274
Wheatstone, Charles, 240
Wordsworth, 252
World War I, 272, 273
World War II, 266
Worms, Concordat, 147
Wu Ti, 93

X

Xenophon, 63

Y

Yajur Veda, 82
Yasodhara, 84
Yoritoma, 99

Z

Zeno, 62
Zero Year, 103
Zoraster, 36, Zorastrianism, 36-37
Zwinglianism, 178-179